Captivology

The Science of Capturing People's Attention

BEN PARR

HarperOne

An Imprint of HarperCollins*Publishers*

HarperOne

The graph on page 148 was redrawn from material originally published in Solomon E. Asch, "Opinions and Social Pressure," in *Readings About the Social Animal*, ed. Elliott Aronson (New York: Worth, 2004). Used by permission.

HarperCollins books may be purchased for educational, business, or sales promotional use. For information please e-mail the Special Markets Department at SPsales@harpercollins.com.

HarperCollins website: http://www.harpercollins.com

HarperCollins®, 👟®, and HarperOne™ are
trademarks of HarperCollins Publishers.

FIRST EDITION

Designed by Level C

Library of Congress Cataloging-in-Publication Data is available upon request.

ISBN 978–0–06–232419–1

15 16 17 18 19 RRD(H) 10 9 8 7 6 5 4 3 2 1

To Kurt Garvin and Matt Ryd

Contents

Introduction:
A Bonfire of Attention

D ug is the naive and adorable talking dog from Pixar's *Up*. While Dug has many admirable qualities—loyalty, unconditional love, and joyfulness chief among them—perhaps my favorite thing about him is his phenomenally short attention span.

> **Dug:** My name is Dug. I have just met you, and I love you. [He jumps on Carl.]
>
> **Carl:** Wha . . .
>
> **Dug:** My master made me this collar. He is a good and smart master and he made me this collar so that I may talk. SQUIRREL! [He looks to distance for a few seconds.]
>
> **Dug:** My master is good and smart.[1]

We are all Dugs. Fifteen hundred years ago, we had the patience to sit in the Baths of Diocletian and discuss the finer points of Roman politics and philosophy. Today, we can't go through dinner without somebody pulling out his or her phone and checking Twitter.

I'm no exception. Like the squirrel-loving Dug, I succumb to distractions all the time. As a product of the texting and Facebook generation, I found it impossible to avoid Reddit, Gmail, and Netflix while I was writing this book. I have no fewer than fifteen windows and twenty-five tabs open on two monitors at any time. I track tech, entertainment, media, and science news across six Twitter accounts in a desktop app called TweetDeck. It whizzes by with a constant stream of updates like a trader's Bloomberg Terminal.

In exchange for nearly instantaneous access to massive amounts of information, I've had to give up a little bit of my attention span. All of us have made this trade-off. We have all acquired new habits and coping mechanisms—e-mail management tools, calendar software, and constant multitasking—to manage the massive amount of information that's coming at us every day. According to researchers at the University of Southern California, the average person in 1986 was exposed to approximately forty newspapers' worth of information daily. In 2006, that number had more than quadrupled to 174 newspapers' worth of information daily.[2] Imagine somebody dropping off 174 newspapers at your doorstep every single day.

Part of the reason for this rise in consumption is due to how easy it is today to create content. In 1986, there were no blog posts, status updates, YouTube channels, or Instagrams. If you wanted people to read your opinion piece, you had to send a letter to the editor of your local newspaper. If you wanted to share a photo with your friends, you had to take the film to the camera store, get it developed, print multiple copies, and physically hand the photos to your friends. Today, the only thing you need to share any content is a keyboard or a touch screen.

Our attention just can't keep up with all this information. The more data available to us, the more our attention has to be divided to consume it. As a result, attention has become a scarce resource. We have the same 1,440 minutes per day our ancestors had but far more information and distractions to fill that time. There are clear limits to how much and how long humans can pay attention. The combination of increased information and our brain's limits has changed our habits—and not necessarily for the better. Many of us have turned to multitasking as a way to keep up.

"There's clearly a tendency for people to attempt multiple, simultaneous—as much as they can—activities," said Dr. Adam Gazzaley, director of neuroscience at the University of California, San Francisco.[3] But research shows that our propensity for multitasking and distractions is a bad thing. According to UC Irvine professor of informatics Dr. Gloria Mark, once you are captured by a distraction, it can take up to twenty-three minutes to get back on track.[4] And since the average person succumbs to distractions an average of every three minutes, it can be difficult to escape.[5]

It's even worse if you are a multitasker. You might think a chronic multitasker would be more adept at switching between tasks, but you would be wrong. A recent study by Stanford professor Eyal Ophir found that "heavy media multitaskers"—those who consumed a large amount of media content—were not only more susceptible to irrelevant stimuli, but they were also significantly slower when it came to switching between tasks.[6] Another study, from the University of Utah, found that people who identified as "strong multitaskers" were in fact the least capable multitaskers of the 310 subjects they tested. Heavy multitaskers are far less capable of inhibiting distractions than those who identify as light multitaskers.[7]

So not only is attention more scarce, but our habits are also making us less efficient at focusing our attention. This isn't good news if you're a startup trying to capture the undivided attention of a user, or a local official trying to rally support for a new library or a much-needed renovation of your city's infrastructure. If you want to capture attention for your ideas, your work, or your product, you will not only have to compete against countless people and companies who are vying for the same attention you are, but you'll also need to fight against the very unproductive habits that we have all developed to manage our attention in the midst of overwhelming stimuli. Attention is scarce and fleeting. You better figure out how it works, what people naturally pay attention to, and why.

And yet, despite the fact that all around us is a fierce competition for attention, there are people who still don't believe they need to put in the effort to break through the noise to get their ideas noticed.

Over the past few years, I've heard way too many people misuse the famous quote from the 1989 film *Field of Dreams*, declaring, "If you build it, he will come." This misappropriated quote suggests that if you simply put your head down and develop a great idea or build a fantastic product, people will eventually recognize it and come to you. It also implies that reaching out to people with your idea or project is not only unnecessary, but also beneath you.

It is the most annoying misuse of a quote ever. I despise when people use this quote this way not only because it's wrong but also because it leads people to believe that attention isn't something you should actively court. This "build it, they will come" mind-set is behind the reason some of history's greatest minds went unrecognized for decades or, worse yet, their work still has never seen the light of day.

Vincent van Gogh, one of the greatest painters of his time, sold just *one* work of art while he was alive. Alfred Wegener, the man who discovered that continents drift ever so slowly on the surface of the Earth, was ridiculed and ignored until two decades after his death. Fortunately, these masters were eventually discovered. But we can only imagine the van Goghs and Wegeners that have slipped through the cracks because they couldn't capture the attention of others.

Then and now, attention has always mattered. Nowadays, if you are a teacher, you have to find novel ways to keep your easily distracted students engaged in your lessons. If you are a marketer, you have to find ways to promote your brands. If you run a charity, you need your cause to be in the forefront of a donor's mind. If you are a scientist, you need to get the attention of those who allocate research grants. If you are an actor, you need to maintain the attention of agents, casting directors, and audiences. If you're a musician, you need your music to stay on people's minds so they'll buy it and tell their friends.

Do you want people to recognize your art? Do you want people to use your product? Do you want others to read or watch your content? Do you want to run for office someday? Do you want to have your research recognized and shared? Do you want to make more people aware of your favorite charity and its cause? Do you want your crush to turn his or her attention toward you? Do you want your students to stop looking at their phones and focus on what you're teaching them?

If you answered yes to any of these questions, then this book is for you.

Why I Wrote This Book

I wrote *Captivology* out of necessity. In my world—the world of technology and startups—attention often means the difference between success and failure. Startups need to catch the attention of busy investors. They need to secure the attention of the press to spread the word about their products. They need to captivate their users long enough to entice them to come back. Startups need to grab the attention of potential hires and keep them engaged once they join their team. Without attention, even a great startup with a compelling product will die. Attention is the fuel that drives great companies, causes, and ideas.

As the managing partner of a venture capital firm that invests in early-stage startups, entrepreneurs come to me to help them get their businesses off the ground and, of course, for money. But when I first started the firm, I noticed that what startups really wanted was our expertise dealing with the press, developing marketing campaigns, building viral products, optimizing customer acquisition, and connecting with Hollywood. In other words, they were coming to us for help getting attention.

This is when I really became deeply interested in the mechanics of attention and how to capture it. I wanted to know: Why are we, as a society, captivated by products like the iPhone or Facebook but couldn't care less about Myspace? Why do some musicians turn into Beyoncé while others never see the light of day? Why do some nonprofits, like charity: water, succeed in getting our donations while other charities are ineffective?

Attention turns a great product or idea into a world-changing one. It turns a talented group of musicians into The Beatles. But attention, I've learned, doesn't simply fall into your lap; you have to ignite it in your audience and add the right fuel to make it grow into a bonfire.

Building a Bonfire of Attention

Adrian Grenier, director of the critically acclaimed documentary *Teenage Paparazzo* and best known for his role as Vincent Chase in HBO's *Entourage*, compares capturing attention to building a fire: "First you need the kindling. You need the little leaves and the twigs, and you get that going, which is easy to ignite. Then you move on to your bigger logs, and eventually a whole big bonfire. At first you need something to ignite the attention, and then you got to keep it going somehow."[8]

Grenier's analogy is spot on: like a bonfire, lasting attention builds up in stages. Three, to be precise.

In the first stage—ignition—you have to capture what I call immediate attention—your audience's instant and unconscious reaction to the world around us. If you hear someone call out your name, you react instinctively. The same automatic reaction happens if you see a giant spider in your bed or smell a delicious batch of chocolate chip cookies. These external stimuli ignite your target audience's attention.

In the second stage—kindling—you're trying to attract what I call short attention—your audience's short-term focus on a specific event or stimuli. When a book, film, speaker, or subject captivates our short attention, we can concentrate and focus on it for a few minutes or a few hours. This is the kindling of attention, and it is the most delicate stage. Just as a strong breeze can put out a kindling fire, a distraction (like almost every notification on your phone) can break your target audience's focus.

In the final stage of attention—bonfire—you're focused on captivating what I call long attention—your audience's long-term interest in an idea, product, message, cause, work, and so on. When our long attention is engaged, we go beyond turning up the radio when our favorite artists are playing to buying their albums and attending their concerts. We go beyond watching *Game of Thrones* to focusing our attention on reading the entire book series. We go beyond aligning with a particular political view to spending time watching TV shows that express it, volunteering time to disseminate it, and donating money to candidates that support it. Long attention is the stage where you've truly captured your target audience's deep and undivided attention. Their attention is roaring into a bonfire that lasts.

The Seven Captivation Triggers

In *Captivology*, I draw on scientific research and interviews with experts in the field of psychology and cognition to examine what it takes to build a bonfire of attention. I also show how masters of attention—thought leaders from film director Steven Soderbergh to Facebook COO Sheryl Sandberg, who excel at capturing attention—move their target audiences through the three stages of attention. They ignite their audience's attention by being distinctive or disruptive; they kindle their audience's attention by keeping them engaged with a unique, novel, and useful message; and they create value for their target audience to generate long-term interest.

Based on my research and personal interviews with masters of attention, I have identified seven captivation triggers—psychological and scientific phenomena that trigger shockingly predictable and quantifiable responses in the mind. These triggers spark our brain's attention response systems by appealing to fundamental aspects of human nature. They are the essential tools for capturing attention for your ideas, products, causes, and more across all three stages of attention. These captivation triggers are the heart and soul of *Captivology*:

- Automaticity Trigger: Using specific sensory cues like colors, symbols, and sounds to capture attention based on automatic reaction to certain stimuli

- Framing Trigger: Adapting to or changing somebody's view of the world so they pay more attention to you

- Disruption Trigger: Violating people's expectations to change what they pay attention to

- Reward Trigger: Leveraging people's motivations for intrinsic and extrinsic rewards

- Reputation Trigger: Using the reputations of experts, authorities, and the crowd to instill trust and captivate audiences

- Mystery Trigger: Creating mystery, uncertainty, and suspense to keep an audience intrigued until the very end

- Acknowledgment Trigger: Fostering a deeper connection, because people tend to pay attention to those who provide them with validation and understanding

Chapters 2 through 8 focus on each of these captivation triggers, the science behind how each works, and case studies of how the masters of attention use the triggers to capture, maintain, and grow the attention of others.

What This Book Is About

While doing my research for this book, I noticed a common trend among the masters of attention—the Bill Gateses, Shigeru Miyamotos, and Sheryl Sandbergs of the world: they don't seek attention for themselves but for their projects and causes. You won't find Daniel Day-Lewis or Adele in the tabloid headlines because they focus on driving attention away from themselves and toward their films, albums, and charities.

"There's attention for the sake of being in the limelight, and then there's attention for the sake of what's extrinsic to you," Susan Cain, the best-selling author of *Quiet*, emphasized to me while I was writing *Captivology*. In her case, she needed to drive attention for her book and to promote the quiet revolution. Cain calls this a "passion-based approach" to capturing attention. As an introvert, she never seeks the spotlight, but she's found ways to bring attention to the things she cares about.

Captivology isn't about how to be loud, seek fame or fortune, or become the center of attention. Nor is this a book about how to keep focused in a world full of distractions or about the rise of ADHD. And this isn't a book on quick-and-easy marketing techniques or a scientific textbook on attention. There are other great books that tackle these subjects or take that approach.

Instead, *Captivology* is an exploration of how attention works, focused on the triggers that can attract the attention of whatever audience you are targeting, in any industry or situation. This book is the story of our relationship with attention and how capturing it can transform everything you do. It's about using science and practical techniques to create a bonfire of attention for your message, cause, product, or idea.

My hope is that by the time you finish *Captivology*, you will understand why certain topics always seem to dominate the news, why Super Mario became an icon while thousands of other video game characters have faded into obscurity, and why the world was obsessed with the mysterious disappearance of Malaysian Airlines Flight 370. Is *Captivology* going to turn you into the next Taylor Swift or Richard Branson? No, but I hope that by the end of this book, you will have the tools and knowledge you need to build long-lasting attention for you and your projects, ideas, and causes.

Above all, I hope *Captivology* resonates with anyone who has ever had a passion they wanted to promote. I hope my book helps you understand how to rise above the noisy crowd and be heard—all without having to shout.

Chapter 1

The Three Stages of Attention

•

S tanford's Jon Krosnick, a political science professor and the director of Stanford's Political Psychology Research Group, has studied hundreds of election results in Ohio and California. In almost every single race he and his colleagues studied—from local alderman elections to the 1996 and 2000 presidential elections—if a candidate's name was listed first on the ballot, it increased the amount of votes that candidate received by an average of 2 percent, sometimes more. Two points may not seem like much, but with a two-point swing, we would likely be talking about how President Mitt Romney would have handled Edward Snowden.

Krosnick's research doesn't show voters are lazy. Instead, it demonstrates just how limited our attention truly is. When we are juggling a job, a family, social and community activities, work e-mails and meetings, we might have enough attention left to learn about presidential or parliamentary candidates but probably not enough time or concern to learn about the candidates for, say, a school board election. With limited information, the human brain automatically looks for shortcuts to help it make decisions.

Being first has a positive association in our culture—first place, first in line, and so on. Thus, we unconsciously ascribe the positive quality of being first to the first name listed on the ballot, even though the candidate's placement on the ballot has nothing to do with his or her qualifications for office.

These mental shortcuts are known as heuristics. They are the quick general rules that guide our attention, consciously and unconsciously, both in the immediate moment and over the course of years or even decades. How do I find Waldo? Search for red-and-white stripes and ignore everything else. Which movie should I watch? Rely on the reviews from Rotten Tomatoes. We only have so much attention to give, and so we look for shortcuts to help us allocate that attention.

Not all attention is created equal, though. Some attention, like the kind you pay when somebody is shouting at a party, is fleeting. Think about what happens once the person shouting at the party stops: everybody simply directs their attention back to their previous conversations. People will turn their heads toward a disturbance, but their focus will fizzle out once the disturbance is gone. We shift our attention from one thing to the next.

For the purposes of this book, there are three types of attention—immediate, short, and long—and the shortcuts we use for each type of attention are different. For example, when we hear a person shout, we quickly (and often subconsciously) determine whether the person is just throwing a temper tantrum or having a medical emergency. If we determine it's the former, our attention quickly shifts away, but if it's the latter, our attention will ratchet to the next level as we focus and decide what to do next to help.

How does our brain help us manage our limited attention? And what role do the three types of attention play in our lives? To answer those questions, we need the help of some hookworm eggs.

Immediate Attention, or How to Analyze a Piece of . . .

At the most fundamental level, attention is our first line of defense against danger and threats. Maintaining an alert state is hardwired into all animals, including humans. We're especially adept at detecting moving people and animals, the most likely threats to our survival.

Researchers at the University of California, Santa Barbara, found evidence to support this notion. They asked subjects to look for changes in complex scenes—images of forests, groups of people in parks, etc. The images would appear, disappear, and reappear over and over again in 250-millisecond bursts until the subjects either identified changes or determined that nothing had changed.[1]

What was surprising was how much quicker and more accurate subjects were at identifying changing animals and people than plants or inanimate objects. After ten seconds of viewing the images, approximately 95 percent of subjects detected changes to people and 81 percent detected changes to animals. In contrast, subjects could detect changes to plants less than 60 percent of the time after ten seconds. That's a significant decrease in our ability to detect changes to people and animals versus changes to plants. This may not be surprising, actually—we're far more likely to be threatened by a pack of wolves than a clump of ferns.

One lesson we can take away from this study is that if you want to blend into the background, you should dress up as an oak tree. But perhaps the more important lesson here is that we are hardwired to search for and identify important changes to our environment. We are constantly shifting our attention from object to object, looking for anything that is dangerous, interesting, or novel until we decide to focus our attention on something. This is the point at which we shift from immediate to short attention.

Immediate attention is a bottom-up process—attention driven automatically, driven by the stimulus instead of by our consciousness. We will instinctively panic and duck at the sound of a gunshot, look up at a sky filled with bright-colored balloons, or gag at the smell of six-month-old rotting eggs, even if it's just for a brief moment. These reactions are controlled by our body's automatic responses and by sensory memory, a system that helps us store sights, sounds, smells, and other sensory inputs for a short period of time. This type of memory lasts no longer than a couple of seconds—just long enough for a smell or sound to be forgotten or moved into working memory.[2]

It isn't just sounds, colors, and smells we automatically react to, though—it's also our near-instantaneous mental and emotional impressions and gut reactions that help drive our immediate attention.

Take the case of Dr. Stephanie J. Krauth and a team of Swiss epidemiologists at the Swiss Tropical and Public Health Institute. They were researching ways to improve the diagnosis of helminth infection and better understand the growth and disintegration of hookworm eggs in human stool. Helminth infections (parasite infections) are rare in Western countries like Switzerland or the United States but are an especially serious problem in Africa and Southeast Asia. The researchers found some tricks for making more accurate diagnoses such as, among other things, icing stool samples, which they wanted to share with a wide audience of practitioners. But they knew that simply publishing the results of their study wouldn't receive much attention outside of the small group of scientists interested in tropical diseases. They needed to do something to captivate the attention of practitioners who could make a difference in affected areas.[3]

So how did they get people to immediately notice their work? By titling their paper "An In-Depth Analysis of a Piece of Sh*t," of course. The provocative and unconventional title alone was enough to get the study's findings published in *Smithsonian*, *RealClearScience*, *VICE*, and *io9*.

The novelty and emotional resonance of the paper's title captured attention immediately. Perhaps it's because the research shows that negative emotions—fear, anger, hatred, etc.—typically trump positive emotions when it comes to capturing immediate attention. Immediate attention is biased toward the perception of threats and novel stimuli.[4]

In the big scheme of things, immediate attention is the simplest type of attention to capture, which is why it's the "ignition" of attention. We are conditioned, for example, to react when somebody calls out our name. You can't control your reaction unless you're already aware somebody is about to call out your name—then you can think about it and ignore it or react consciously. Conscious focus and reaction, however, require a greater level of attention.

Short Attention and Novelty

Clive Wearing, a seventy-six-year-old gray-haired musician from the United Kingdom, may have the shortest attention span in the world.

In 1985, Clive was a successful conductor and keyboardist. He made music for the BBC Radio 3 and was a leading expert on Lassus and other Renaissance composers. That would all be taken away from him when he contracted herpes encephalitis. The disease attacked his brain, literally boring holes through the temporal, occipital, parietal, and frontal lobes of his brain. It completely destroyed his hippocampus, which is the part of the brain that coordinates the transfer of short-term memory into long-term memory.

"Clive really only has less than thirty seconds of memory, and sometimes it's as little as seven seconds," his wife, Deborah Wearing, states in a BBC documentary about his life and his condition. "It's as little as a sentence."

Clive now suffers from irreparable retrograde and anterograde amnesia. He can't form new memories, and his past is cloudy. He will forget what you asked him during his answer to your question. Every time he sees his wife, he jumps up, lifts her in the air, twirls her around, and kisses her. It's as if he's seeing her for the first time after a long trip, every single time.

His conversations go something like this:

Clive: How long have I been ill?

Deborah: Four months.

Clive: Four months? Is that F-O-R or F-O-U-R (ha-ha!)?

Deborah: F-O-U-R.

Clive: Well, I've been unconscious the whole time! What do you think it's like to be unconscious for . . . how long?

Deborah: Four months.

Clive: Four months! For months? Is that F-O-R or F-O-U-R?

Deborah: F-O-U-R.

Clive: I haven't heard anything, seen anything, smelled anything, felt anything, touched anything. How long?

Deborah: Four months.

Clive: . . . four months! It's like being dead. I haven't been conscious the whole time. How long's it been?[5]

Wearing is a famous case among memory researchers—he's the man without working memory. Without it, he is capable of only quick sensory and emotional reactions that last for a few seconds before he essentially resets. He is unable to move to the second stage of attention. He is unable to focus.

Short attention is all about focus. It's when we, at some conscious level, decide to allocate some of our time and concentration toward something. It is often triggered when we want to fixate on something new or novel; it's how we learn about our world, whether it's in the classroom, the conference hall, or the forest. This span of attention can be as short as a YouTube clip or as long as a *Lord of the Rings* movie. Most of the time, however, our short attention only lasts until the next distraction makes its appearance.

Why the focus on novelty? The answer may be as simple as dopamine, the neurotransmitter that controls the brain's reward centers, especially as it pertains to achievement or completing tasks. In a study on the role of dopamine in motivation and learning, Dr. Kent Berridge and Dr. Terry Robinson of the University of Michigan found that blocking dopamine in rats didn't stop them from "liking" something, but instead stopped them from "wanting" something. When Berridge and Robinson suppressed the dopamine of their rats, they found that the rats could still feel pleasure from eating a tasty snack, but they had zero motivation to do so. Dopamine is so vital to motivation that, without it, the rats didn't even want to eat and began to starve.[6]

In other words, a lack of dopamine doesn't inhibit pleasure, but instead affects motivation. This indirectly leads to less pleasure, of course—you can still enjoy chocolate without dopamine, but you might not be willing to leave your house and drive to the store to get it. That's why it's no coincidence that our brains release dopamine whenever we are exploring anything new or novel. It is absolutely necessary to our survival—without dopamine, we wouldn't be motivated to learn anything new. Short attention is the direct result of motivation. Without dopamine, the motivation to focus disappears.

"We seek novelty because novelty—and that type of exploratory behavior—allows you to find resources and mate and not be stuck in a rut," said Dr. Adam Gazzaley of the UCSF Neuroscience Imaging Center.[7] "That type of behavior presumably confers survival advantage."

To understand short attention, we have to understand the cognitive system that manages it. To do that, we have to explore one of the most fascinating aspects of our brain: working memory.

"Attention is the way we direct working memory resources," Dr. John Sweller of the University of New South Wales, a leading researcher in education psychology and cognitive load, told me. "The way you direct working memory, that's what you're attending to."[8]

Working memory is the cognitive system that manages short-term memories. It does this through a decision-making "central executive" that 1) chooses where to focus attention and 2) decides which short-term memories become long-term memories.

Under the central executive's command are three "slave systems"—auditory memory, visual memory, and an episodic buffer—that process and store short-term memories until the central executive can decide what to do with them.

The first two slave systems are dedicated to helping us temporarily remember what we hear and what we see. The first makes it possible to remember a phone number you heard until you have a chance to write it down. The auditory slave system is also called the phonological loop because remembering a set of numbers, a sound, or a sentence requires you to repeat it in your head over and over again until you no longer need it.[9] Short-term visual memory, on the other hand, tends to rely on prominent features—a color, a unique hairstyle, or in the case of *Where's Waldo?*, a striped red-and-white outfit. This is because working memory can store a finite number of visual details before we start forgetting details or start getting them wrong. Try remembering the facial features of your mother or significant other, and then try to do the same thing with a crowd you saw at Disneyland, and you can start to see where this becomes a problem. Enhancing unique features and removing distractions are key to visual attention.

The final slave system—the episodic buffer—takes the things you see, hear, and already know (past memories) and turns them into cohesive stories the mind can understand. Imagine if you watched *Return of the Jedi* without the audio or the backstory of the previous movies—it would make far less sense. The episodic buffer adds the context and ties everything together.[10]

What's important to remember about working memory is that it's only temporary storage. Just as a powerful breeze can blow out kindling, a powerful distraction can quickly erase everything in working memory, before any knowledge can be transferred to long-term memory. This defeats the entire purpose of attention, because memory drives attention, and attention drives memory.

If a teacher gives a lesson on calculus to amnesiac Clive Wearing, it will be as if the lesson never happened because Clive will remember absolutely nothing about it the next day. The same can be said for a student who daydreams through an entire lesson—she's going to fail the next test just as badly as someone with retrograde amnesia.

As William James, declared by many as the father of American psychology, wrote in his landmark 1890 text *The Principles of Psychology*, "We cannot deny that an object once attended to will remain in the memory, whilst one inattentively allowed to pass will leave no traces behind."[11]

As the ignition of attention, short attention is a vital component of our attentional system, but just like a small, sputtering fire, it dies out if there aren't more substantial logs nearby to fuel it. That's where the third type of attention—long attention—comes into play, when the things we learn during short attention become the long-term memories that guide our interests and our actions.

Long Attention, or Why Do We Buy Beyoncé Albums?

On December 13, 2013, Beyoncé Knowles-Carter dropped a bomb-shell that changed the music industry. With zero marketing and promotion, Beyoncé released her fifth studio album exclusively on iTunes, announcing it with a single photo on Instagram on a Friday at midnight.

The result of her surprise album shocked the establishment. In three hours, Beyoncé's self-titled album sold 80 thousand copies. In one day, it sold 430 thousand copies. By day three, it had broken iTunes records with an astounding 828,733 digital copies sold, topping the charts in 104 countries in the process.

"I miss that immersive experience; now people only listen to a few seconds of song on the iPods and they don't really invest in the whole experience," the music legend declared when asked about her surprise album launch. "It's all about the single, and the hype. It's so much that gets between the music and the art and the fans. I felt like, I don't want anybody to get the message, when my record is coming out. I just want this to come out when it's ready and from me to my fans."[12]

Record labels typically spend millions of dollars on the marketing and promotion of albums. Labels release singles, drive up preorders, spend on radio promotion, and get their artists to perform on *Saturday Night Live*. Beyoncé did none of these things, and she was able to beat the likes of Lady Gaga, Eminem, Kanye West, and Robin Thicke.

Why was Beyoncé able to perform this seeming feat of wizardry? There are some factors that clearly stand out. For one thing, the novelty and disruptiveness of her surprise album launch generated massive media coverage, along with 1.2 million tweets in under twelve hours. The album came with a whopping seventeen music videos, making it even more enticing to buy. Fans also couldn't buy singles individually—they had to buy the full album. And finally, the album itself received critical acclaim from most reviewers.[13]

These are all good deductions. But out of all the explanations for the success of Ms. Knowles-Carter's fifth album, *Variety* columnist and respected music industry analyst Bob Lefsetz had the most poignant explanation: "Beyoncé has put in years of hard work and hit tracks to get to the point where people pay attention." In Lefsetz's opinion, the success of Beyoncé's newest album stemmed from the years of hard work and audience building she has done to get to the point where millions are willing to pay attention to her *by default*.[14]

The media loves to talk about overnight successes. Pinterest, *Angry Birds*, and Psy's "Gangnam Style" all seemed to come out of nowhere to become billion-dollar companies and international superstars. But what if I told you Pinterest was founded in 2008, three years before it became an "overnight sensation"?[15] Did you know *Angry Birds* was the fifty-second game released by game studio Rovio?[16] And did you know that Psy had been topping the charts in South Korea for nearly a decade before his horse dancing swept the globe?

The truth is that most "viral" moments are years in the making. Beyoncé doesn't go for quick wins—she has carefully developed her craft, her image, and her reputation to create long-term interest in everything she does, from her albums to her commercials to her clothing line. While other celebrities resort to "leaked" sex tapes and crazy antics to even get mentioned by the media, the Mark Zuckerbergs, Tom Hankses, and Beyoncés of the world have built attention that will last the test of time.

Long attention is our ability to focus our attention and interest for a prolonged period of time on a person, product, or idea—the way fans have developed long-term interest in Beyoncé. A fan may not pay attention to *Angry Birds* on a daily basis, but when Rovio releases a new game, you can bet it'll shoot to the top of the App Store charts. All Apple has to do in order to launch a frenzy is send a few invites out to the media.

Why? Why does our attention seem to fixate on a small group of interests? The answer lies, once again, in our brain's miraculous memory structure. Long attention is influenced by the knowledge and experiences that reside in our long-term memories. They help guide our attention and interests.

"What you already know directs what you attend to," Sweller said. He used the smartphone as an example. "If you know how to use a smartphone," Sweller noted, "the way in which you use that smartphone is directly different than someone trying to learn how to use it. . . . If you're dealing with something you're familiar with, attention comes from long-term memory."[17]

Unlike short attention, familiarity is the key to long attention. We build shortcuts for the activities and ideas we're familiar with. In some cases, these familiar occurrences and daily routines become instinctive habits. You don't have to think in order to brush your teeth or take a shower, but you know you need to do both, and you know how to do them almost automatically. We know which of our friends are fans of soccer or football from years of experience, so we know who to call when the World Cup or the Bears-Packers game is on.

The secret to creating a successful lesson plan, advertising campaign, or long-term relationship is finding effective ways to capture short attention and then transitioning into long attention. As the masters of attention I interviewed for this book will attest, it's not enough to have an audience watch an entertaining ad—it has to generate followers, fans, and most importantly, sales. You can't make a bonfire with just kindling—you need plenty of logs and patience too.

To better understand the three types of attention and how the masters use them to capture attention for their causes, it's worth looking at how one particular company successfully leveraged them to build a bonfire of attention for its popular product: Super Mario.

The Immediate, Short, and Long of Mario

Shigeru Miyamoto is a slender, sixty-two-year-old Japanese man with a childlike smile and a head full of black hair that parts on his forehead. He may not seem like it on first glance, but this quiet and unassuming man is one of the world's most successful masters of attention. Among gamers, he is known as one of the fathers of modern video gaming.

In the late 1970s, Miyamoto joined Nintendo as an artist, back when it was still moving away from its origins as a playing card company and toward its future in video games. He helped build one of the company's first games, *Radar Scope*, which was successful in Japan but not in the United States. He then moved on to create the two characters that would change his career: Donkey Kong and Mario.

I wanted to uncover why Mario, a chubby plumber with a thick mustache and an endearing Italian accent, had become one of the most recognized and popular characters in all of fiction, so I went directly to the source. When I first met Shigeru Miyamoto in a white room in Los Angeles, he wore a simple pair of black jeans, black shoes, a T-shirt with the characters from Nintendo's Pikmin series—which Miyamoto created—and a gray-patterned jacket with the Pikmin logo. It was lunchtime at Electronic Entertainment Expo—more commonly known as E3, the largest and most prominent of the gaming industry conventions—so he had brought a rice roll with him to eat, while his translator had a far more American meal: chicken wings and pulled pork.

The first stage of attention—immediate attention—is all about reaction, recognition, and standing out. So I asked Miyamoto what made Mario so recognizable and distinctive. In other words, why does he stand out? Mario's unique features, I learned, weren't simply by chance.

"The origin of Mario came from the limitations of the hardware at the time," Miyamoto told me through his translator. "We only had sixteen dots by sixteen dots to draw Mario."

The first Mario needed to look human and attract attention with just 256 total pixels. So Miyamoto and his team added a few features that would make his human features stand out. The first was a big nose, "to give him a distinctive flair," and a mustache to define that nose. Next was his head. Creating unique hair was almost impossible with 256 pixels of space, so the Nintendo team gave him a red cap. And finally, to make him stand out even further, Mario received red overalls instead of a shirt. Mario would trade his red overalls for a blue pair after *Super Mario Bros.*

The unique look has stuck. His big nose, red cap, and blue overalls are iconic and instantly recognizable. But having a distinctive character is only the beginning. Miyamoto also traces the plumber's success to the new styles of gameplay that each generation of Mario game promotes.

"He is representative of what is the latest and greatest of every generation of hardware," Miyamoto said. As you might recall, short attention relies on focus and novelty. A game that cannot keep a player's focus isn't a game worth playing. Typical Mario games have the player focus on achieving an immediate task—reach the flag pole, defeat one of Bowser's minions, etc.—and immediately rewards the player for each achievement. One hundred gold coins mean a new life, and seventy stars will let you fight Bowser in *Super Mario 64*. The dopamine flows almost immediately.

The best game designers are masters of short attention. They find ways to motivate players to reach an achievable goal and then go to the next one. It only takes a few minutes to get through a single stage in Mario. Imagine how many people would quit if it took an hour or even a day to complete a level.

Gameplay alone doesn't make a player loyal to the Mario franchise, though. The final stage of attention, long attention, relies on interest and a certain level of familiarity.

"The other element of Mario that helped make him more popular was the fact that we didn't want to make him into a superhero," Miyamoto explained to me during our conversation. "He was more an everyman. You can see that in his character design—he's just some guy, you can't tell how old he is. That appealed more to people."

In his book *Super Mario: How Nintendo Conquered America*, author Jeff Ryan points out that Mario is a "one-size-fits-all hero." He's simple and relatable. He's often mute in his game, allowing us to envision Mario as "our eternal alter ego."[18]

Mario games are also familiar, despite the new gameplay mechanics that appear in each game. His mission is often the same: save the princess from the evil Bowser. Mario's powers—his jumping ability, his fire flowers, and his mushrooms—are constants. So are the goombas, gold coins, stars, and koopas. Just enough things are different from game to game to capture short attention while certain elements are familiar enough to retain long attention over the course of years. Different games, same hero.

I came across this pattern time and time again during my years of research for this book. Mario's eye-popping features capture immediate attention; novel and enjoyable gameplay and attainable rewards stimulate working memory and capture short attention; likable characters and familiar figures keep Mario in our long-term memory and thus capture long attention. Miyamoto patiently built his bonfire over decades until it could be seen on the other side of the world.

Harnessing the Three Types of Attention

When you're trying to capture the attention of others—whether it's a classroom full of students or dispersed readers of your blog—you must remember that they can only pay attention to a small number of people and ideas. With thousands of distractions and priorities competing for your audience's attention, it's easy to see why their focus can be so fleeting.

To build a bonfire of attention for your message, you have to capture your audience's immediate, short, and long attention. First, you need to elicit a reaction by being distinctive or disruptive. Once you have your audience's immediate attention, you need something unique, novel, and useful to keep their working memory focused on your message. Having secured their short attention, you must create value for your audience to capture their long-term attention.

The captivation triggers I describe in the next seven chapters are ideal tools to use to capture these three types of attention. The triggers—Automaticity, Framing, Disruption, Reward, Reputation, Mystery, and Acknowledgment—will help you build a bonfire of attention by progressing from capturing your audience's immediate attention to mesmerizing their short attention and finally to captivating their long attention.

Keep the three types of attention—and the three stages for building a bonfire of attention—in mind as you read the rest of this book. Doing so will help you better understand not only how to capture the attention of others but also how your own attention works.

Chapter 2

Automaticity Trigger

•

Ophrys apifera, like many flowering plants, pollinates by attracting insects and hoping those insects spread its pollen—a process called entomophily. Better known as the bee orchid, *Ophrys apifera* is unique because it relies on the assistance of just one species—the long-horned bee—to spread its pollen for reproduction.[1]

Flowering plants find many ways to attract bees, wasps, and other insects to their pollen. Most use bright colors to advertise that they have nectar—an important food for most insects. But the bee orchid uses a more thorough tactic to attract the long-horned bees. The center of the orchid's flower, between its beautiful pink-lavender petals, hosts a furry protrusion that has the colors, shape, smell, and even texture of a bee—more specifically, a female bee.

By mimicking the pheromones of the female bee, the bee orchid attracts eager male bees in order to convince them to land and attempt to mate with their flowers. The short, furry, and smooth hairs running along the flower's protrusion further signals to the male bee that it has found a willing female bee. Once the bee has attempted to do its business, or has figured out that its female bee isn't a bee at all, it flies off to another bee orchid and spreads the orchid's pollen.

The bee orchid uses this tactic—pseudocopulation—in order to trick bees into mating with it. In fact, the entire genus of *Ophrys* is incredibly adept at using pseudocopulation to spread its pollen. The bumblebee orchid's protrusion is darker and fatter; the fly orchid is thinner and has what look like wings; the early spider orchid is a darker brown and contains distinctive markings that make it look like an arachnid. Each one has found a way to use sensory cues to attract its insect of choice.

All plants and animals—humans included—rely on sensory cues for focusing, directing, and misdirecting attention. Fireflies rely on bioluminescence to attract potential mates, while the bright yellow of a wasp is an instantaneous warning for us to back away and keep our distance. The leaf insect purposely shuns attention by hiding in plain sight. Some even have frayed edges that look like bite marks; when it comes to fooling predators, the details can mean the difference between life and death.

While we humans don't use illuminating rears to attract mates or bright colors to ward off predators, we rely heavily on sensory cues hardwired into our brain to help us direct our attention. More often than not, this happens unconsciously and in unexpected ways. Men will sit closer to a woman and ask more intimate questions solely because she is wearing the color red,[2] and if you want people to better taste the sweetness of a drink, all you have to do is drop some green food coloring in it.[3]

What's happening? How does something as simple as a color or a shape influence the way we pay attention?

The Automaticity Trigger

If I were to show you a picture of a lion and a picture of an antelope, which one would you pay more attention to?

In fact, this is what Jessica Yorzinski and her collaborators at Duke University and University of California, Davis, tested. They tracked the eye movements of subjects as they looked at sets of images. One set had lions and antelope; another had snakes and lizards. Subjects were asked to identify a target animal in a three-by-three square array of images. They included one target animal and seven "distractors"—the middle box was left empty. It looked something like this:

Antelope	Antelope	Antelope
Antelope		Lion
Antelope	Antelope	Antelope

The result? Yorzinski and her team found that subjects not only located dangerous animals faster but also that their gaze lasted longer on the lions and snakes, even when they were asked to search for antelope and lizards. Their attention automatically focused on potential threats and ignored everything else.[4]

This is how our brain is programmed. We ignore everything that isn't necessary to our goals, because if we didn't, we'd quickly succumb to directed attention fatigue (DAF)—a phenomenon that occurs with exposure to too many stimuli. When people experience DAF, they start feeling mentally fatigued, are more distracted, make more mistakes, and are generally more irritable. Imagine if everything you saw, felt, or touched was processed by your consciousness, morning and night, with no capability to focus or concentrate—you'd go insane too.

That's why we rely on salient sensory cues to warn us of danger and alert us to new situations that require our attention. Our brain is always looking for these sensory cues—colors, movements, sounds, textures, smells, and other sensations—to help us figure out what we need to pay attention to throughout the day.

Not all cues are made equal, though. A man wearing a black suit in a crowd will be far less effective at generating attention than a man wearing a red suit. We have a tendency to shift our attention toward cues that stick out from the crowd. Is that rustling in the brush just the wind, or is it a predator preparing to pounce? We need to be aware of disturbances in our environment so we can investigate and decide if we need to fight, flee, or go back to our daily business. At its core, looking for cues that stand out is a survival mechanism. As a result, we are more likely to remember *isolated* or *unique* sensory cues. This is known as the Von Restorff effect, named after psychiatrist and pediatrician Hedwig von Restorff.[5]

The following is a list of foods. I want you to take twenty seconds and attempt to memorize these words, then write down as many of these as you can on a piece of paper.

Celery

Zucchini

Mango

Cheese

Mary Poppins

Milk

Broccoli

Eggs

Meat loaf

Quinoa

Apple

Sushi

Blueberry

Chocolate

Salmon

Coffee

Pineapple

It's incredibly difficult for most people to remember a list of items this long, especially if they're only given twenty seconds, but I bet two items made your list: mango and Mary Poppins. Why? Because isolated items—things that stand out—are more likely to be encoded to memory. In this case, mango stands out visually and Mary Poppins stands out contextually (it doesn't belong on this list of foods). In a world where we must function with scarce working memory, instinctive cues are often the first thing our attention encounters.

This is where the first captivation trigger comes into play. The Automaticity Trigger is our unconscious tendency to shift our attention toward the sights, sounds, and other sensory cues important to our safety and survival. The bright yellow of a nest of wasps or the loud bang of a gunshot activates our attention automatically because we need to respond quickly to potential threats and opportunities.

The Automaticity Trigger is what sparks the first stage of attention—immediate attention. It's the jolt that forces people to turn their attention toward you. Because of that, it is essential to harness the power of this trigger if you want to start capturing attention for your ideas or products.

The Automaticity Trigger can capture our attention in two distinct ways. The first is through contrast—when a sensory cue captures our attention because it simply stands out. Contrast is, for example, why mango stands out in the list from earlier—the word visually contrasts with its environment. Contrast is the reason why our eyes are naturally attracted to a flashlight in the darkness and why a loud boom on a quiet afternoon diverts our attention.

The second way the Automaticity Trigger captures our attention is through association—when a sensory cue draws our immediate attention because of a mental association (or lack thereof) we have with that cue. Mary Poppins stands out on our previous list because we don't associate that term with foods, and thus it sticks out like a sore thumb. A wasp's yellow or the deep crimson of blood activates our attention because we know both colors are associated with danger at a subconscious level.

Throughout the rest of this chapter, we will explore how the Automaticity Trigger works and how you can leverage it by appealing to key aspects of your audience's senses, especially sight, hearing, and touch. To do that, we need to first explore the most powerful visual sensory cue of them all: color.

What Is the Color of Attention?

You're hiking through the forest when unexpectedly you fall into a small river and lose your cell phone. You need it—that's how you were going to call your ride home! You're far away from where you started, so you make your way to a nearby road. Now you need to wave a car down to make a phone call before it gets dark. What color shirt should you wear if you want somebody to pull over? Does it even matter?

In a study published in *Color Research & Application*, French professor Dr. Nicolas Guéguen asked five women in their early twenties to pose as hitchhikers and attempt to get unsuspecting drivers to stop and pick them up. The key variable: the color of the

T-shirt each woman wore changed. Guéguen and his team tested black, white, red, blue, green, and yellow to see if any color had a discernible advantage on the attention of drivers.[6]

The results were fascinating. Female drivers noticed and stopped for a female hitchhiker 9.6 percent of the time if the hitchhiker wore a yellow shirt and 9 percent for a red shirt. But a hitchhiker wearing a green shirt would only get stops 5.28 percent of the time. Black, at 5.98 percent, didn't fare much better (blue was 6.69 percent and white was 7.12 percent).

More interesting, though, was how male drivers responded to the female hitchhikers. Red was in a league of its own. 20.77 percent of male drivers—one in five—stopped to pick up the female hitchhikers in red shirts. Yellow (14.89 percent) was only marginally higher than blue (14.11 percent) and white (13.98 percent), while black and green once again performed the worst.

Guéguen's study perfectly demonstrates the two elements of the Automaticity Trigger: contrast and association. When female hitchhikers tried to get the attention of female drivers, the reason those drivers pulled over seemed to be about contrast. Red and yellow simply pop out visually when you place them against the backdrop of gray roads. On the other hand, contrast didn't seem to play much of a role when it came to female hitchhikers capturing the attention of male drivers. In the latter case, the unconscious association the male drivers had between romance and the color red likely kicked in, drawing their eye almost automatically.

The color red is particularly adept at capturing attention in romantic situations. Another study conducted by Dr. Andrew Elliot at the University of Rochester found that simply placing a thick red border around a photo of a person increased how attractive a stranger perceived the person in the photo.[7] In other words, all it takes to make the opposite sex think you're more attractive is to put on some red. The theories for why we feel more attraction to those wearing red vary wildly, but some psychologists suggest it's due to the fact that humans often flush red when they're sexually aroused or interested.

Perhaps the first lesson we can take away is that, when you're building any type of campaign that involves romance or sex, red is the color of choice—both because it pops out to the eye (contrast) and because it stimulates us unconsciously (association). But the more important lesson here is that, when it comes to color and attention, you have to consider both whether a color stands out amongst its surroundings and what mental associations we have with that color.

Let's dive deeper into contrast and how we can leverage color contrasts to unconsciously direct attention.

Contrast: Albino Animals Don't Survive Long in the Wild

In 2010, Canadian user experience (UX) designer Dan McGrady started CareLogger, a pet project to make it easy for diabetics to track their health. The project was bootstrapped, so maximizing sign-ups was key for CareLogger to become sustainable. McGrady, like all good UX designers, tested every little detail of his landing pages through A/B testing—a methodology for testing the impact of small changes to a website or app by randomly giving different users either the current design or the "new" design to see which has better conversion or engagement. In one fascinating A/B experiment, McGrady tested only the color of his sign-up button. One button was green, and the other was red. Both buttons were placed on a light-gray background.[8]

Did something as simple as color affect the attention of potential customers? The answer was a resounding yes—the red button converted 34 percent more sign-ups than the green button. The outcome was eye-popping.

This result won't surprise user experience and user interface designers—they're profoundly aware of the impact a single color change can have on user behavior. Marketing optimization firm WiderFunnel once worked with enterprise giant SAP to improve its pay-per-click advertising conversion rate for its software trial download landing page. SAP wanted to improve conversions by 20 percent. WiderFunnel made a series of changes to the software site's landing page, including the addition of a giant orange "Download Now" button, which boosted conversions by 32.5 percent.[9]

WiderFunnel likes to call this button BOB—the Big Orange Button. Most website designers will tell you that, when you want somebody to click a button, it should be red, orange, or yellow—one of the warm colors. If you need to direct your audience's attention to a specific button, link, or icon, using bright colors to strongly contrast a key item with the rest of the page is always the wise course of action. The reason why this works has to do with our natural physiology.

Dr. Peter König, a German professor of neurobiopsychology at the University of Osnabrück, was curious about how humans visually process color features and, more importantly, what factors make a color distinctive to the human eye—especially when it comes to natural scenes. Previous research had indicated that color saturation—the vividness of a color—was the best indicator for predicting which objects we fixate our attention on, but König and his team of researchers wanted to go a step farther. They wondered, *Which color contrasts attract attention the most?*

Over the course of three experiments, König and his team showed subjects a series of unaltered photographs of the Ugandan rainforest along with photographs in which various colors were either removed or manipulated. These scenes had no man-made objects—just berries, leaves, trees, and other scenes from the Kibale Forest. In the first experiment, three types of photos were presented to subjects—unaltered, photos with the red and green removed, and photos with the blue and yellow removed. Subjects in the second experiment were shown twelve different scenes with different color hues. The final experiment tested the original images from the first experiment but with the colors altered and with subjects who had partial color blindness. The researchers used eye-tracking software to measure the level of attentiveness of each subject and to track where their visual attention shifted.[10]

The results are hard to dispute, especially when you actually see the photos with your own eyes. One photo with prominent red berries hanging from a bush, for example, became even more vivid when blue and yellow colors were removed. In the photo with the red and green colors removed, however, it's completely impossible to spot the berries and it's incredibly difficult to distinguish any discerning features in the photograph.

The experiments confirmed this effect—saturation and contrast were higher with images missing blue and yellow hues (red was easier to distinguish), making it easier for participants to spot important items like the berries. Participants fixated on the same locations far more often with images lacking blue and yellow than they did with images lacking red and green—or even the original images. Even partially color-blind subjects showed a greater tendency to fixate on the same points when the images lacked blue and yellow— being red-green color-blind didn't stop them from spotting important information like the berries.

Color contrast is how our brain finds and attends to relevant stimuli. In the wild, life-giving red berries stand out against the green of grasses and forests. If leaves were naturally purple instead of green, then red would be a terrible color for capturing attention. This also explains why red, yellow, and orange website buttons stand out—they contrast better against the white and gray backgrounds that make up the vast majority of websites. All you need to do to confirm this is open up a product page on Amazon.com, known for its optimization techniques, and find the yellow "Add to Cart" and orange "Buy Now with 1-Click" buttons.

Animals, of course, have jived with the attention-grabbing power of color contrast for centuries. The cuttlefish has the unique capability of mimicking the complex color patterns of its surroundings despite the fact that it is completely color-blind. It's nearly impossible to see one on the sea floor because it will turn not just brown but sandy brown, complete with different shades of brown to mimic different grains of sand. When an animal—or a hunter in the woods, for that matter—wants to go unnoticed, it utilizes camouflage to blend in with its surroundings, color being the key feature.[11]

On the other hand, when Pope Francis released two pure-white "peace doves" from his window, they were immediately attacked by a hooded crow and a yellow-legged gull—an event some called a bad omen. In reality, the doves stand out against backgrounds of green and brown, and most every other color the ground or buildings around them might be, making them easy prey. In general, albino animals don't survive as long in the wild because they stick out like a sore thumb in their natural environments.[12]

So what do you need to do if you want to capture attention by utilizing color? The answer is to pick the right contrast. If you want to capture attention for your product, create packaging with colors that pop against the colors of the products you're likely to be stocked next to (Everyone else is blue? Go with orange!). If you want people to notice you at a bar, wear bright colors that contrast with the typical dark lighting of most bars (red is your friend in these situations). If you want people to pay attention to you at a professional conference, try refraining from wearing a powder-blue collared shirt—from my personal experience, it's the color all finance people wear under their suits (I personally like purples and pinks).

And if you want to get people to buy your stuff, pick a color that is the opposite of your website's background color. In one of its many client case studies, optimization firm Unbounce changed a dark-blue "Add to Cart" button on a gray background to bright green—

not orange or yellow—as an experiment for a large European retailer. The result: the bright-green "Add to Cart" button, which anybody would say pops out on the page, improved conversions by an incredible 35.81 percent. If you want something to stand out, find the one item you want people to focus their attention upon, and give it the most prominent contrast of color. In most cases, bright colors with high saturation and warm tones will do the job.[13]

There are great online tools for checking color contrasts if you don't trust your eyes. Das Plankton's contrast tool not only lets you visually see the contrast of various color combinations, but it also tests for color deficiencies and lets you know the contrast ratio (a measure of how much contrast there is) of the colors you're testing.[*] WebAIM has a simpler tool for checking the contrast ratio of two different colors and whether they pass or fail the Web Content Accessibility Guidelines.[**]

Of course, contrast is just one element to consider when it comes to color. After all, you can't wear orange or bright green everywhere—you're going to eventually piss people off or wear people out. And the reason for that leads us to the powerful and unconscious associations we have with color.

Associations: The Difference Between the Red Pill and the Blue Pill

Whenever I can, I like to fly Virgin America. It's among the most enjoyable experiences available in the skies. For me, though, it isn't the onboard entertainment or Wi-Fi that sells me—lots of airlines

---

[*]   You can find the actual Das Plankton contrast tool here: http://www.dasplankton.de/ContrastA/.
[**] Here's the URL of the WebAIM contrast checker: http://webaim.org/resources/contrastchecker/.

have those. It's the purple mood lighting that envelops the cabin that I love most.

Mood lighting isn't just something that makes you feel good—it's something that can literally save your life. In Nara, Japan—a few hundred miles west of Tokyo—the local officials were looking for a solution to a growing crime problem. Nara's city officials had a plan, though. After hearing about the impact blue lights had on crime in Glasgow, Scotland, the city installed a series of blue lights at crime hot spots and train stations. The result was a 9 percent drop in crime, but more astounding was that suicides at Nara's train stations completely ceased. Between 2006 and 2008, zero people committed suicide under the blue lights.[14]

There likely isn't one single reason why blue lighting stops crime and reduces suicides. Several studies since the 1970s have found that subjects exposed to red and yellow scored high on the State-Trait Anxiety Inventory, a psychological test to measure a subject's anxiety, but scored far lower when exposed to blue and green. Another study found that narrow-bandwidth blue light proved effective at treating seasonal affective disorder. Another theory states that blue, a color commonly associated with police and law enforcement, may also serve as an unconscious deterrent to crime. Across cultures, blue is the color of calm.[15]

Nara's blue light experiment demonstrates the profound effect color has on our psyche, but how do we apply this knowledge to effectively capture other people's attention? Should we be coloring our offices blue? The answer to that question isn't as simple as choosing the right color contrast. You also have to consider the associations a color has with your audience, or you may end up capturing the wrong kind of attention.

Take red for example. While red's association with romance and sex is common across most cultures, red also symbolizes purity in India, good luck in China, and death or vitality in certain parts of

Africa. And while green reminds Westerners of nature and tranquillity, it represents exorcism and infidelity in China. Seriously, don't use the color green for your product packaging in China.[16]

With all that said, there are some general rules for using color that apply universally. We already talked about the first a little: blue is the color of calm. In a study published in the *Journal of Experimental Psychology: General,* Patricia Valdez and UCLA's Albert Mehrabian found that blue, blue green, green, purple blue, red purple, and purple were perceived as the most pleasant colors or color combinations, while green yellow and yellow rated as the least pleasant. The results were "highly consistent," and the relationship between colors and their emotional reactions were "highly predictable."[17]

The second general rule is that if you want to increase excitement, stimulation, or arousal, warm colors are the tools you should use. Scientists at the University of Amsterdam found that a patient's reaction to a drug—even a placebo—was affected by just the color of the drug. Red, yellow, and orange pills had more stimulating effects, while green and blue pills had a more sedative effect on patients. The *mere perception* of a drug varied by its color, and that was enough to influence its effect on the body. If you want to make your friends feel more energetic, you might want to expose them to more red and orange.[18]

You see this kind of color cuing all the time in nature. The golden poison frog clearly stands out from its muddy surroundings (it lives in damp rainforests), but predators know that its bright-yellow skin is a warning to avoid it at all costs. After all, ingesting just one milligram of its poison will not only kill you, but it will take out a dozen of your friends as well.

Color associations don't just affect our moods—they also affect our perceptions of a brand, so considering what each color means to the average person is vital when you're making artwork, advertisements, or websites. In a study published in the *Journal of the Academy of Marketing Science*, researchers found that a person's assessment of the likability, familiarity, and sincerity of a brand dramatically varied by simply manipulating the color of a fictional logo. The study found the following positive correlations between colors and brand associations. Each color list is ordered from strongest to weakest positive correlation:

Sincerity: White, pink, yellow (Orange was the least sincere color.)

Excitement: Red, orange, black (Brown had the largest negative correlation.)

Competence: Blue, red (I was surprised to learn that yellow had the strongest negative correlation with competence.)

Sophistication: Black, purple, pink (Orange was the least sophisticated color.)

Ruggedness: Brown (The correlation is off the charts. On the other hand, purple had the largest negative correlation, followed by yellow.)[19]

It's important to note that this particular study consisted of students who primarily identified as Americans—71 percent identified with American culture, 16 percent identified with Asian cultures, and 13 percent identified with other cultures. The most attention-grabbing colors—at least mentally—can vary from culture to culture. You have to not only pick attention-grabbing colors but find ones that match your audience as well.

How do you pick the right colors, though? While there is no sure-fire solution, David McCandless's book *Information Is Beautiful* has one of the most complete charts mapping the correlations between colors and their emotional associations across cultures. It's the best color-correlation chart I've been able to find, and it serves as a great reference. I've embedded his chart, a link to his book, and a simple color-correlation tool at www.Captivology.com/color.

And finally, it isn't just the color that matters when it comes to leveraging the Automaticity Trigger to capture attention—the brightness and saturation matter as well. The Valdez/Mehrabian emotion-color study also found that increases in color saturation correlated with an increase in arousal and dominance (emotions like anger). Increases in brightness, on the other hand, correlated with increases in pleasure and sharp decreases in dominance. And the *Academy of Marketing Science* study came to a similar conclusion: high saturation increased a brand's perceived excitement, competence, and ruggedness but was negatively correlated with sophistication and sincerity.

If you want to capture people's attention by making them experience the feeling of control and dominance, then use colors with high saturation—whether it's in the packaging of your products, in the clothes you are wearing (I suggest this when you try to persuade your boss to green-light one of your ideas), or in the promotional collateral that you design for your next campaign. If you want to capture their attention by increasing their sense of pleasure, then increase the color brightness of any color cue you use.

When it comes to color, contrast is the best tool for capturing attention, but considering the way your audience will respond to the saturation and brightness of color is critical too.

Colors aren't the only visual cues that matter when it comes to attention, though. Other visual cues have the power to simplify a complicated message through the power of association.

Why Did a Symbol Make Us Care About Heartbleed?

Software bugs aren't inherently interesting to the general public. They are often technical, and all the user has to do is wait for the developers to issue an update with the fix. Very few of them really deserve your attention. But a vulnerability in OpenSSL—the open-source protocol that provides security for the sensitive communication of information between your browser and the servers of Facebook, Google, Yahoo, and many of the largest websites in the world—is different.

Researchers at Google and cybersecurity firm Codenomicon found such a bug in OpenSSL. It allowed a developer with basic software knowledge to read the memory of a server through an extension of OpenSSL that sends pings between a browser and a server during a secure connection—also known as the heartbeat extension—to keep that connection alive. Theoretically, a hacker could use the bug to retrieve user passwords, credit card numbers, and even a server's private keys. Worse yet, the bug had been hiding in the OpenSSL code since early 2012. People needed to know about the bug so they could change their passwords and website owners could update their servers to a bug-free version of SSL. Otherwise, the consequences could have been catastrophic.[20]

The bug's official name—CVE–2014–0160—isn't exactly memorable, though. So Codenomicon did something unique—it gave the OpenSSL bug its own branding. This involved three things: a name, a symbol, and a website. One of the engineers dubbed it "Heartbleed"—referencing the leak in the heartbeat extension— and quickly created a simple, symmetrical blood-red heart with five blood drips coming from its base. The accompanying site— Heartbleed.com—was filled with a straightforward Q&A on the bug, how it worked, and why it was a serious threat to Internet security.

"This huge vulnerability needed a striking mark," Codenomi-con's Leena Snidate, who designed the logo, told *Fast Company*. "The colour choice was immediate for me—deep blood red."

When the bug was publicly announced, the news spread every-where. The logo—red, simple, distinctive, and symmetrical—was embedded on almost every major news site and blog in the world. Within a week, thousands of sites had patched the Heartbleed bug, and millions received the warning that they needed to change their passwords. Not since the infamous Y2K problem had a software bug captured the attention of the public so vividly and quickly.

Symbols are another visual cue, much like color, that capture our immediate attention. They captivate us through the associations we have with those symbols (unlike color, which relies more on con-trast). One study conducted by researchers at Duke University and the University of Waterloo, demonstrates this phenomenon. The re-searchers briefly showed one group of subjects the iconic Apple logo and another group IBM's blue-striped logo. The researchers then asked the subjects to come up with as many possible uses they could for a brick and write them down.[21]

Even brief exposure to the logos had a major impact on creativ-ity. Subjects exposed to the Apple logo were able to come up with significantly more uses—up to 33 percent more on average—for the brick than the people who saw the IBM logo, even after a short break between seeing the logos and doing the brick brainstorm. In a follow-up experiment in the same study, the researchers exposed subjects to the Disney Channel logo and the E! Channel logo and administered a social norms test. Exposure to the Disney Channel logo, which was rated by pilot-test participants as an honest and sin-cere logo, increased the number of honest responses. It's surprising on one level that these associations had an impact on behavior, but what's even more surprising is that subjects were making these as-sociations subconsciously.

This is known as the priming effect. In his book *Thinking, Fast and Slow,* famed psychologist Daniel Kahneman explains that our brain is an "associative machine" that attaches meanings and associations unconsciously to different words, ideas, images, and even colors. If I were to make you read a paragraph about aging, balding, and the state of Florida, you might find yourself walking slower and more gingerly, Kahneman argues.[22] If you're a reader of books like *Blink,* you already know that there are a lot of unconscious influences that affect our thinking and behavior. We know that Apple is creative, red is romantic and dangerous, and Florida is filled with old people (sorry, Floridians!). Symbols pull several of these associative machines into one place.

There are two ways to grab attention with symbols. The first is to harness preexisting associations. In the case of Heartbleed, a deep-red logo dripping with blood screams, "Danger! You need to pay attention to this bug!" better than any blog post ever could have. Our associations with red and dripping blood fill in the blanks automatically.

Our deep-seated associations with popular symbols is also the reason why you shouldn't reinvent the wheel when it comes to web or mobile design. The play button, the camera icon, the red notification bubble—we've already learned these associations through the use of hundreds of web products. Trying to be clever by creating your own symbols can backfire when people are expecting a video to start playing when they click a sideways triangle.*

The second method for capturing attention through the power of symbols is to develop new associations through consistency and branding. The Apple logo didn't originally stand for creativity and great design, but it gained that association through years of subtle

---

* The Noun Project (www.thenounproject.com) is a collection of thousands of simple, beautiful, and attention-grabbing symbols and icons for almost anything you can think of.

branding and successful product launches. Building long-term brand loyalty and positive associations is a subject we'll cover in the chapter on the Acknowledgment Trigger, but suffice it to say, there is no shortcut to great branding.

There is, however, a shortcut to getting people to like you. And that leads us to how to use touch, the most intimate and personal sensory cue of them all, to capture people's attention.

Why You Should Always Buy Someone Coffee

OCD super genius Sheldon Cooper isn't known for his empathy in the hit CBS show *The Big Bang Theory*, but he does know that, when somebody's upset, you offer him or her a hot beverage.

> **Sheldon:** Did you offer him a hot beverage?
>
> **Leonard:** No.
>
> **Sheldon:** Leonard, social protocol states when a friend is upset, you offer them a hot beverage, such as tea.
>
> **Howard:** Tea does sound nice.
>
> **Sheldon:** You heard the man, Leonard. And while you're at it, I'm upset that we have an unannounced houseguest, so make me cocoa.[23]

It may just seem like a common courtesy—after all, grabbing coffee with friends is a time-tested ritual—but Sheldon may actually have a scientific reason for offering hot beverages to his distressed guest, because researchers have shown that simply holding a hot object can generate positive feelings about others.

A study published in *Science* asked forty-one students to fill out a personality impression questionnaire regarding a hypothetical person. They had to rate the person on ten personality traits. Before entering the room to fill out the questionnaire, though, someone would meet the students, complete with two textbooks, a clipboard, and a cup of coffee, and ask them to hold his or her cup of coffee up the elevator to the testing room. Unbeknownst to the students, some of the cups were hot and some were cold.[24]

The result was astounding: students who held the hot cup of coffee rated the hypothetical person as having a significantly warmer personality than the ones who held the cold cup of coffee. The study was performed a second time with fifty-three students, but instead of coffee, the researchers gave Icy Hot packs to the participants to hold as a "product evaluation." Afterward, they were given the option of receiving a Snapple or a one-dollar gift certificate for ice cream as a thank-you for participating. The one-dollar gift was framed as a way to treat a friend, while the Snapple was framed as a personal reward.

The students who held the cold pack chose the Snapple 75 percent of the time. But the majority of students who held the warm pack chose the gift for a friend (the one-dollar gift certificate), at a rate of 54 percent. Another recent study published in the *Journal of Evolutionary Psychology* came to the same conclusion: holding a warm object brings up our emotional feelings of warmth, leading to positive attention and more cooperation.[25]

As this story demonstrates, touch can be an important sensory cue when it comes to grabbing people's attention. But just as a warm object brings up our emotional feelings of warmth, leading to positive attention, pain can demand our attention and bring up strong negative reactions. Chris Eccleston, the director for the Centre for Pain Research at the University of Bath, and Geert Crombez of the University of Ghent, have researched the link between pain and attention for most of their careers. In their model for pain and attention, Eccleston and Crombez find that pain is "an inescapable fact of life: Pain will emerge over other demands for attention."[26]

The reason we pay attention to pain is the same reason we pay attention to the sound of a gunshot, a bright-yellow sign, or deep-red blood: we're primed to avoid pain for our survival. That's why pain redirects our attention, even if it's only for a brief moment. Burn your tongue on hot coffee, and your lovely coffee chat quickly gets sidelined. This is why it can be torture for people with chronic pain to concentrate on complex problems—the more attention-demanding the task, the more likely pain is to punch a hole in their concentration.

The key to capturing attention with touch is to hone in on the positive associations that come with touch. It's especially useful for building intimacy, trust, and connection with somebody. A fascinating study conducted by Judee Burgoon of the University of Arizona found that the sensation of touch correlated with composure, intimacy, trust, informality, and equality. The type of touch subjects experienced mattered too—face touching and hand holding created more intimacy and informality, while handshakes conveyed the most trust of any type of physical sensation. Another study found that eye contact and mutual touch between randomly paired strangers of opposite genders correlated with elevated heart rates and increased desire.[27]

Touch grows attention by creating intimacy. Of course, social context means everything. It's appropriate to hold hands on a date but not with a stranger you meet in line at Costco. The reason is simple: because touch is intimate, it cannot be forced upon someone. It has to be mutual. Use other sensory cues like color and sound to capture attention; reserve touch for when it's appropriate to build deeper attention and intimacy. So if you are going on a sales call and want to ensure a buyer's attention, bring them a hot cup of coffee. If you are out with friends and want to get the attention of someone you know, touch them on the shoulder. And be careful with cues like touching the face, holding hands, or touching the thigh—this requires a very high level of comfort between both parties to already exist.

So far we've uncovered how you can use the Automaticity Trigger to capture attention through sight (color and symbols) and touch, but we have one last sensory cue that is vital to our attentional systems: sound.

Why Can We Hear Our Names in a Crowded Room?

In many self-defense classes, instructors teach their students—especially women—not to yell, "Help!" or "Rape!" when they are under attack. Instead, women should scream, "Fire!" to catch the attention of anybody nearby. I know I've heard this advice multiple times. I was curious: Is this advice sound? And if so, why do whistles and fires catch our attention more than yelling for help in a dangerous situation?

Kate McCulley, a twenty-something travel blogger, would say the answer to the first question is yes! McCulley was once leaving her Boston gym at ten P.M. with a spring in her step and her headphones securely in her ears. (Reminder: never wear headphones when walking in a city late at night.) As she turned to go home on Charlesgate East, a hooded attacker grabbed her from behind and wrestled her to the concrete ground as he tried to pry her iPhone from her hand. She screamed, "Fire!" and bit him before he took off with her iPhone. People quickly came to her aid, including a girl who came over just because she was curious about the fire.[28]

The problem with "Help!" is that it can mean anything from "I'm under attack!" to "I'm lost" or "I locked my keys in my car." In addition, some people don't want to risk themselves if there is actually an attack in progress. A fire, on the other hand, is a very specific situation that won't threaten you with a knife or a gun, so people are less likely to think they'll be hurt if they help.

We encounter literally thousands of sounds on a daily basis, and most of them don't even register a blip on our radar. So why does screaming "Fire!" break that barrier, even if we're concentrating on something completely different when we hear someone scream that word?

Our brain reacts automatically to two types of auditory stimuli: unexpected, novel sounds like a loud firecracker on a quiet summer day; and salient, semantic sounds like somebody calling out our name. (Screaming "Fire!," because it's unexpected and salient, would qualify as both.) In fact, the middle frontal cortex and the middle and superior temporal cortices of the brain immediately activate when someone says your name. Even the brains of sedated infants respond automatically when they hear their name. It doesn't matter whether you are concentrating on another task—these two types of sounds find a way to redirect your attention, if for a brief moment. Loud sounds or unique frequencies (like my least favorite sound in the world, nails slowly screeching down a chalkboard) capture our attention because they stand out from the other sounds around us, often warning us of danger. Other sounds, such as a name, a police siren, or the first notes of our favorite song, stand out because of the mental associations we have with each of these sounds. This is contrast and association at work.[29]

The reason unexpected sounds and salient words or noises capture our attention has to do with the fundamental purpose of our auditory system. According to Dr. Michael Posner, an expert in human attention, auditory attention is strongly linked to maintaining our alertness. Unlike visual cues—colors and symbols—auditory attention serves as a 360-degree detection system to the information and threats around us. If a car is squealing its tires and racing toward you while you're crossing the street, it's your auditory alert system that warns you to run like hell.[30]

The fact that we are always processing the sounds around us makes auditory attention fundamentally different from the other kinds of attention. For example, you will not only hear your name when someone calls it out (whether you want to or not), but you also automatically attempt to pinpoint its location. Even when we're in a noisy room, we have the ability to identify a single noise or conversation in space and tune in. Our ability to focus on a single conversation in a noisy room is a well-known phenomenon called the cocktail party effect.

In the 1950s, British cognitive scientist Dr. Edward Colin Cherry, the man who first discovered the effect, found that subjects had little to no difficulty "rejecting" unwanted speech when attempting to hone in on a specific conversation. In his widely cited study, Cherry had a group of subjects wear headphones that simultaneously played two different messages from the same voice. In the first experiment, both voices played through both sides of the headphones, while in the second experiment, one voice was fed to each ear separately. The task: subjects had to concentrate on just one message, speak it aloud, and write down that target message.[31]

Cherry found that subjects could eventually discern a target message when two messages were played in both ears at the same time, though it became nearly impossible when one of the messages was filled with illogical gibberish. But in the second experiment, with one message in each ear, subjects could easily hone in on the target message and tune out the other message. This is much like a cocktail party, where we use not only the frequency of somebody's voice but also its location to quickly tune in. Cherry also found that pretty much all the speech occurring in the unattended ear went unnoticed—subjects didn't even recognize when the unattended message changed from English to German. We're very, very good at focus when we want or need to be—often at the expense of everything around us.

Subsequent experiments by Princeton's Dr. Anne Treisman revealed that we indeed ignore sounds in one ear and listen to speech in the other, though our brain will automatically remember certain sounds, even if we're not directing our attention in any way toward those sounds.[32] For example, if someone says your name, your attention will shift even if you weren't paying attention to the person who said your name at the time. It's a process known as attenuation theory. But even so, you're likely to miss most of the story if you don't direct your attention to that source. In another experiment published in the *Journal of Experimental Psychology: Learning, Memory, and Cognition,* researchers found that just one-third of all test subjects recalled hearing their names if they were intently listening to something else.[33]

When you use the Automaticity Trigger, you have to consider your audience's preconceptions about certain sounds in addition to the sounds' distinctiveness and contrast. Unexpected sounds capture our attention best, but we also need to have a positive association with them. The shrill of the vuvuzela horn was certainly unexpected for Americans and Europeans watching the 2010 World Cup, and so it captured attention. Then again, I don't know a single person who enjoys that sound and would treat you kindly if you walked into a room playing one. But if I walked into a party and heard someone playing a harp, I would both notice and appreciate it.

Where does this leave us? What sounds are inherently attention grabbing? The answer—the real answer—is that it depends on what you're doing and what you consider important or salient. In the case of the German army of World War II, that was the sound of tanks and artillery.

How Artists Helped Win a War

Brest, France. It's August 1944—a few months after D-Day. Allied forces are closing in on France's westernmost port city. Hitler's forces control Brest. It is one of the epicenters for Germany's U-boat operation. The Allies need to take the city in order to bring in more supplies to troops in the European theater, but it is a well-fortified position; the Germans aren't giving the city up without a fierce fight.

Luckily, the Allies have thousands of troops, tanks, and artillery surrounding the city. The German Wehrmacht unit defending Brest can hear the sound of artillery fire, tank engines, and Allied officers shouting orders. They can see the light of artillery and mortar fire and troops. The more than thirty-five thousand soldiers, led by General Gerhard Ramcke, decide to hold their positions and counter fire instead of risking an attack against the Allies.

What Ramcke and the Germans don't know is that they aren't firing on an Allied army. The sound of tanks and moving soldiers isn't real. Neither is the artillery fire—that effect is from flash canisters being set off by the 23rd Headquarters Special Troops, a top-secret unit composed of artists, fashion designers, and some of the most creative enlisted soldiers at the disposal of the Allies.[34]

The 23rd—better known today as the Ghost Army—were masters at diverting attention. Their clever and highly detailed deceptions fooled not only German forces but were even convincing enough to confuse friendlies too. By mid-September, the town of Brest fell into Allied control, thanks in part to the efforts of the Ghost Army.

The Ghost Army had just around 1,100 men from four companies, but time and time again, the 23rd fooled Hitler's forces into thinking it was a far more fearsome force. Flash canisters, inflatable tanks and planes, spoof radio messages, and dummy parachute drops were their weapons of choice. When the Allies crossed the Rhine in 1945, the Ghost Army faked a crossing to divert attention away from the 9th Army. With six hundred inflatable tanks and artillery, the 23rd successfully drew Axis fire, leading to a decisive victory for the 9th Army with limited casualties.

Their efforts in the last years of the war remained a closely guarded secret until half a century later, when their contributions to the war were declassified. Thanks to their captivating tactics, they were able to save countless lives.

Why was the Ghost Army so successful in accomplishing its feats of deception? The 23rd certainly wasn't the first to utilize misdirection on the battlefield, but its efforts are among the most effective diversions in military history. I'd argue that their success in capturing the enemy's attention really boils down to contrast and association.

There's no denying that German troops saw and heard the Ghost Army, who moved over thirty trucks with massive loudspeakers that could be heard fifteen miles away and whose flash canisters lit up the night sky. But just in case, some of the actors would stumble into bars and loudly discuss their "orders." Seeing and hearing the soldiers stumble around certainly grabbed the German army's attention.

However, it was the intricacy of the deception that made it believable. The sonic unit of the Ghost Army—an eight-man operation—painstakingly prepared the recordings that played to the Germans with every sound an opposing army would expect to hear. They didn't just record the sounds of troops' movements; they also recorded every sequence of bridge-building operations, tanks starting and stopping, trucks on dirt roads and highways, and soldiers as they started and stopped, chatted and marched. The sonic unit then mixed these sounds into "soundscapes"—thematic sound scenes appropriate for each situation. Different soundscapes were played when troops were on the move, when troops were resting, and for multiple situations for the theater of war.

The visual component of the 23rd Headquarters Special Troops was just as elaborate. While a lieutenant commanded the unit, he would sometimes wear the stars and decorations of a general, just to add to the deception that this was a large unit approaching the Germans. During the Ghost Army's final operation at the Rhine, the troops mixed real tanks with their intricately painted fake ones and camouflaged them well enough to fool German reconnaissance planes.

They gave the Germans exactly what they were looking for—or more specifically, what they were primed to pay attention to. Imagine if you were a German soldier on the move to the next battle—what sounds are going to catch your attention? You can only imagine how salient the sound of tanks or the sight of parachuting troops would be for soldiers, generals, and recon officers. The Ghost Army successfully caught immediate attention with salient sounds and held it through short and long attention.

Moving Beyond Immediate Attention

My goal in this chapter has been to highlight the impressive automaticity with which our senses process the world around us and direct our attention, long before we're even conscious or aware of them. The subconscious influences that color, sound, touch, and other sensory experiences have on our attention are necessary mechanisms for our survival. This influence happens automatically, before we—or our audiences—have a chance to think.

That's why the Automaticity Trigger—our tendency to pay attention to certain sensory cues because of their contrast or the unconscious associations we have with those cues—is so good at capturing our attention—or interrupting our concentration. Certain stimuli become more attention grabbing in the right contexts. We will pay attention to a lion before an antelope. We will pay attention to a gunshot over the chirps of robins. And we will usually look at red before blue, especially if romance or sex is involved.

We cannot deny that danger, lust, and pain capture our attention, but they don't control it or maintain it. To truly capture, maintain, and grow attention, you have to enter somebody's consciousness. You not only have to capture someone's immediate attention and elicit a reaction, but you also have to capture someone's short attention and make him or her focus on you, your idea, or your message.

The rest of the captivation triggers deal with short and long attention—the two types of attention that operate at a conscious level. The Framing Trigger is the first of the triggers that help us move from capturing someone's immediate attention to capturing their short and long attention.

Chapter 3

Framing Trigger

●

In the early 1900s, antiperspirants and deodorants were not the $18 billion commodity they are today. Mum, a deodorant, and Everdry, an antiperspirant, were both on the market, but they weren't in every bathroom. Women of the era used a combination of perfume, dress shields, and cotton pads to keep perspiration at bay, while sweat was a sign of manliness and strength for men in the early 1900s, when labor and farming jobs still dominated. Many people of the era thought that blocking sweat was unhealthy. More importantly, though, it was considered uncouth to talk about your bodily functions, so the market remained nascent.[1]

This didn't deter Edna Murphey, a teenage entrepreneur from Cincinnati, though. She knew that her surgeon father had invented a million-dollar product—liquid antiperspirant. Originally created to keep her father's hands dry during surgeries, Edna soon realized that it kept her armpits fresh and free of sticky sweat.

Determined, Edna Murphey borrowed $150 from her grandfather, and in 1910, she built a sales force of women and launched her antiperspirant, Odorono. It didn't take off like she imagined it would, though—the old habits and beliefs about hygiene and anti-

perspirants were simply too much for her to overcome. Antiperspirants had a reputation problem.

After her confidence was boosted by some mild success at the
1912 summer exposition in Atlantic City, Edna turned to James
Webb Young, a copywriter at J. Walter Thompson Company, for
help breaking her product out. Young, a former Bible salesman,
knew that it wasn't Odorono itself that was holding sales back—it
was the market's perception of all antiperspirants. He knew they had
to use some clever advertising to change that.

Young and Murphey first tackled the claim that stopping perspiration with an antiperspirant was unhealthy. This one wasn't difficult. With an advertising campaign that highlighted the fact that
Odorono was developed by a doctor, they were able to double sales.

The real magic, however, occurred in 1919, when Young decided
to stop focusing on Odorono's virtues and reframe society's attitudes
toward antiperspirant. Young's taboo campaign, "Within the Curve
of a Woman's Arm: A Frank Discussion of a Subject Too Often
Avoided," ran in *Ladies' Home Journal*. The controversial ad cuts
right to the point:

> Many a woman who says, "No, I am never annoyed by perspi-
> ration," does not know the facts—does not realize how much
> sweeter and daintier she would be if she were *entirely* free from it.

According to *Smithsonian* magazine, two hundred women can-
celed their subscriptions to *Ladies' Home Journal* because of the
offensiveness of the ad. (Several of Young's female friends stopped
talking to him as well.) The controversy was well worth the price,
though—sales of Odorono skyrocketed by 112 percent to $417 thou-
sand in just one year. By 1927, that number broke $1 million.

In 1929, after two decades of blood, sweat, and more sweat, Edna
Murphey sold the company she'd started with a $150 loan. James

Young would eventually become vice president at JWT, the first chairman of the Advertising Council, a professor at the University of Chicago, and one of the greatest minds in the history of advertising.

Why did Odorono take off when so many other attempts to popularize deodorant and antiperspirant failed? And what attention-grabbing techniques can we learn from Murphey and Young's savvy campaigns?

The Framing Trigger

While attention is often triggered by an event, a smell, or some other stimulus, most of our attention is goal driven: we make a conscious decision to focus on an assignment because our goal is to complete it and receive a good grade, and we check our text messages because our goal is to find out what our friends are saying. Where we direct our attention is a choice, and the decision of how we allocate it determines which people we choose to date, which movies and shows we watch, and which ideas live or die.

Frames of reference help us make these choices. They help us draw on our experiences and previously acquired knowledge to make sense of the world: "We process information in a way that uses our existing frames of reference," said Dr. Dietram Scheufele, a communications scholar at the University of Wisconsin—Madison. "We don't start from scratch every single time."[2]

To explain what Scheufele means here, indulge me for a moment in a little thought exercise. For this exercise, take out a piece of paper and draw a tree. That's it.

What did you draw? I bet you drew something with branches, leaves, a tree trunk and bark. If I had included crayons with this book, I suspect the leaves would be green and the trunk would be brown. You were able to do this because you already know the basics of a tree. When you encounter an object with a thick brown trunk and thousands of green photosynthetic organs, you can immediately categorize it as a tree—or even more specifically as a palm tree or a pine tree—because you already have knowledge of trees and what they are supposed to look like.

Everybody has a general idea of what a tree is supposed to look like, just as everybody "knows" what vanilla should taste like or a purring cat should sound like. These mental structures—schemata—help us understand the world and identify the objects around us. Years of experiences have helped us build mental frameworks, preconceptions, and opinions about how the world should work. Address books should be organized in alphabetical order, and climate change is either a proven fact or a work of fiction. These are our frames of reference.

Our past experiences, biological wiring, cultural expectations, interests, opinions, and current moods influence our frames of reference. They are the context in which we make our choices or react the way we do, because no choice or reaction is ever made in a vacuum. If you develop a fear of dogs because you were bitten as a child, you will choose to be far more aware of dogs in your vicinity because you perceive them as a threat. If you're exhausted, hungry, or emotionally distressed, you're not going to care about your professor's lecture on the ancient Peloponnesian War or my panel at the South By Southwest conference (which is why I prefer to deliver presentations at the beginning of the day or right after lunch).

To help us direct our attention, we rely both on our frame of reference when we encounter an idea or message, and on how a message or idea is framed—the framing effect.

The framing effect is a cognitive bias that affects the way we perceive a piece of information based on the way it is presented to us. We often make different conclusions about the same information when the explanation is changed even slightly. One of the most famous examples of the framing effect comes from Dr. Elizabeth Loftus and Dr. John Palmer, researchers at the University of Washington who in 1974 asked forty-five students, in five groups of nine, to watch a series of clips depicting car accidents. After the students watched the videos, they were asked a simple question: "About how fast were the cars going when they collided with each other?"[3]

Well, not quite. Each group received a slightly different question. While one group was asked how fast the cars were going when they *collided*, another group was asked how fast the cars were going when they *bumped* each other, and so on. The verb changed from group to group, and it was shown that a simple verb change drastically changed the students' answers. Groups asked how fast the cars were going when they *smashed* into each other estimated they were going 40.8 miles per hour, while groups asked how fast the cars were going when they *contacted* each other estimated a speed of 31.8 miles per hour, a giant 22 percent difference, despite the students watching the exact same car crashes.

Frames of reference aren't set in stone, though. Like Edna Murphey and James Young, you can change and influence the frames of reference of others. At first, Murphey and Young couldn't sell their product because nobody was willing to talk about perspiration. So Murphey and Young reframed the national conversation around antiperspirant. Instead of trying to force a product few women wanted, they attacked the taboo association of not just Odorono, but *all* antiperspirants. The result was a dramatic shift in social bias. Just a few years after the 1919 campaign, antiperspirant had become a necessity for women—those who wanted to be dainty and alluring wore antiperspirant. Other antiperspirant and deodorant companies started running their own ads linking sweaty armpits to "aloneness" and man repellent. This only increased the size of the pie, making Odorono that much more successful.

The Framing Trigger is all about changing how you present an idea to someone to make him or her more receptive to your message. Politicians use framing all the time to affect the attention and reactions of their constituents. For example, a politician will get entirely different reactions depending on if he frames a law restricting ownership of certain kinds of guns as "gun control" or as "gun safety." The former sounds like government intervention; the latter just seems obvious. Of course, the political leanings—or frames of reference—of the politician's audience matter just as much. It doesn't matter whether the politician frames a law restricting guns as gun control or gun safety to an audience full of members of the National Rifle Association: that politician will have captured his audience's attention all right, in the sense that he will quickly become the least popular person there. Tell a hardcore gun control advocate about how the Second Amendment allows you to carry an assault rifle, and you will get a similar reaction. And of course, there are people who simply don't care about the politics of guns and will tune out, no matter how the politician frames the law. Each of these groups has a different frame of reference.

The Framing Trigger, however, is not as easy to leverage as it may seem—especially since people tend to hold on to their old frames of reference fiercely, a phenomenon I call the inertia of ideas. To change someone's frame of reference and make them more receptive or attentive to your message, we have to understand why our frames of reference are so hard to change in the first place.

The Inertia of Ideas

Over the course of a year, Dr. Marianne Bertrand and Dr. Sendhil Mullainathan of the University of Chicago and MIT, respectively, sent five thousand résumés in response to ads seeking people to fill clerical, customer service, and sales jobs. One set of résumés had higher-quality credentials, while the other set had less-impressive ones.[4]

The only thing Bertrand and Mullainathan changed on each résumé was the name on the top. Some résumés had traditionally Caucasian names (Emily, Brendan, etc.) while others had traditionally African-American names (Aisha, Latoya, Tyrone, etc.). The result was a shocking gap in callbacks. Despite having nearly identical résumés, the ones with African-American names received 50 percent fewer callbacks than the résumés with Caucasian names. The change in qualifications showed a similar bias: the résumés with Caucasian names received 30 percent more callbacks, while those with African-American names received only 9 percent more, despite having the same improvement in résumé quality.

Despite the progress we have made over the past century, prejudice still exists and isn't going away anytime soon. This is because stereotyping leads people to make snap judgments about individuals from certain groups, even when they know little to nothing about the individuals in question. We can come to different conclusions about a person based on something as simple as his or her name.

These stereotypes stick around because it's incredibly difficult for us to change how we view the world—our frame of reference. Even when we know our frame of reference is flawed, it's surprisingly challenging to give up.

Our attention, over the long term, tends to focus on the same few ideas, people, and patterns. This leads to what I call the inertia of ideas: once our frame of reference is set, it is incredibly difficult to change. Like concrete, our opinions on political issues or our beliefs about the world solidify over time and become harder and harder to break. Inertia—the physical resistance that objects have to changes in their state of motion—applies to our ideas as well.

The inertia of ideas occurs because we don't have the mental energy to constantly change our frames of reference—and thus where we place our attention. In a strange way, it makes sense—if you've already looked at the evidence and believe that the Earth is round, then why would you use your precious time and energy every time a crazy person declares our planet is flat, a pentagon, or secretly filled with lizard people? In this case, the inertia of ideas is good, but it has also caused our society to hold on to terrible beliefs and systems like slavery, racism, and sexism for far longer than we should. Incorrect or outdated beliefs don't go away just because you place evidence in front of a person.

The inertia of ideas is why charities struggle all the time to make their various causes a priority among the public—charities must convince thousands of people to adopt a social cause they aren't familiar with and donate money to that cause, when it is easier to donate to a charity they are already familiar with (or not donate at all). Even the most influential figures have a difficult time changing the agenda. Even when there's a spike of interest in a charity cause or a political agenda, it quickly dissipates and society returns to the status quo. Edna Murphey and James Young had to decisively break social taboos to make deodorant acceptable. It took a book and a multimillion-dollar foundation for Facebook's Sheryl Sandberg to make a discussion about women at work and in leadership positions a priority among the public—and we are still far from workplace equality.

If you're trying to capture attention with the Framing Trigger, then you have to be prepared to face the inertia of ideas, because it prevents your audience from being exposed to new ideas, products, and people that can improve their lives. People will unintentionally dismiss your ideas or your work because they don't fit their frames of reference or preconceptions. Pandora, the billion-dollar online radio giant, was famously rejected by not one or two but *three hundred* investors. Some didn't believe Pandora could make money, others didn't believe it had enough traction, and yet others were bearish on the music industry, which was consistently shrinking as the era of the CD came to a close.[5] While a frame of reference built on experience helps investors avoid repeating past mistakes, it can also blind investors to new opportunities that seem absurd on the surface. (IBM's Thomas Watson famously said in 1943 that "there is a world market for maybe five computers."[6])

The inertia of ideas isn't all-powerful, though—you can capture attention despite people's frames of reference. Through the course of my research, I've discovered two tools for tackling an audience's frame of reference and getting them to pay attention using the Framing Trigger. These are adaptation and agenda setting. Adaptation is about identifying your audience's frame of reference and adjusting to it. Agenda setting is a phenomenon that makes a specific topic more salient and important in the minds of your audience, and thus changes their frame of reference to pay more attention to that topic whenever it comes up.

First, let's talk about adaptation. To do that, I need to tell you the story of two violinists and how one was able to capture more attention than the other.

A Tale of Two Violinists

For forty-three minutes on a cold January morning, master violinist Joshua Bell played six timeless masterpieces on his one-of-a-kind Stradivarius violin for a thousand people in Washington, D.C. Just three days earlier, the thirty-nine-year-old played history's greatest masterpieces in front of a crowd of 2,500 in Boston.[7]

As one would expect, Bell sold out the Boston Symphony Hall with relative ease, where good seats went for a hundred dollars a pop. His performances moved the audience to tears, something he has been able to do since he was four. He's even the proud recipient of a Grammy Award.

His performance in Washington, D.C., on the other hand, was a completely different story. There was no price of admission for this concert. But despite the incredible price, nobody stayed to listen. Nobody cried tears of joy or applauded enthusiastically. Nobody paid attention to one of the world's greatest musicians.

What was different between his Boston concert and his D.C. performance? For one thing, Bell wasn't playing in a crowded symphony hall. He was, instead, playing Bach's Chaconne in the open at L'Enfant Plaza, one of the central transportation hubs in Washington, D.C. 1,070 people walked by him during the morning rush hour. Instead of wearing a tux and bow tie, Bell wore a baseball cap and jeans. Instead of announcing his presence, he went incognito.

Out of the 1,070 who saw him, a grand total of twenty-seven gave him money. Even more shocking: just seven people stopped to listen to his concert for more than sixty seconds. Only one person, Stacy Furukawa, recognized him. (She, unsurprisingly, was shocked and dumbfounded to find Bell in the subway.) One of the world's most brilliant musicians could only get 0.7 percent of the people who passed by him to stop and listen.

You've probably heard this story before—it's a famous experiment conducted by *The Washington Post* to see how many people would recognize the work of one of the world's greatest musicians outside of a concert hall. The answer: not very many. But the experiment does not necessarily prove that violinists are unpopular attractions in subway stations. They can, in fact, attract lots of people to listen to them play.

I met Susan Keser on a sweltering and muggy summer day in New York City, trudging through Grand Central Terminal, focused on finding the train back to my friend's place on the Lower East Side. But as I made my way through one of the station's long hallways, I couldn't help but hear the sound of violin music. As I walked, it got louder, until I eventually found a middle-aged woman, centrally located in the long hallway, playing her violin for a small crowd that had gathered.

Susan wore a black-and-blue-striped tank top, comfortable black pants, and gray tennis shoes. She wore her half-blond, half-gray hair in a bun. Like me, her face was drenched in sweat. But there she was, playing Vivaldi's Concerto in B Minor, promoting her craft. (I knew this because she had a giant sign announcing which song she was playing next to her.)

Susan is a fifty-five-year-old professionally trained violinist who has played for world-class orchestras in Germany, Italy, and Turkey. She spent years going back and forth between Europe and the United States, but she never found a permanent home in an orchestra. ("Orchestras want younger performers," she once proclaimed in an interview.[8]) When she moved to New York City in 2006, though, she decided to try a different path. While Joshua Bell may famously have played once in a subway station, Susan does it two to four times a week, throughout the year, through heat waves and blizzards.

"I feel like an ambassador for classical music, trying to promote it to the masses," Susan tells me.[9]

Susan is a common sight around New York's subways and next to the Christopher Columbus statue in Central Park on the weekends. I later learned that it wasn't uncommon for forty to eighty people to be sitting on the benches of Central Park, listening to Keser play a variety of classical masterpieces mixed with pop songs like Coldplay's "Viva la Vida" and Jason Mraz's "I'm Yours." She's even been featured on *The Today Show*. She makes a decent living off her street and subway performances—more than many professional musicians—through a combination of CD sales and private gigs that are booked as a direct result of her public demonstrations.

So why did Joshua Bell, an internationally recognized violin master, only get seven people out of a thousand to listen to his music for over a minute, while Susan Keser attracts crowds ten times that size on a regular basis? The answer lies in Susan's ability to adapt to her audience's frames of reference.

In a blog post analyzing Bell's subway performance, Susan's son offers the most plausible explanation for Bell's failure to attract crowds. He points out some important flaws in the Joshua Bell *Washington Post* experiment, starting with the most obvious one: Bell was playing his violin during rush hour.[10]

I want you to place yourself in the frame of reference of a subway commuter in each situation. As you read each scenario, think about how you'd feel in the moment and what you would do if you were in their situations:

> **Lois Lane:** It's rush hour in D.C., and Lois needs to get to work— there's an important Senate hearing she needs to cover for the *Daily Planet*. She's walking through the doors of the subway station and most likely fiddling around for her transit card so she can get to the train on time. By the time she's swiping her card, she hears the sounds of Bell's violin, but she's already past the gates.

> **Clark Kent:** It's after rush hour, and Clark's heading to the other side of the city to meet up with a friend for a casual lunch in New York City. As he's walking through one of the subway's long corridors, he starts hearing the sound of echoing music, and it's getting louder. As it grows, he starts looking for the source of the sound, eventually spotting a woman violinist with long locks of gray hair. His curiosity grows as he gets closer. He can now see a music stand next to her with a piece of paper declaring, "Now Playing: Vivaldi's Concerto in B Minor," on it. He stops for a moment to listen.

While the morning rush hour may technically have the most foot traffic, and thus the most potential eyeballs and ears to sway, commuters are simply *not in the right frame of reference to stop and listen.* Polls consistently show that people are at their most stressed during rush hour, and when people are stressed and focused on getting to work through busy crowds, they don't have the mental capacity to focus on anything else.[11] This is an important lesson Susan Keser learned through trial and error. She plays in the subway stations in the late morning. She never plays during rush hour, and she rarely performs in the tunnels after two P.M.

"After two P.M., the atmosphere changes everywhere," Susan claims. "People are more negative."[12]

No matter what Susan Keser does, she'll always get a better response after rush hour. And no matter what she tries, she won't get teenagers to respond to Chopin's classics like they will to American Top 40 hits. That's why she often plays songs familiar to the masses, especially in the afternoon.

"Some people are just very receptive," Keser said of her music. She said that their moods, the weather, and other things can make people listen in. "And other people are just . . . not going to pay attention to any musician at all. Some people just don't like music."

If you look at the video footage of Joshua Bell's hour in the subway, you may also notice that Joshua Bell has situated himself in a peculiar spot—he's playing near the exit of L'Enfant Plaza, just past the turnstiles. Compare that to our street violinist Susan Keser, who always finds a spot in a tunnel or a long passageway in the subway system. In these long passages, people have more time to be exposed to her music as they walk. She learned early on that playing near entrances and exits had the worst returns, so she adapted and moved herself to prime locations where potential listeners would be more likely to stop and listen. Over the years, Keser has figured out the frame of reference of her potential audience at different times of the day, and she has adjusted where she plays, when she plays, and which songs she plays based on her now-intuitive understanding of their frames of reference.

Adaptation, at its essence, is the process of understanding how your audience thinks and how your audience will react to your message (their frame of reference, in other words), and then changing the delivery of that message to fit your audience's frame of reference. With Odorono, for example, Murphey and Young learned about customer misconceptions about the medical safety of antiperspirants and adapted by addressing the concern (rather than just ignoring the problem) in their advertising. Doing so was instrumental to boosting their sales. Understanding your audience's frame of reference is vital to capturing attention. "Knowing [your audience's] history, knowing what kind of people they are, that is important to use to guide their attention to something that's important, that you want them to focus on," David Copperfield, the master illusionist, said when I interviewed him.

To captivate others using the Framing Trigger, you have to think through your audience's frames of reference. And while there are many considerations when it comes to understanding this, three stand out as the most important. First, determine the receptiveness of your audience. When is your audience at its most stressed and least stressed? When and where will they be the least distracted? What kind of words and topics will automatically shut down their message?

Second, understand your audience's concerns. What will their natural objections be to your message? What words or arguments will make them immediately become defensive? One tactic that works well when you're trying to get the attention of somebody who disagrees with you is to find a small piece of common ground to agree upon before making your more substantive arguments. People hold tight to their frames of reference, so you're not doing yourself any favors if your target audience is already on the defensive.

And third, know the cultural norms and traditions of your audience. What would offend them or make them squeal with delight? Branding and messaging has to adapt to each culture's frame of reference. This is something brands forget all the time. Cosmetics giant Revlon once promoted a camellia-scented perfume for women in Brazil. A fragrance imitating the sweet-smelling flower is no problem in Western countries, but in Brazil and most Latin American countries, the camellia flower is prominently used for funerals. I don't know about you, but I wouldn't want people to think about funerals and death when they smell me. As you can imagine, the fragrance landed with a thud.[13]

Adaptation—whether it's to your audience's immediate needs and condition, to their cultural norms, or even to their political views—is essential to capturing attention. But adaptation is only the first part of the story when it comes to using the Framing Trigger. It's time to talk about the surprising and incredible power of agenda setting.

How Do Politicians Set the Agenda?

In 1997, a few years after Newt Gingrich's "Contract with America," revered Republican pollster Frank Luntz dropped a bombshell 222-page memo. The memo, "Language of the 21st Century," outlined everything from talking points to the things Republican politicians ought to say and not to say to their constituents. For example, Luntz suggested politicians say "Washington" instead of "government" when being critical of the federal government. (People consistently show disdain for Washington and its inaction, but like their local governments, Luntz said.) He also recommended Republican members of Congress refer to the "estate tax" as the "death tax" because polls showed that a full 10 percent more of the American public believed the death tax was unfair compared to the estate tax, despite the two being the exact same thing.[14]

As the subtitle of his 2007 book, *Words that Work*, proclaimed: "It's not what you say, it's what people hear."

Luntz is famous for his approach to political communications. He regularly holds focus groups that help him hone the messages of his clients—many of them top politicians at the state and national levels. He tests different phrases over and over again until he finds the ones that carry the most emotional resonance. Luntz sometimes takes his approach to the extremes—he famously used his techniques to reframe the word *Orwellian* as being clear and succinct instead of being destructive to the fabric of free society. Luntz himself is framed by party identification. If you're a Republican, you're more likely to think he's a brilliant strategist. If you're a Democrat, you're more likely to perceive him as a villain finding ways to manipulate the public.

Let's be clear: Luntz isn't the only one to manipulate talking points to set an agenda. It happens on both sides of the aisle and in almost every country and political process. But regardless of your political leanings, Luntz proves that a simple change of words can have a dramatic effect on where and how we direct our attention. And by keeping those words on the top of the news, politicians can make them salient in the minds of voters.

You see this happen every day when you turn on your television and watch Fox News, CNN, CNBC, BBC, or any other cable news channel. When you open up CNN.com and the top story is another celebrity being arrested (instead of a story with far more important global consequences, such as uprisings and protests in Ukraine or Thailand), your perceptions of what's important—and thus where to place your attention—are being framed. It's a self-fulfilling prophecy: the more the media covers a story, the more the public demands information on the story. It doesn't stop until the story has reached its conclusion or the public has lost interest.

Agenda setting is the act of changing the importance or salience of a specific topic in the minds of an audience. Agenda setting most often happens in the media. During the 2014 "Bridgegate"—when New Jersey Governor Chris Christie's administration was engulfed in

controversy for closing lanes on the George Washington Bridge as ret-
ribution against a mayor who didn't endorse the governor—MSNBC
(a left-leaning cable news network) and CNN covered the story for a
whopping 142 minutes on the day the e-mails and texts were released.
Fox News (a right-leaning cable news network) spent just fourteen
minutes and thirty seconds on the story that day.[15] Which audience
do you think was most likely to dismiss the Bridgegate story?

Agenda setting goes farther than just reordering the priorities of
the public, though. If I tell you that even Albert Einstein failed his
math classes (contrary to popular lore, he didn't), and repeat it often
enough, you will start believing it's true—even though the fact that
I'm repeating it has absolutely no impact on its validity. It's a cognitive bias called the illusion-of-truth effect, and it is a powerful after-
effect of clever agenda setting.

In the 1970s, researchers from Temple and Villanova Universities
gave a group of forty college students a series of 140 plausible asser-
tions in politics, sports, medicine, and other topics that wouldn't be
familiar to most students, such as:

1. Tulane defeated Columbia in the first Sugar Bowl game.

2. French horn players get cash bonuses to stay in the U.S.
   Army.

3. Lithium is the lightest of all metals.

4. Outside of New York and Chicago, the tallest building in
   America is found in Dallas.

5. Australia is approximately equal in area to the continental
   United States.[16]

Half of these statements were true, while the other half were lies
given to the students. (Which two statements from the list above do
you think are the lies, by the way?)[17]

Students were asked to assess sixty of these statements at a time for their validity, and to rate their validity on a scale of 1 to 7. This was done a second time two weeks later and one last time after another two-week break. The catch: twenty of the statements, randomly chosen, were repeated to the participants on the second and third occasions.

The researchers found that the students consistently rated the statements that were repeated as more true and valid every time they were repeated. It didn't matter whether the statement was true or false—for some reason, students would give statements a higher truth rating than the last time they heard it. This is despite the fact that repeating a statement has absolutely no impact on whether it's true or not. Seeing the same statements multiple times gradually changed their frames of reference enough that they started believing that what they were reading was true.

This effect has been studied many times by cognitive scientists. The familiarity of a statement seems to have an impact on our assessment of its validity. Now imagine what happens when you apply the illusion-of-truth effect to everyday life. Plausible statements like "Climate change will have severe consequences for the planet's future" and "Global warming has plenty of skeptics in the scientific community" become more believable every time we hear them on the news, on the radio, or on social media.

Repetition and the illusion-of-truth effect amplify agenda setting and thus the amount of attention we give toward one side of a debate versus the other. This is why agenda setting is a powerful tool for capturing attention—it changes the frames of reference of your audience. Repetition—in moderation—is the key to setting your agenda and making your cause more important to your audience.

In advertising, repetition to set an agenda is known as effective frequency—the number of times an audience has to be exposed to a message before either a response is made or the repetition becomes worthless. Repetition creates familiarity, salience, and credibility (the latter through the illusion-of-truth effect). But repetition is only effective when people aren't paying much attention to you.

One study published in the *Journal of Personality and Social Psychology* found that repetition did indeed increase the persuasiveness of an argument—even a weak argument—but only "when little processing of messaging content occurred."[18] But once you've captured your audience's attention—and they are listening—your arguments had better be strong, because additional repetition will start decreasing the strength of an argument. Once you have somebody's attention, repetition can backfire, changing your audience's frame of reference to be more negative or more annoyed. Only use repetition when your audience is barely aware of your existence.

Agenda setting isn't just a tool politicians can use to sway the frames of reference of voters, though—it's also a powerful weapon for changing the frames of reference of customers and users.

Why Is Everybody Buying Twinkies?

Twinkies—the sponge cakes with a white cream filling—have been a staple food on the shelves of grocery stores and big retailers for decades. I personally don't like them, and I can't say I know a lot of people who *love* them. But in late 2012, Twinkie sales took off like a rocket ship.

Why? It wasn't because Twinkies had become any tastier or because the company launched a new marketing campaign. Instead, after years of strikes and managerial incompetence, Hostess Brands—the owner of the Twinkie—announced that it was going out of business. The snack cakes would grace store shelves no more, so people rushed to their local stores and bought all the Twinkies they could. Photos of empty shelves stormed the web.[19]

When we believe an opportunity is about to disappear, we suddenly start paying attention, even though nothing else about the situation has changed. It's because we have a natural fear of missing out and an aversion to loss. In the case of the Twinkie, its sudden end drove up its value, even though nothing had changed about it but its scarcity. Scarcity and the fear of missing out are powerful tools for changing somebody's agenda.

The fear of missing out drives a lot of deals in the tech industry too. In my work as a venture capitalist, when portfolio companies decide they're going to raise a new round of funding, I coach them to set up as many investor meetings in a row as possible. The reason I suggest this to my startups is because investors typically don't want to make the first move—they often wait to see what other investors are going to do and to gather more information. If a funding round is moving slowly, investors have few incentives to agree to terms. But if one or two investors say yes, and an entrepreneur tells the other fifty investors she's met with that she has already raised $500,000 of the $1 million she is raising to fund her startup, investors will suddenly return her calls. I've seen fellow investors make ridiculous, overpriced offers just because a deal is about to close. I'm guilty of it too.

The fundamentals of my portfolio companies haven't changed—just the scarcity of access. Scarcity is yet another form of agenda setting, because scarcity changes the importance of a topic and thus changes our frame of reference. Which startups investors will pursue dramatically change simply due to perceived scarcity.[20] When investors view an opportunity as suddenly scarce, their attention and receptiveness increase. It's a concept known as commodity theory—first proposed by T. C. Brock in 1968 and further expanded by Dr. Robert Cialdini in his classic 1984 book *Influence: The Psychology of Persuasion.*

The premise of commodity theory is simple: the scarcer something becomes, the more we value it. But the reason for why something becomes scarce matters. In one experiment conducted by Theo Verhallen of Tilburg University, 230 female subjects were asked to evaluate three recipe books from the same editorial series and choose one. Verhallen gave subjects some information on each book, letting the women know that two of the books were "abundantly available" and the third was in limited supply. For the third book, some were told that it was limited in supply because of accidental circumstances, and others were told it was limited due to popularity.[21]

What Verhallen found was that, while all groups chose the limited-supply book more often, their frames of reference for doing so differed. Subjects evaluated a book that was in limited supply due to production issues as more costly and more unique, but when subjects evaluated a book limited in supply due to its popularity, their evaluation of its worth didn't change—just its uniqueness. Framing something as popular doesn't change its worth; framing something as inherently limited in supply does.

Compare the following two statements to see what I mean:

Our cookies are made with the finest chocolate chips and organic ingredients. We always sell out because people love them so much!

Our cookies are made with the best ingredients, but the ingredients we use are about to go out of season. We will only be selling them this week. After that, they won't be available until next year.

Which cookies do you think you're more likely to buy *at that given moment*? The ones that are about to disappear for a year, of course. It's exactly what happened with the Twinkie. And when the scarce cookie makes its return the next year, you can bet people will be lining up to grab a box. When the Twinkie made its return to store shelves in July 2013 (after Hostess was acquired out of bank-ruptcy), sales jumped by seven times their historic levels.[22]

If you're trying to capture attention using the Framing Trigger, then having a scarce product is useful. But there are multiple ways to create scarcity without having an actual shortage. Woot.com, one of the original daily deals sites, creates scarcity by selling only one item at a time and having it available for only twenty-four hours, after which time it disappears. (Amazon acquired Woot in 2010 for $110 million.)

You can also simply present something as scarce, like the cookies we just discussed. In fact, a 1975 study found that, if you present people with two identical glass jars—one with ten cookies and another with just two—they will assign a much higher value to the cookies in the jar with just two. Any cues that demonstrate the scarcity of the product will have an impact on attention.[23]

You can also create scarcity by simply limiting access. When Google first launched Gmail, for example, it made its e-mail service scarce by only offering a small number of invites to the public at a time. This created a frenzy—I remember people offering one hundred dollars or more to buy my first batch of Gmail invites. It placed Gmail at the top of message boards and news stories. Nowadays you'll find lots of startups that implement invite systems to increase the attention on and perceived value of their product.

Commodity theory and the fear of missing out also apply when it comes to information, and perhaps they're part of the reason why we check Facebook, *Politico*, or our text messages every day—or multiple times a day. Josh Elman, a partner at venture firm Greylock Partners and a former product manager at Facebook, Twitter, and LinkedIn, argues that the fear of missing out drove the success of all the major social networks.

"One of the big reasons [Facebook] attracts your attention is it has information you can only get there, and if you're not getting that information, you're missing out," Elman explained. "If I'm not paying attention to Facebook, then I'm totally missing out." He emphasizes that the fear of missing out drives daily interaction.[24] It helps explain why LinkedIn, for example, added LinkedIn Today, a portal with the most important professional and business news. Making people feel like they will miss out if they're not using your product or listening to your ideas is yet another way to create scarcity, set the agenda, and capture attention.

Now that we have a firmer grasp on adaptation and agenda setting, let's see how one of the masters of attention utilizes these techniques to command audiences.

How Magicians Manipulate Frames

"So here's the card," Jon Armstrong, a baby-faced man with a distinctive pair of black glasses, says to me. We are seated near a window in the famous Magic Castle of Los Angeles. In his hand is a deck of cards. He shows me the king of diamonds from the top of the deck. "So I have this card, and I'm going to change the card." Armstrong simply turns the card in his hand and, without any hesitation, transforms it into the four of spades. I begin to laugh. I tried, but I couldn't follow his subtle movements.

"Let me explain something to you," Armstrong declares. "If I turn the card over in such a way that it seems suspicious, like putting my hand over it or something," he says as he places his hand on the top of the card to hide it, "even though I'm not doing anything, suspicion arose, right?" Armstrong pauses for a moment. "And I can use that because I can say, 'Here's the card. Here, hold on to it,' and now all your attention's on this card. And yet I haven't done anything to the card. But then that's when I am going over here in the deck," he says as he shuffles the fifty-one cards in his other hand, "to do my dirty work."

Armstrong is a master of harnessing the Framing Trigger, using both adaptation and agenda setting to amaze his audience. As chairman of Magic Castle and the Academy of Magical Arts, Armstrong is among the elite when it comes to close-range magic. He is a master at manipulating his audience's attention so they never can figure out the secret to his magic. The result is a flawless performance and a sense of delight.

Much of Armstrong's craft doesn't come from the card tricks but from his intimate knowledge of how his audience thinks. His goal is to instill an "unwilling acceptance of the unbelievable" in his audience. For example, if a magician begins to perform a trick and, just before the big reveal, the magician's assistant suddenly loses her top, and when you look back at the trick there's an elephant, you won't accept the trick. Why? Because you know something must have happened while you were looking away. It was a ruse. You didn't accept the unbelievable. However, if you place a volunteer into a box wheeled on stage and, without any obvious distractions, an elephant pops out, you will accept it. Yes, you know that person didn't actually disappear, but you can't fathom how the magician pulled off the trick.

In some cases, members of Armstrong's audience will be dead-set on figuring out the secret to one of his tricks (their frame of reference is to figure out his trick). He will quickly pick up on his audience's intent and adapt to that fact by changing the trick. If somebody keeps staring at the deck of cards in his hands, for example, he changes the trick so the actual "dirty work" occurs away from the deck. Sometimes he removes the key cards from the deck, making the deck a decoy that distracts his audience. They don't suspect a thing because their attention is focused in the wrong direction.

But perhaps Armstrong's best trick comes from his ability to set the agenda by setting low expectations and wildly exceeding them. Armstrong often starts his routine with a bit of fumbling and nervousness—to make the audience think he is not in complete control. Every time he does this, he's utilizing agenda setting and repetition to make his audience think he's simply a fool. Viewing Armstrong as a bumbling fool is now their frame of reference. But when, suddenly, he defies the expectations he's set by pulling off one of his tricks with complete mastery, the audience's expectations all go out the window and they become far more receptive and attentive to the rest of his show.

"They're caught off guard by it, and that sort of sets the bar—and that happens very, very early on," Armstrong explained to me. "Now they're like, 'Well, wait a minute—I just thought this was going to be kind of lame, but now this—that's a really good trick.' And they're already put off guard."

Armstrong is a master of framing. He uses adaptation to keep his audiences guessing, and he uses agenda setting and repetition to set and break their expectations. The key is that Armstrong, through years of shows and research, has come to intuitively understand his audience's frames of reference, much like Susan Keser has in the streets of New York City or Edna Murphey did when she found a way to change the agenda when it came to deodorant.

The Final Word on Frames of Reference

The Framing Trigger is different from the other captivation triggers because it sets the stage for all the others. The Framing Trigger has a major impact on both our short attention (our short-term focus) and our long attention (our long-term interests). By using the Framing Trigger, you can get on your audience's radar and either adapt to or change their frame of reference so they become more receptive to you and your message.

People don't change their frames of reference on a dime, though, and for good reason. If we kept changing our opinions and listening to every argument somebody threw our way, we'd be overwhelmed. This is why we have frames of reference in the first place—they help us understand our world through the lens of our past experiences.

So you need to take the time to first understand your audience's frames of reference before choosing a strategy for capturing attention. Your audience is not keenly aware of the reason why they reject a résumé, put on deodorant, donate to a political campaign, or coast by Susan Keser the violinist on their way to work, but you now are. And you can use that to your advantage.

Forcing people out of their frames of reference—harnessing the Framing Trigger—is a subtle and nuanced way of capturing attention. But sometimes it's necessary to take a more direct approach. In the next chapter, we'll explore how the next captivation trigger— Disruption—can help us capture attention.

Chapter 4

Disruption Trigger

•

Black Friday is the American shopping event of the year. Year after year, without fail, millions of Americans line up in the cold to get their hands on T-shirts, toys, TVs, and tablets. Americans purchased over $14 billion in merchandise over the 2013 Thanksgiving weekend alone.[1]

Brands are doing everything they can to encourage the masses to shop even more. Walmart has started opening their doors to shoppers at six P.M. *on Thanksgiving Day.* The airwaves and magazines are filled with ads from Macy's, JCPenney, and other retailers touting their specials. The more buying fervor they can generate, the more they benefit.

Patagonia, a small, high-end outdoor clothing company started by avid climber and environmentalist Yvon Chouinard, decided to try a completely different route. On Black Friday 2011, the company bought a full-page ad in the *New York Times* with a simple but shocking headline:

DON'T BUY THIS JACKET

Instead of touting its Black Friday discounts or the quality of its line of premium outdoor gear, Patagonia asked consumers to buy *less* for the long-term health of the environment.[2]

"The environmental cost of everything we make is astonishing," the company said in its ad, explaining that the process to create its most popular jacket uses up 135 liters of water—enough for a person to live off of for forty-five days. The ad then encouraged consumers to buy only what they need and to repair their gear before buying replacements. Patagonia, for its part, pledged to do what it could to reduce its environmental footprint and help its customers repair, reuse, or recycle their gear.

The message—an anti-consumerist message on the most consumer-driven day of the year—attracted attention like moths to a flame. It quickly struck a chord with both the press and the public. Patagonia's Black Friday ad and its subsequent campaign to convince consumers to buy only what they need have been covered in everything from *Bloomberg* to *Fast Company*. More importantly, though, Patagonia's sales skyrocketed by 40 percent the two years after the campaign. Instead of buying less, consumers bought more!

Patagonia disrupted our expectations for how a brand is supposed to act on Black Friday. Every November and December, brands are supposed to convince you to buy as much of their stuff as possible. They are supposed to promote big discounts and deals. Patagonia did the exact opposite, and that's why its campaign captured so much attention. It effectively utilized the power of disruption.

The Disruption Trigger

In Silicon Valley, disruption is the mantra that entrepreneurs live by. The companies they're building are upstarts. Their challenge is figuring out a way to displace bigger, slower, and less innovative companies in their respective industries. When they succeed, they will have changed and displaced not just their competition but also entire industries or, in some cases, the very way we live. Try to think about life before the web browser or the iPhone.

Disruption is about *changing the status quo*. Craigslist, the bare-bones but still-popular classifieds website, hasn't needed to change for a decade because nobody has successfully found a way to knock it off its perch as king of the classifieds. Walmart and Barnes & Noble, on the other hand, were blindsided by Amazon.com, whose free shipping, vast selection, and ease of use have made it the largest online retailer in the world. These companies were forced to change in order to remain relevant and to compete with Amazon. They were disrupted.

Disruption isn't just a Silicon Valley phenomenon, though. Unless you live in a germ-free hamster ball or your mother's basement, you've likely experienced some form of it yourself.

Let's say you're sitting in a coffee shop and, out of nowhere, a parade of colorful clowns walks in. Guess what? You're going to shift your attention to them. You might ask yourself questions like, "Why are they all dressed up?" or "Where did they come from?" I'm betting the question you're most likely to ask yourself, though, is, "What the hell?!" Your short attention has been triggered because you didn't expect clowns to walk into your coffee shop. Surprise!

While short attention is triggered by novelty, novelty alone won't hold somebody's attention for long. Hundreds of new people walk into your favorite coffee shop all the time, and you will never re-member who they were or what they looked like. Not only does something have to be novel to catch your eye, but it also needs to *violate and disrupt expectations*. Clowns barnstorming your favorite coffee spot effectively disrupts who you expect to walk into a coffee shop, and thus it captures your attention.

A study by researchers at Haverford College found, for example, that musical cues that violate expectations have a dramatic impact on our ability to remember scenes from films and television shows. The researchers took several twenty- to thirty-second clips from *Alfred Hitchcock Presents* and *The Hitchhiker* and played them to a group of participants. The twist: the music was either congruent or incongruent with the mood of the clip. Imagine if happy, bouncy music started playing during the darkest scenes of *Schindler's List*, and you'll have an idea of what an incongruent clip felt and sounded like.[3]

The researchers also tested music placement. One set of clips had the music play at the same time as the clips, while another set of clips played the music for fifteen to twenty seconds before the start of the clip. The latter essentially acted as congruent foreshadowing (happy music followed by a happy clip) or incongruent foreshadowing (happy music followed by a sad clip).

Once the subjects had seen the clips, they were tested on their ability to recall the clips. The result: accurate recall of movie and television scenes jumped when there was congruent accompanying music and dropped when the music was incongruent. In other words, subjects became confused when fast and happy music played with a slow clip, making it difficult to encode into memory. On the other hand, music that accentuated and reinforced the emotional impact of the clip improved memorization and recall.

This shouldn't surprise anybody—attention drops when you're forced to concentrate on more than one thing.

When it came to the clips that played music before the start of the clip, though, *the opposite was true*: subjects remembered clips preceded by incongruent music far better than clips preceded by congruent music. Why was this the case? While playing depressing music alongside a happy clip confuses the mind and divides attention between two competing ideas, playing sad music *before* a happy clip made subjects remember it better because the incongruity stood out.

The incongruent music is an example of the Disruption Trigger in action. The Disruption Trigger is an event—a person's behavior or a change in our environment that disrupts or violates our expectations of how the world should work. It is this violation of our expectations that forces us to pay attention—we focus on the disruption until we know whether it is a pleasant surprise or a potential threat. The Disruption Trigger is the reason why the subjects of the Haverford study remembered the film clips with incongruent music, and it's why consumers paid attention to Patagonia's "Don't Wear This Jacket" campaign.

Expectancy violation theory helps us understand how the Disruption Trigger works. Coined by Dr. Judee Burgoon of the University of Arizona, expectancy violation theory states that people make unconscious predictions about what they expect to occur in a specific situation. When something violates these expectations, we are forced to pay greater attention to the violation and to assign a positive or negative connotation to that violation.[4]

One key aspect of expectancy violation theory is that, when someone or something is disruptive, we immediately assign a positive or negative value to it. Imagine that you're on a first date at a fancy restaurant by the ocean. Got the picture in your head? Now imagine if a total stranger pulls up a chair and sits down at your table. This isn't normal or expected behavior, and thus we pay attention to the person and immediately decide whether it's a positive or negative disruption. In this case, you're likely to have a negative reaction because the person violated a cultural norm by interrupting your date. But if instead a friend unexpectedly interrupts your date and starts talking positively about you to your date, you're going to have a positive reaction because you know and like your friend.

The Disruption Trigger captures our attention by using three key elements—the three S's of disruption—surprise, simplicity, and significance.

Statistics + Finger Paints = A Surprising Lesson

Scott Goldthorp, a handsome sixth-grade teacher with dirty-blond hair and a fit physique, sought a way to convey the key concepts of statistics to his middle school students in a way that wouldn't bore them to sleep. He didn't want to simply teach his students about median, mode, central tendency, and variability—he wanted his students to understand why they were important.[5]

How do you get sixth graders excited about statistics and histograms, though? With finger paints and jumping, of course.

Goldthorp divided his students into three rotating groups. He asked one group to paint their hands and make two handprints: one while standing and one while jumping as high as they could. They would slap their hands onto pieces of chart paper taped to the walls. Once this was completed, a second group would measure the results using a meter stick and record the results. A third group would be cleaning their hands before getting back into the painting and recording cycle.

On the second day of the lesson, Goldthorp asked his students to create graphs to display the data they had collected from the day before in order to compare the standing versus jumping results. He also asked his students to calculate the mean, median, mode, and range of a sample set of the data.

This simple but innovative approach to teaching statistics turned out to be a major success. Students got excited about calculating the math and learning that, for example, taller students don't necessarily jump higher than shorter ones. Goldthorp does this sort of unexpected, interactive teaching for many of his math lessons.

"When I first started doing it [teaching interactive lessons], the students seemed a little apprehensive: This is math class, we should just be calculating numbers!" Goldthorp told *Scientific American*.

"At the beginning of the year, they might be out of their comfort zone. But after they get used to it, they love it."

Goldthorp, who received the 2013 Rosenthal Prize for Innovation in Math Teaching, disrupted his students' expectations by using surprise—the first S of the Disruption Trigger. The students had an expectation for how math is taught—to sit down with some lined paper and solve equations. That's how you're supposed to learn math, right? Instead, the Cherry Hill teacher surprised the students by using art and physiology to deliver his message. It made for a far more captivating and memorable lesson.

Any type of surprise that violates our expectations—like a teacher using exercise and art to teach a math lesson—captures our attention and sticks in our memory. Researchers at Purdue, Furman, and Duke Universities proved this by giving subjects forty-eight sentences with three nouns each and asking them later to recall the nouns. One set of sentences was simple and straightforward (e.g., "The maid spilled ammonia on the table"). This set of sentences constituted the control set. The other set of sentences, however, changed certain words so that the sentences became surprising and sometimes just plain bizarre (e.g., "The maid licked ammonia off the table").[6]

Some of the subjects got a healthy mix of common sentences and surprising sentences, while others received unmixed groups of just common sentences or just surprising sentences. The researchers learned that bizarre sentences did indeed stick in the minds of subjects . . . but only if they were mixed with common sentences. For something to catch our attention, it has to stick out like a sore thumb—a lesson we learned from the chapter on the Automaticity Trigger.

Our response to surprise is brief and comes in many valences— the positive or negative emotional impact we feel. We can have a positive response to a surprise, like Goldthorp's students had to his unique teaching style. We can have an ambivalent response to a surprise, even if it does startle us. And yes, we can have a negative response to a surprise as well.

The valence of a surprise matters when utilizing the Disruption Trigger to capture people's attention. While any type of surprise captures people's attention because it catches them off guard and thus violates their expectations, positive surprises are the best ones for keeping attention. Patagonia, for example, surprised consumers with a message they wanted to hear—don't buy this jacket until you absolutely need it, and in the meantime we'll do what we can to repair your existing gear. It's a pleasant surprise, so we keep Patagonia front and center in our mind. Next time we absolutely need to buy a ski jacket, we'll think of Patagonia first.

Of course, a negative or unpleasant surprise can capture attention as well. Controversy, for example, violates our expectations of what a prominent person or brand is supposed to say or do, and thus it garners greater interest from the media and the public. During an on-air television interview in St. Louis, former Missouri Congressman Todd Akin, a pro-life Republican campaigning in 2012 for a seat in the U.S. Senate, was asked whether he thought women who became pregnant due to rape should be able to get an abortion. Akin captured plenty of attention with his misguided and scientifically inaccurate response: "If it's a legitimate rape, the female body has ways to try to shut that whole thing down." By putting his foot in his mouth, he ignited a media firestorm that instantly doomed his Senate aspirations. He lost to Claire McCaskill, 54.7 percent to 39.2 percent.[7]

Some brands, however, have found ways to court controversy and use it to their advantage. In the 1990s, Wonderbra put out a series of billboards with model Eva Herzigová in the company's undergarments, with just two words: "Hello Boys." The campaign reportedly stopped traffic and caused fury in the United Kingdom for being plastered outside. It was racy for its time, but the proof is in the pudding: Playtex (which manufactures Wonderbra) sold twenty-five thousand per week in the months after the campaign launched (a 41 percent boost in sales).[8]

Surprise is a powerful element of the Disruption Trigger, but which type of surprise you use to be effective depends on the tone of your brand and message. We expect rappers to push the envelope and make controversial statements—there's a counterculture element to what they do and say that appeals to their audiences. On the other hand, we expect our senators to be well-informed and to use discretion—a test that Todd Akin failed. A surprise appearance at a fund-raiser or at a community event is an appropriate way for a senator to use disruption. You need to understand both what your brand represents and what type of surprises will appeal or turn off your target audience.

A few years ago, I was the host for a hackathon—an event where developers build brand-new apps from scratch over the course of twenty-four or forty-eight hours. During the final presentations, one of the developers decided it would be a great idea to lean next to one of the judges—prominent venture capitalist Dave McClure—and yell as loud as he could into his ear. It was his idea of an attention-grabbing stunt. This scream was loud enough to make me cover my ears—I can only imagine the ringing it caused in McClure's head.

The presenter was hoping his stunt would capture everybody's attention, but the result was that McClure understandably became angry and needed to step out to calm down. The developer did *not* win the competition, as he demonstrated a clear lack of judgment to the judges—a group of prominent investors and entrepreneurs he hoped to raise money from. This is an example of when surprise captured attention but clearly led to a negative outcome.

Skillful use of the Disruption Trigger relies on surprise, but you have to think about how your audience will react to that surprise and what opinion your audience will form about you based on the attention you receive from that surprise.

But surprise is just the first component of the Disruption Trigger, which leads us to the second S.

Why Are the World's Most Popular Products So Simple?

Mike Evangelist, a young product manager, sat patiently with his team in a boardroom, thumbing through pages of mock-ups, prototype screenshots, and documentation they had prepared in just three weeks. Evangelist, along with the rest of his team from Astarte GmbH, had recently been acquired by Apple and put in charge of building a new product for burning DVDs. At the time, in the mid-2000s, the market was filled with complicated pieces of software that were great at ruining blank DVDs but mediocre at actually burning movies or music onto them. Evangelist was one of the product managers in charge of designing a piece of software that would stand above the rest.[9]

When Steve Jobs finally entered the boardroom at Apple headquarters to discuss the project, he didn't show much interest in any of Evangelist's screenshots. Instead, he grabbed a marker and drew a rectangle on the whiteboard. Only a rectangle.

"Here's the new application," Jobs told Evangelist and his shell-shocked team. "It's got one window. You drag your video into the window. Then you click the button that says *burn*. That's it. That's what we're going to make."

This isn't how programs are supposed to operate. They are supposed to have menus, icons, and multiple windows. They are supposed to have countless options to cater to all types of power users. But Jobs, with his deep appreciation for the simplicity of the Bauhaus style of architecture and obsession with user experience, would have none of it. Evangelist and his team built the product as Jobs instructed, eventually resulting in iDVD, a core piece of the Apple iLife suite for the next decade.

"I still have the slides I prepared for that meeting, and they're ridiculous in their complexity," Evangelist once told *Fast Company*. "All this other stuff was completely in the way."

Simple ideas capture attention better than complex ones, which is why simplicity is the second *S* of disruption. Time and time again, Jobs proved that simplicity trumps complexity when it comes to building disruptive products that capture people's attention. The first iPhone had just one button, instead of the hundreds of buttons PDAs and keyboard-laden phones had at the time. The iMac G3 was a colorful but powerful computer encased in a single piece of translucent plastic. Steve Jobs was notorious for cutting unnecessary features to get the simple interface he wanted.

Other entrepreneurs have since followed his lead. The popular blogging platform Tumblr, acquired in 2012 by Yahoo, had a long-standing policy of not adding a new feature to its core product unless another feature is removed. It made for interesting discussions of just how necessary a feature truly is.

Most people subscribe to the belief that more is better: If I add more features, more people will want to use my product. If I add more statistics, my argument will be more convincing. If I have more choices, I will be happier.

None of these things are true. A study by researchers at Yale University and the University of Innsbruck found that stock traders with more financial and market information did not perform better than their counterparts. Instead, the quality of the information mattered more. In their research, they learned that well-informed traders— specifically insiders—clearly had the best financial performance, not because they had the most amount of information but because they had the *best* information.[10]

The belief that the more information you present, the stronger your arguments become is something I like to call the complexity trap. I once had an entrepreneur send me a hundred-plus-page pitch deck for his startup. It discussed every possible avenue for growth, along with what seemed like every graph he could muster—plenty of them irrelevant. While a novice entrepreneur may think that this is a smart approach to pitching a venture capitalist, it is actually counterproductive. It demonstrated a clear lack of focus and an inability to trim down extraneous work and ideas that wouldn't be directly beneficial to the growth of the startup.

I had to turn the entrepreneur down because he fell for the complexity trap. A pitch deck a fifth of the size he sent me would have retained my attention and been more persuasive. Simplicity always trumps complexity when it comes to grabbing people's attention—not just in the world of startups, but also in everything from education to politics. The reason for this is quite simple: complex ideas take more energy for us to process and increase something known as cognitive load.

Cognitive load is the amount of mental workload that an attention-consuming task requires of working memory. The more cognitive load a task requires, the more likely it is to cause attention fatigue. The result is a lack of attentional control, forgetfulness, lapses in concentration, and an increased propensity for errors.

"You can look at many sources of information, like webpages and books, and you find that they're loaded with information that misdirects attention and working memory resources," said Dr. John Sweller of the University of New South Wales. It's this increase in misdirection and working memory use that leads to the complexity trap. As tasks become more complicated, our attention deviates and quickly shifts to less cognitive-intensive tasks. Useful buttons, popups, and callouts soon become distractions and lead to less attention.[11]

So how do you make something simple so it can more effectively capture attention?

In some cases, complexity is unavoidable. Calculus is inherently complex and requires a lot of concentration and attention to master. The same is true of solving difficult puzzles, mastering complex sonatas, or writing books. This type of cognitive load is inherent to the task and known as intrinsic cognitive load. You can't control the inherit difficulty of learning calculus or mastering chess. However, you do have control over *how you present* that information to someone. To demonstrate, I have a challenge for you. Pretend you're a middle school music teacher and you've prepared a discussion on Beethoven's "Für Elise." You forgot your laptop with Beethoven's classic tune, though. Your challenge is simple: write a verbal explanation of Beethoven's "Für Elise."

Okay, that wasn't so simple, right? In fact, it's unproductive to try to explain a song verbally. You could talk about how the piece is set in A minor and in a 3/8 time signature, or you could try to explain the emotions you feel as you listen to the piece. Or you could just borrow somebody's laptop, open up YouTube, and play the song instead. It's easy to recognize a song when you play it, but it's a lot more difficult to recognize or understand if you try to explain it verbally. The same is true of tutorials and manuals: a confusing, poorly written manual with complex explanations can turn something relatively simple—like putting together furniture—into your personal nightmare.

"Some material is complex because of the way it's presented," Sweller explained to me. "If you're looking at something with the intention to learn something about it, the way that information is structured changes how much we learn."[12]

Cognitive load is extrinsic if that cognitive load is due to the way a piece of information is presented. Teaching "Für Elise" without the music adds unnecessary complexity. Math teacher Scott Goldthorp, on the other hand, simplified his explanation of statistics to his sixth graders by using finger paints to make the concepts applicable to the real world. This made a complicated subject simpler to understand because the students could use what they already knew about the world and apply that frame of reference to better understand the role that statistics play in our world. The simpler the explanation, the more likely it will stick.

The attention of your audience is fickle, so it's important to decrease cognitive load and simplify your ideas, products, or concepts. This will make it easier for your audience to pay attention and remember the message you're trying to deliver. Your goal should be to find ways to reduce complexity due to cognitive load to ensure that your audience focuses their attention exactly where you want them to direct it.

There are two key ways to reduce complexity and thus increase the focus and attention of your audience. The first is to remove everything that isn't vital to the integrity of your message, idea, or product. Steve Jobs did this with every product he touched, cutting unnecessary features until he had only the functionality he wanted. On the other hand, presentations filled with bullet points are the antithesis of simplicity and rarely add value to a presentation. They add complexity by forcing your audience to both read what is on the screen *and* listen to what you have to say at the same time. Trying to keep track of multiple bullet points on every single slide becomes a chore, increasing cognitive load and increasing the chance they'll pull out their phones and start playing games. You will never find a single bullet point in any of my presentations for this reason. I convey my message almost entirely through images and photographs that are easy to understand and add to the key points I'm discussing.

The second method of removing complexity is to make the information you're trying to present easier to find and access. Reduce the amount of searching or sleuthing your audience has to conduct. In journalism schools, aspiring journalists are taught to avoid "burying the lede." The lede is the first paragraph of a story, and it is a journalist's chance to snag the attention of readers and intrigue them enough to continue reading. If a journalist's headline or lede doesn't provide critical information about what the article is about, though, the reader will drop off because it requires too much cognitive load to search an article for its key points when there are thousands of other articles that present key information and facts in their ledes.

The same rule—making your message more accessible to your audience—is true of presentations as well. Many presenters wait until near the end to present their key points, making the incorrect assumption that their audiences are patient enough to keep listening until they get to the point. That's why my friend Jeremiah Owyang of Crowd Companies always starts his presentations with what his audience will learn in his talks, giving them an essential outline that makes it easier for them to follow his presentations.[13]

Whether you're trying to build an attention-grabbing product or create a disruptive and memorable lesson plan, simplicity is bliss. But there's still one more S of the Disruption Trigger we need to cover: significance.

Keeping Things Significant

You have fifteen or fewer seconds to capture somebody's attention.

"The first fifteen seconds matter most," Rachel Lightfoot Melby, a strategist and researcher for Google's YouTube division, explained to me as we sat in a spacious office at YouTube's headquarters. Her job is to understand why millions of people click on certain videos and not others, and to teach the next generation of video stars how to build their audiences and keep them there.[14]

Statistically, it's in these fifteen seconds that YouTubers need to convince a viewer to watch more. We're a very fickle audience. Four out of five viewers will bounce away from a video if it stops to buffer even once.[15] The decision to pay attention after we've been exposed to a video, idea, or event happens in those first few seconds.

A common mistake many YouTubers make, Melby tells me, is not immediately addressing the reason viewers came to their videos in the first place. Imagine you're searching for videos of the Chelyabinsk meteor that exploded in the Russian sky in February 2013. You find a video appropriately titled "Meteorite Crash in Russia!!" with a thumbnail of the meteor. But when you click, you're treated to thirty seconds of some random person trying to explain the meteor's origin first. It's boring, painful, and inconsistent with the expectations of YouTube's audience.

While a video titled "Most Badass Meteor Explosion Ever!" will catch our eye, if the video's content doesn't meet our expectations or align with our interests, our attention will immediately drop off in favor of something else. Significance—the third and final S of the Disruption Trigger—is finding a way to make a disruption meaningful for your audience. If you want to capture somebody's attention with a video in those first fifteen seconds, some element of your initial video has to have some measure of importance, relevance, or salience to your audience. You must violate expectations to capture attention, but not so completely as to alienate your audience. There's a fine-tuned balance, but if done right, harnessing significance can violate expectations and thus capture attention.

If you keep in mind what is significant and meaningful to your audience, your disruption will resonate. But if your message goes against their values, the opposite result can occur. In 2008, Motrin came out with a series of ads targeting moms who use baby slings and may be experiencing back pain as a result. Any hope that the message—that Motrin can help mothers with back pain—would resonate with moms was lost when the ad suggested that "wearing a baby" was a fashion statement and that moms who wear baby slings look "tired and crazy." This assertion that moms who wear baby slings are doing it as a fashion statement, rather than a parenting choice, outraged a large group of moms. The backlash was a Twitter and YouTube uprising by offended mothers that resulted in a quick apology from Motrin. The result was a failed campaigned that, instead of addressing the real issues that mothers face, marginalized mothers.[16]

The ad was inconsistent with the real values of mothers, and Motrin paid the price. Instead of Motrin's campaign being positive and meaningful to its target audience, it became a point of contention. Motrin didn't fully understand its audience and released a badly targeted campaign, and it backfired.

And there are plenty of even more painful examples. Quiznos' use of freaky-looking rodent creatures to promote its sandwiches—because, you know, rodents and sandwiches aren't a completely disgusting thought (Quiznos filed for bankruptcy in 2014) is one. And the phrase "toilet to tap" has held back real innovation in the implementation of water purification technology because of the instinctive gag reflex "toilet to tap" creates. In both cases, the campaigns became insignificant because they ended up disgusting their target audiences instead of captivating them.[17]

Disruptions that aren't significant and consistent with an audience's values always lead to trouble and distract from the message you're trying to deliver. But when surprise, simplicity, and significance all come together, the result is something that not only captures attention but also keeps it.

Why Did We Fall in Love with the Old Spice Guy?

In the early 2000s, Old Spice was the number-two player in the deodorant market, behind Right Guard. A new competitor, Axe, had just entered the U.S. market and was quickly gaining market share, thanks to its sexualized ads targeting teenage boys and its implicit promise that using Axe products would get you laid by beautiful women—it was "sex in a can." It played on the base instincts of teenage boys, and it was starting to work.[18]

At first, Old Spice tried to copy Axe's game plan with ads that attempted to capture its competitor's edgy sex appeal. But instead of reclaiming market share from Axe, it ended up being an awkward face-plant for the decades-old brand. "It was embarrassing," said Mark Fitzloff, executive creative director at Wieden+Kennedy, the advertising firm that worked with Old Spice to fix its branding problem. "It was literally like watching your grandfather dance. Nobody wanted to see that."

The campaign failed in part because the Axe campaign had made the Old Spice brand seem like the deodorant of your grandfather. Axe owned the market on edgy, sexy ads targeted toward teenage boys, and Old Spice's copycat strategy came across as the dad who tries to be cool but instead ends up awkwardly embarrassing himself. Even Old Spice's name didn't help: How could something be new and hip if it literally had *old* in its name? The Old Spice campaign lacked significance or surprise, and thus it failed to disrupt the market.

In 2007, with its market share slipping, Old Spice turned to Wieden+Kennedy, the masterminds behind dozens of marketing campaigns, including Nike's "Just Do It" campaign. Mark Fitzloff and his colleagues were in charge of revitalizing the Old Spice brand. Their first goal was simple: to create a campaign that was truly consistent with a brand that had been around for eighty years. It couldn't imitate Axe.

Wieden+Kennedy began its makeover of Old Spice with a magazine ad that didn't feature teenage girls in bikinis or contemporary stars like Mila Kunis. Instead, the first Wieden+Kennedy ad featured Faye Dunaway, the award-winning actress who transformed into a star and sex symbol after she starred in the 1967 film *Bonnie and Clyde*. The magazine ad features a young Dunaway seductively stretched out in front of a fire. The headline: "If your grandfather hadn't worn it, you wouldn't exist. Experience is everything."

The Dunaway ad changed what it meant to be "old." Instead of associating old with stodginess, the campaign connected old with experience and wisdom—like how a younger brother looks up to his older brother. The campaign hit all three S's of the Disruption Trigger: it had a simple message, it had a surprising twist, and it remained significant by appealing to our collective desire for experience and wisdom.

Wieden+Kennedy's most disruptive campaign for Old Spice, however, came a few years later with Isaiah Mustafa, a former NFL wide receiver who is better known as the "Old Spice Guy." Mustafa's character exuded wisdom and experience in a way that didn't take himself or Old Spice too seriously. In the course of thirty seconds, Mustafa, speaking to the ladies in the audience (who often influence personal-care buying decisions), magically appears on a boat, finds an oyster, gives you two tickets "to that thing you love," turns the tickets to diamonds, and somehow ends up on a horse. He does this all while talking about how Old Spice body wash will make their men smell like him, even if they can't be him. It consistently disrupts and violates expectations by placing Mustafa in completely unexpected and unconventional situations. (By the way, if you can find me a man who can turn tickets into diamonds, I'll give you a horse.)[19]

The ad, along with the videos that followed, made for a new and delightful series of surprising situations (like Mustafa putting on a wig and pretending to be your mom or Mustafa facing off against Fabio) that contained the same message—using Old Spice will make you, in some way, as cool and interesting as the Old Spice Guy. This message was meaningful and significant to

Old Spice's audience—who doesn't want to be cool and interesting? It didn't need to be sex in a can to sell. The result was one of the fastest-growing viral campaigns in history. The original ad has garnered over 50 million views on YouTube, and many of Mustafa's videos, including dozens created on the fly as responses to celebrities and fans, have over a million views. But most importantly, the Wieden+Kennedy campaign drove sales. In the three months after the Old Spice Guy made his debut, sales skyrocketed by 55 percent.

The Old Spice campaign worked because it not only violated expectations, but it also followed the three S's. Subsequent campaigns have had the Old Spice Guy do everything from serenading celebrities on YouTube to eating a bowling ball sandwich as if it were no big deal. But in every campaign, he's surprising, he's engaging, and he's consistent with his quirky and positive persona.

Simplicity, Surprise, and Significance in Context

Game of Thrones—both the series of books and the popular HBO show based on them—has been raking in readers, viewers, and awards for years. The show is now the most popular show in HBO history, with an average gross audience of 18.4 million viewers per episode and rising.[20]

One of the reasons *Game of Thrones* has been so successful is its penchant for disrupting expectations. How does it do this? By unexpectedly killing off lead characters, oftentimes in shocking and brutal fashion. Authors of popular book series are not supposed to kill off main characters, but George R. R. Martin does it anyway. These dramatic and unexpected moments are examples of the Disruption Trigger in action. I won't spoil the books or the show for you, but let's just say that these disruptive moments (e.g., the infamous Red Wedding) are the ones that fans of *Game of Thrones* talk about the most.

When you look deeper, you can see the three *S*'s of disruption in action. It's impossible to predict whom Martin will kill off next (surprise), and the deep connection many fans build with these lead characters makes their deaths that much more meaningful and important to the fans (significance). And while the world of Westeros isn't simple, its underlying themes are. A BBC article argued that "Author George R. R. Martin's web of characters and lineages may be confusing, but there's a moral simplicity to *Game of Thrones* that attracted audiences to it."[24]

Surprise, simplicity, and significance just can't be ignored when using the Disruption Trigger to capture attention, because if you ignore even one, your message simply becomes less captivating. If someone were to surprise me with a football jersey, I'd pay attention and be thankful. But a gift with significance will be more attention grabbing. I would be far more excited about a Chicago Bears jersey (my favorite team) than I would be about the Oakland Raiders (I couldn't care less about them). Each *S* reinforces the other until you have something that cannot be ignored.

The Disruption Trigger is just one trigger, though, and its strength is in capturing attention for a brief period of time rather than maintaining it over long periods of time. It's primarily a tool for capturing short attention, and it can quickly fizzle out if you don't follow up with the other captivation triggers.

This leads us to the next set of captivation triggers. These are the triggers that help us maintain long attention. They are the tools for maintaining and growing attention for days, weeks, years, and even centuries.

Chapter 5

Reward Trigger

A few years ago, I was dining with a group of tech industry friends at an upscale restaurant in San Francisco. Our out-of-town friend Milana had come to visit us, but despite the fact that we rarely got a chance to see her, none of us were paying attention to her. Instead, we were locked in a constant staring match with our smartphones. Texting. Scanning Twitter. E-mailing. Checking in on Foursquare.

That's when Milana suggested we play the phone stacking game. Each of us placed our iPhones and Android phones on top of each other. (Milana, being the workaholic nerd she is, put three phones in the pile.) None of us were allowed to look at our phones. The first one to touch the pile had to pay for the entire table's tab.

Nobody touched their phones for the rest of the night. Our attention had instantly transferred from our vibrating devices to our vibrant conversation. I've been suggesting the phone stacking game at group dinners ever since.

Approximately 70 percent of managers say they check their phones within an hour of waking up, and 56 percent say they check their phones within an hour before bed.[1] Here's a crazier stat, though: the average person checks their smartphone 110 times per day.[2] Sadly, I probably check my phone twice as often. We're a society addicted to our phones.

Actually, it's not the smartphone itself that's addicting. The real culprits are the e-mail, text, and app notifications, because they grab our attention by triggering a complex mechanism in our brain that powers our motivations and desires. It is this mechanism that makes us pay attention to everything from our smartphones to the McDonald's arches.

But how does this mechanism work? And how can you harness it to capture attention?

The Reward Mechanism

All animals—including humans—are creatures developed specifically for accomplishing goals and seeking rewards. Sex allows us to procreate and rewards us with pleasure; hunting allows us to find food and is rewarded with sustenance; solving a difficult puzzle rewards us with personal satisfaction. Our body is constantly training us to develop certain habits that it thinks are either pleasurable or beneficial to our well-being and survival.

Eating a delicious treat like a chocolate brownie, for example, seizes our attention for the same reason clearing our phone's notifications makes us feel better: our brain rewards us for these behaviors. I suspect most of you are familiar at some level with dopamine. It's a neurotransmitter in the brain that helps send or block signals to nerve cells. Most people have heard that when dopamine is released in the body, it stimulates pleasure centers in the brain, causing us to feel happiness while we eat a cupcake or relief when we reach inbox zero.

But this perception of dopamine is a misconception. As we learned in chapter 1, recent research has shown us that while dopamine is related to pleasure, it doesn't actually cause pleasure. Studies have shown that you can take away dopamine from a rat and it will still feel pleasure. What it will lose is its motivation to do anything pleasurable. In fact, a rat without dopamine won't even be motivated to eat.

"If you suppress dopamine, you suppress the attractiveness of all rewards," said Dr. Kent Berridge of the University of Michigan, an expert in affective neuroscience and the brain systems that control motivation, pleasure, and reward. He told me that there are, in fact, two key systems involved in rewarding us for desired behaviors.[3]

The first system—wanting—is the system that gives us the motivation to act and is powered by dopamine. It gives us desire. When you crave a cupcake, sex, or a drug, dopamine is flowing through your brain. On the other hand, the second system—liking—is the system that actually rewards us with pleasure and satisfaction, completing the reward cycle. Liking is controlled by another set of neurotransmitters known as opioids.

This dual system for rewards explains why we're obsessed with our phones. Imagine you're locked in a room for an hour and you have only two options to pass the time: you can either play with your phone, or you can solve a complex jigsaw puzzle. Which one do you think you're going to spend more time playing with? Sure, you might try the jigsaw puzzle, but when that phone vibrates, you're going to check to see what notification just popped up on the phone. Is it an e-mail? A news article? A tweet?

Dopamine is released both when we're looking at a phone and when we're solving a puzzle, but the trigger to release dopamine comes much quicker and more often with the phone. Dopamine triggers wanting, which leads to seeking—it makes us want to investigate new things and solve puzzles. The phone offers this in spades—new texts and e-mails come in seconds, reactivating our reward systems. The puzzle, on the other hand, isn't changing or getting solved anytime soon. Our natural reward system is optimized for novelty and the search for new information.[4]

Dopamine and the body's reward system are vital to our attention. Our body releases dopamine whenever it thinks there's a potential reward at the end of the rainbow—this gives us the motivation we need to achieve that reward. Rewards also have the unique ability to distract us, even long after the promise of a reward has disappeared.

Brian Anderson, Patryk Laurent, and Steven Yantis—neuroscientists at Johns Hopkins University—trained a group of participants to search for a red target or a green target (circles, squares, etc.) in a sea of colorful shapes over the course of one thousand trials. Every time the subjects identified the red or green target, they received a small amount of money—either a penny or a nickel—as a reward for the correct response. What they didn't know was that one group had an 80 percent chance of receiving a nickel and a 20 percent chance of receiving a penny, while a second group's reward probability was reversed: they had only a 20 percent chance of earning a nickel.[5]

Then the subjects were asked to complete 480 more trials in which they were asked to look for a unique shape in a sea of shapes. In this round, the participants received absolutely no reward. The shapes were never red or green for the control group. However, the other group had shapes of all colors, including red and green—the colors they had looked for in the previous experiment—but these were absolutely irrelevant to their current task of finding unique shapes.

The fact that the second set of trials had no monetary reward didn't matter to subjects' attentional systems, though. Thanks to the monetary reward of the previous experiment, their response times slowed significantly in the shape-searching task. Their attention was now trained to focus on the red and green shapes automatically, thanks to their association with monetary rewards. In addition, the subjects with the higher monetary rewards from the first experiment were the slowest to react in the second. More money turned into more attention for red and green shapes, even though they had no monetary value in the second set of trials.

The Reward Trigger activates our desire and motivation for a reward—the wanting mechanism. Once we want something, we pay attention until we achieve the reward we desire—the liking mechanism.

The rewards we desire come in two flavors: extrinsic and intrinsic. Extrinsic rewards are tangible rewards we receive for accomplishing something. Things like money, food, trophies, and a perfect score on a test fall into this category. Intrinsic rewards, on the other hand, are the intangible rewards that provide us with feelings of internal satisfaction and accomplishment. It's the satisfaction and joy you feel when you nail your instrumental solo during a concert, solve a difficult puzzle, or finish a great book.

Just like rewards, the motivations we have to achieve those rewards can also be extrinsic or intrinsic. If you're reading *Captivology* because you will be quizzed on the book in class, you're extrinsically motivated because you're motivated by an extrinsic reward. If, however, you're reading this book because you have a desire to learn and become more captivating, then you have intrinsic motivations because the reward for accomplishing the task is intangible and intrinsic.[6]

As we'll see throughout the rest of this chapter, both types of rewards (and the motivations behind them) have a powerful influence on people's attention, but the types of attention each reward effects are different. If you're looking to capture immediate and short attention, extrinsic rewards (like the pennies and nickels of the Johns Hopkins experiment) can be extremely effective. However, if you're looking to build loyalty and long attention, then intrinsic rewards are far more helpful. Identifying the right rewards to activate the right motivations in the right situations is central to using the Reward Trigger effectively.

It's time to dive deeper into the two main types of rewards, starting with extrinsic rewards.

Extrinsic Rewards, or Why You Should Wrap Your Money in Bacon

Most companies offer a standard array of benefits and rewards to attract and retain employees. You're familiar with them: health and dental insurance, pay raises, cash bonuses, vacation days, flexible scheduling, paid paternity leave, etc. But none of these particularly stand out. These are rewards that you can find at almost any company that cares about its employees. Even more luxurious bonuses, like on-site meals, gym memberships, and massages, are becoming more and more common among startups trying to catch the attention of in-demand engineers and designers.

But there are a couple of companies that don't do the typical perks, and they stand out as more distinctive and thoughtful than the rest. Scopely, a Los Angeles–based mobile and social game publisher, decided to parody the "Most Interesting Man in the World" campaign from the popular Dos Equis commercials. Rather than simply giving recruits a cash bonus for joining the company, Scopely gave new recruits and the people who referred them a briefcase filled with a year's supply of Dos Equis, a custom tuxedo, cigars, a spear gun, Sex Panther cologne (popularized in the movie *Anchorman*), an oil painting of the recruit, and last but not least, eleven thousand dollars in cash wrapped with bacon. Yes, bacon.[7]

Overboard? Sure. Effective? Absolutely. The company received more than a thousand résumés from the creative campaign and was able to convince multiple engineers from hyper-competitive Silicon Valley to move south for Scopely.

Scopely used clear extrinsic rewards to capture attention and successfully recruit high-value employees. But any person or company can offer extrinsic rewards like cash and gifts (assuming they have those rewards on hand). What Scopely did was different, though, and it snowballed into a heap of attention. So why were its extrinsic rewards so attention grabbing?

We are used to extrinsic rewards in nearly every facet of our lives. Did your kid get a perfect score on her spelling test? She gets a gold star and an A! Did you outperform sales projections? You get a performance bonus! But in many cases, these run-of-the-mill extrinsic rewards only capture fleeting moments of attention.

"If-then rewards and extrinsic motivators like money and fame . . . absolutely, unequivocally, get our attention," said Daniel Pink, the best-selling author of *Drive* and *To Sell Is Human*, when I interviewed him. "They get our attention in a very fixed way. They're extraordinarily effective at times." But, Pink said, there is a caveat to these types of rewards when it comes to attention.[8]

"What [rewards] don't necessarily do is get our attention in a sustained way, because you have to offer another one in order to reclaim that attention."

Extrinsic rewards work best to capture attention when you only need to grab someone's attention once or twice to accomplish your goal. If you need to motivate your audience to recommend star employees for your company, extrinsic rewards work. But extrinsic rewards are far less effective once that star employee joins your company. A comprehensive analysis of multiple studies found that the correlation between money and job satisfaction is very weak. This is because intrinsic rewards like happiness, purpose, and self-satisfaction are better motivators than extrinsic ones like bonuses and vacation time, at least when it comes to long-term employment at a company.[9]

We clearly pay attention to tangible rewards for short-term tasks, but it's also clear that not all extrinsic rewards are equal when it comes to our attention. Plenty of companies offer referral and signing bonuses to attract engineering talent, but most of them aren't as adept as Scopely at using those rewards to captivate potential recruits. So what separated Scopely's rewards from thousands of others?

The answer isn't which extrinsic rewards Scopely offered, as one might expect, but the way in which Scopely *presented* those rewards. Researchers at Emory and Baylor Universities, testing the impact of rewards on the pleasure centers of the brain, squirted either water (meh) or fruit juice (tasty!) into the mouths of twenty-five subjects. In one run, subjects knew that the two drinks would alternate at fixed, predictable intervals. In the other run, the order and timing of the sensations were randomized.[10]

As expected, the subjects in both runs experienced pleasure when they tasted the fruit juice—its sweet taste activated their brains' nucleus accumbens, an area of the brain deeply involved in pleasure and reward. The MRI scans the researchers conducted, however, found that the subjects' pleasure centers became much more active for the subjects who participated in the randomized water/juice test. It didn't even matter whether the subjects preferred water or fruit juice—either way, their brains would light up more intensely when they were surprised.

Surprise and unpredictability are the keys here. The reward centers of the brain became more active when subjects were surprised by extrinsic rewards. The less predictable a reward is, the more pleasurable it becomes. If you recall from the chapter on the Disruption Trigger, our brain is wired to pay attention to anything that violates our expectations, so the correlation between surprise and rewards makes sense.

In the case of Scopely, the company understood that everyone expected a cash bonus if they referred an engineer to the company. However, nobody expected to get that money wrapped in bacon. The fact that Scopely also included uncommon rewards with its bacon-wrapped money—when's the last time a company offered you a harpoon gun?—only enhanced the surprising nature of the primary reward (the eleven thousand dollars in cash) and thus the attention Scopely received.

We can safely conclude that uncommon extrinsic rewards capture people's attention because they surprise them, and people are wired to pay attention to surprises. Even if you're offering a common reward like money, finding a creative, unique way to present those rewards will make them more attention grabbing. But it's not just surprising extrinsic rewards that matter when it comes to capturing people's attention—how and when you deliver those rewards also matters.

How to Deliver Extrinsic Rewards

Imagine you're running alongside the beautiful Sydney Harbour, trying to keep in shape while exploring Australia's largest city during a visit. You have your phone with you for the music, but you've also opened up your favorite running app to track your miles and log your route so you know how to get back to any interesting sights. As you finish your run, you check and see that you broke ten miles— absolutely one of your best runs.

Your running app buzzes, congratulating you on your accomplishment. But more importantly, it's just offered to send you a free pack of Gatorade and a pair of gym shorts for your achievement. Nice! You didn't expect that at all. You were running for other reasons, but these rewards for your achievements made your day.

This is the secret sauce of Kiip, a fast-growing platform for mobile rewards. If you're playing a puzzle game and you beat your friends' high score, a message powered by Kiip may just pop up, letting you know that you just earned a freebie, a discount, or some other type of achievement-based reward. Brands love it because it puts their product in front of targeted users during their happiest moments or moments of need, and apps love it because it provides an extra dose of happiness for the user and a source of income that doesn't depend on banner ads.

Brian Wong, the company's cofounder and CEO, said there are two ways to offer somebody a reward. The first is one we're all familiar with: incentives. If you do something, I will give you something in return. Incentives are everywhere in the economy through loyalty programs and added bonuses. Buy our credit card and you'll get twenty-five thousand miles free. The user is rewarded for changing their behavior. It's dangling a carrot.

Wong isn't a fan of incentives, to say the least. "It's essentially micro-bribery," he said.[11]

His company specializes in another type of reward: post-action rewards. This is when the user isn't expecting to receive anything but is given a serendipitous reward for an achievement. It not only surprises the user (activating the pleasure centers of his or her brain, as we just learned), but it also treats people as human beings with worth, rather than Pavlovian dogs that can be trained.

"Consumers respond much more highly to something that isn't dangled in front of their face as an incentive," said Wong.

Are people more motivated by a surprising reward based on achievement than an incentive? Kiip measured how consumers responded to incentives versus post-action rewards. When Kiip offered a reward as an incentive, they found that less than 15 percent of consumers redeemed the reward Kiip offered. But when the product offered a serendipitous reward—one offered after an achievement—the redemption rate grew to north of 20 percent. That's a big difference if you're trying to get your product in the hands of potential customers, and it's a far less intrusive method for reaching a target audience. Perhaps that's why more than 350 brands and 2,100 apps are using Kiip.

"In the original version of rewarding and loyalty, it was to define the behavior," explained Wong. "But it's now about the behavior defining the reward."

There are many ways to give somebody an extrinsic reward. Yu-kai Chou, an expert at gamification (a discipline that uses game mechanics and rewards to increase user engagement), breaks reward delivery into six general categories. We've already learned about two types: incentives (offering a reward in return for completing a specific action) and post-action rewards (providing an unexpected reward after completing a specific action). But there are a few others Chou outlines:

- Collections: Giving users only a piece of the overall reward in the hopes they will be incentivized to complete the collection. McDonald's has done this for years with its Monopoly Game, where you have to collect two to three separate pieces to qualify to win everything from a vacation to a million dollars.

- Lottery: Offering a reward based on chance.

- Random Rewards: Users know they will receive a reward after completing a task but don't know what that reward will be. This is different than Kiip's post-action rewards, which never promise you'll receive a reward after completing an action (instead, Kiip's rewards are total surprises).

- Gifting: Having other users give you a reward. This is used all the time in social games like *Candy Crush Saga*, *FarmVille*, and their successors. Users can send their friends extra lives or special items. This is clever because these rewards could just as easily come from the game itself, but instead this approach involves your friends, giving you the feeling of validation.

All six ways of giving rewards—incentives, post-action rewards, collections, lottery, random rewards, and gifting—captivate users in the right situations. A random reward is captivating because users don't know what they're going to get (surprise). On the other hand, gifting is effective because people feel validated by friends giving them gifts (a concept we'll discuss further in the chapter on the Acknowledgment Trigger).

The main lesson to draw here, though, is that surprising somebody with a reward is more effective at capturing attention than offering a fixed reward. Any time you can add a level of unpredictability to a reward, you should. Post-action rewards and random rewards are the most effective methods for delivering rewards in this case.[12]

We've covered the power of extrinsic rewards on our attention, but I did say earlier that extrinsic rewards are limited to capturing immediate and short attention. When you need to capture sustained attention that lasts over the course of months or years—long attention—intrinsic rewards are the way to go. To better understand why intrinsic rewards captivate our attention over the long term, let's turn our attention to a Canadian hero.

Intrinsic Rewards, or How One Man's Motivation Changed the World

In the 1970s, a curly-haired college athlete returning home crashed into a pickup truck, totaling his car. He was okay except for a sore knee. That soreness would come and go until 1977, when he could no longer ignore the pain and went to the hospital. He received a far more somber diagnosis than he expected—cancer. More specifically, doctors diagnosed him with osteosarcoma, an aggressive tumor that often starts in the bones of the legs and knees. The doctors had to amputate his leg in order to save him.[13]

If you're a Canadian, this story will be familiar. In 1979, Terry Fox, now outfitted with an artificial leg, began training his body. He started with a half mile on the track at Hastings Junior High School. Then a week later, he ran his first mile. Through the training, pain, and countless blisters, Fox persevered and his strength grew, despite his chemotherapy. By the end of the year, he completed his first marathon, eliciting cheers from the crowd. But his real plan had just begun. His true goal: run across all of Canada in order to raise awareness and a million dollars for cancer research. Even his mother thought he was nuts, but he insisted.

Inspired by Fox's story, Ford of Canada gave him a camper van, Adidas gave him running shoes, and other sponsors came out of the woodwork, offering flights, gas money, and living expenses. The Canadian Cancer Society agreed to help promote the run.

"I've seen a lot of disability, people who were really shut in and away from life and who couldn't do anything," Fox once told *Montreal Gazette*. "I want to show that just because they're disabled, it's not the end. In fact, it's more of a challenge."

In April 1980, his run across Canada began. Despite gale-force winds and a lack of visibility in the beginning, he pushed forward, running approximately a full marathon's length every single day. Port aux Basques. Nova Scotia. Montreal. And while the donations weren't rolling in just yet, he continued. Eventually he caught the attention of Isadore Sharp, the founder of Four Seasons who lost his son to cancer just two years prior. He and his company rallied hundreds of other corporations to donate two dollars per mile that Fox ran, and this kept Fox going.

As he kept running, his story kept spreading. People were finally turning out for Fox. Ten thousand people rallied for the marathoner when he made it to Toronto, raising a hundred thousand dollars in a single day for cancer research. In Ontario, hockey legend Bobby Orr presented him with a twenty-five-thousand-dollar check. The endeavor captured the attention and the hearts of not just Canadians, but people all across the world.

By the time his journey ended 143 days later, Terry Fox's Marathon of Hope had changed the game for cancer research. And while he never made it across Canada, his run raised $1.7 million. A national telethon organized a week later in his honor helped raise an astounding $10.5 million more. The cancer and his amazing run took their toll on his body, though. By June 1981, Fox had developed pneumonia and passed away. An entire nation mourned.

Fox's Marathon of Hope made cancer research a priority. The Terry Fox Run, an event that now spans four continents, continues to raise millions to fight cancer. So why did Terry Fox capture the hearts and minds of millions of Canadians during his run? More importantly, why is his work still making an impact, decades after his death?

For Fox's supporters, they were rewarded for their commitment with long-term personal satisfaction and the knowledge that they helped make the world better—there was no short-term reward for their support. Even the actual goal of Fox's Marathon of Hope—to find a cure for cancer—is still a long way from fruition. No amount of short-term, extrinsic rewards was going to motivate the Canadian people to keep paying attention.

"What fifty years of social science tells us very clearly is that if-then rewards are pretty effective for simple, short-term kinds of tasks," Daniel Pink explained during our interview. "What they don't necessarily do is get our attention in a sustained way, because you have to offer another one in order to reclaim that attention."

If-then rewards are extrinsic rewards—specifically incentives (if you do something, then you get a reward in return). We already know that, if you want someone to pay attention to a single task or idea, extrinsic rewards can be effective. But once a task or idea becomes more complicated, extrinsic rewards lose their effectiveness. This is because receiving a reward completes the dopamine-opioid cycle of wanting and liking. Once we have our extrinsic reward, there is no longer any incentive to continue to pay attention. To restart the cycle, Pink said, you have to offer another reward.[14]

Pink also said that organizations use incentive rewards too often. The result is that work gets done, but employees have no reason to excel, and job satisfaction tanks. Imagine a workplace where you had no companionship and no love for your job or your company's business. The only reason you stuck around was because of the salary and the bonuses. But these are just enough to get you to do the minimum work—you have no additional incentive to go above and beyond the call of duty.

I suspect a fair number of you have either experienced this scenario once in your life or have a friend in this situation. It's a terrible work environment for employees and a terrible way for employers to conduct business. A study conducted by Dr. James Harter, Gallup's chief scientist of workplace management and well-being, found low job satisfaction was correlated with a future drop in the bottom line. In other words, unhappy employees eventually lead to declining profits.[15]

This is where intrinsic rewards come into the picture. They are the intangible, internalized feelings of satisfaction and joy we feel when we accomplish something or do something we love. When I was a kid, I would read books about outer space and the solar system in the library (I was a true nerd). But I didn't devour these books because I had a test. I read these books for the sake of learning. I did it because I inherently enjoyed learning about how comets and stars form.

The difference between extrinsic and intrinsic rewards is all in the motivations we have to achieve each type of reward. Extrinsic rewards motivate us to do something or to pay attention to something in order to receive that reward. We will listen to our teachers to get good grades or work overtime for extra money. But intrinsic rewards are for their own sake—we're motivated to pay attention or take action because something is simply worth doing, and we don't really care if we earn any extrinsic reward for our effort.

The key here is that our motivation to achieve intrinsic rewards like satisfaction is a long-term phenomenon. We know that we cannot master chess or piano in a single sitting—it takes years of dedication, but many of us master these skills anyway. Our brain develops a long-term relationship with the things that motivate us intrinsically. This long-term motivation, activated by the wanting mechanism of the dopamine system, makes us pay attention to the things that will help us achieve the intrinsic rewards we crave. Thus, if you help provide people with the motivation to achieve an intrinsic reward, you also capture their attention.

"Progress in the world comes down to motivating other people and motivating oneself," Sheryl Sandberg, the author of *Lean In* and COO of Facebook, told me when I interviewed her. When I asked her what she thought the key to capturing attention was, her reply was simple: "Motivation."[16]

Intrinsic motivation leads us to intrinsic rewards that will make us pay attention to things that no amount of extrinsic rewards could ever provide. Take Canada's reaction to Terry Fox as an example. There were no tangible rewards for Canadians to support his cause and donate. Donors didn't get job promotions for their donations. Instead, the rewards were intrinsic—the satisfaction that their donations were going toward a worthy champion and a worthy cause was more than enough of a reward. Plus there is something inherently joyful and satisfying about supporting an underdog like Fox; I know I feel joy when I hear about an underdog overcoming the odds to succeed.

How to Deliver Intrinsic Rewards

It's clear that the right intrinsic rewards lead to long-term attention. But what qualifies as an intrinsic reward? And how can you provide intrinsic rewards to motivate others and get them to pay attention?

You can't simply offer an intrinsic reward to somebody like you can offer money or other extrinsic rewards. Intrinsic rewards come from a person's internal desires. It boils down to two questions: What gives your audience personal satisfaction? And what does your audience like to do just for the sake of doing it?

While the answers to these questions vary, there are a couple of intrinsic motivators that are, in general, common across all people. Ohio State University Professor Emeritus Steven Reiss, for example, places intrinsic motivations in sixteen categories: power, independence, curiosity, acceptance (from others), order, saving (or collecting), honor, idealism (social justice), social contact (having friends), family, status, vengeance, romance, eating, physical activity, and tranquillity (safety).[17]

Reiss is not the only one who has categorized intrinsic motivators. Daniel Pink believes that there are three key motivations that drive our behavior and our decisions: autonomy (the freedom of self-direction), mastery (becoming better at something), and purpose ("Knowing why you're doing something, rather than simply how to do it," Pink said).[18] These are poignant and powerful motivations, especially when it comes to providing motivation in the workplace.

Phew! That's a lot of motivations. Before you start highlighting this section and memorizing all of these different motivations, let me make something clear: all of these motivations are simply *different paths people take to achieve an intrinsic reward*. It's important to make the distinction between intrinsic rewards and intrinsic motivations. Intrinsic rewards are simply the happiness and satisfaction we feel from personal accomplishment. Intrinsic motivations—e.g. mastery, honor, social contact—are the reasons we have for taking an action (in this case, to achieve an intrinsic reward). Some people feel that sense of satisfaction by hanging out with friends. Others find it when they find purpose in their careers. And yet others feel joy as they feed their curiosities.

So while there are many paths to an intrinsic reward, the most important thing you can do to give that to your audience—and thus capture their attention—is to understand the key motivators of your audience and then help facilitate their journey to an intrinsic reward. You can't "give" somebody personal satisfaction in their job, for example, but you can give them the freedom they need to achieve that intrinsic reward. Google's famous 20 percent—where engineers have the freedom to spend up to a day per week on a project of their joy—promotes autonomy, independence, and curiosity—all motivators that lead to intrinsic rewards.

In the 1980s, when Ricardo Semler took over as CEO of Brazil's Semco Group—a manufacturing company at the time—he instituted a series of radical policies. He eliminated organizational charts, time sheets, job titles, and expensive micromanagers. The result is that Semco has grown from $4 million per year to north of $200 million per year in a little over two decades. Without all the restrictions present in many other companies, Semco's employees were free to innovate and flourish. They were given the opportunity to achieve intrinsic rewards, and that translated into millions in sales.[19]

For the previous few sections, we've covered the two types of rewards in depth, but we still haven't talked about another important component of the Reward Trigger: How do you make somebody desire a reward? How do you activate the wanting mechanism? To answer that, we will have to take a trip to Thailand.

Seeing Is Wanting

What would you do if a boy and girl, both six years old, walked up to you with cigarettes in their mouths, asking you for a light?

Two Thai children in Bangkok did exactly that. "Can I get a light?" the children ask two young women with cigarettes in their hands. "They drill a hole in your throat. Aren't you afraid of surgery?" one of the women replies to the little girl. "You know it's bad, right? Smoking causes lung cancer and emphysema," a man tells the children.[20]

The children simply ask back, "If it's so bad, why are you smoking?" The kids then hand the adults a piece of paper that says, "You worry about me. But why not about yourself?" and walk away.

The children weren't actually smokers. It was actually a campaign called "Smoking Kid" for the Thai Health Promotion Foundation. In the two-and-a-half-minute video, the children subtly remind strangers on the street of the true dangers of smoking. They make the dangers of smoking real by asking the adults for a light. It's one thing to be given statistics about smoking; it's another to actually see children with cigarettes in their hands.

The video, created by Ogilvy & Mather, was a sensation from the moment of its debut. It generated over 5 million views and twenty thousand antismoking comments on YouTube in just ten days, and it was hailed by everyone from Upworthy to *Reuters* to the local Thai news as one of the best antismoking ads ever made. More importantly, though, phone calls to the Thai Health Promotion Foundation's smoking hotline increased by 40 percent. The children with cigarettes in their mouths provided a vivid, visual cue that triggered the wanting response—"I want to be healthy. I want to quit." Thousands of people saw both the consequences of smoking and the rewards of quitting. All of this motivated people to call the hotline.

So how did they—and how do you—activate the wanting mechanism that activates our attention? The answer is imagery, because
imagery motivates people to go after rewards more intensely than
any other motivator. We're horrendous at visualizing statistics or
abstract goals, but if you show someone a picture of a chocolate
chip cookie or a starving child—imagery—you are far more likely to
catch their attention.

"When we think vividly of a reward . . . it activates the reward
system directly," Dr. Kent Berridge said. "The worst thing an addict
should do is to vividly imagine that drug. . . . The wanting grows."[21]

Visualizing a reward—whether it's an extrinsic or intrinsic reward—is among the best ways to increase your audience's desire and
attention for that reward. Suparna Rajaram and Maryellen Hamilton, researchers at SUNY Stony Brook and Saint Peter's University,
respectively, asked a group of eighty-three students to look at a list of
eighty words. For half of the words, they were asked to simply read
each word that appeared on the screen (the "non-imaged" set). For
the other set of words, however, the subjects were asked to "form a
mental image" of the word before moving on (the "imaged" set).

The subjects were next tested with eighty general knowledge
questions and told the questions were related to a different experiment. Half of the questions had answers unrelated to the first study.
However, the other half of the general knowledge questions had
target answers that the subjects had encountered in the earlier study.
Of these forty questions, half came from the non-imaged word set
and the other half came from the imaged word set.[22]

When Rajaram and Hamilton tallied up the results, they found
that the students had a far greater percentage of right answers (about
45 percent) for the questions related to the imaged words than for
either the non-imaged (about 30 percent) or the new words (about
25 percent). Just imagining the words helped significantly with both
memory and recognition. This effect is well known among teachers

and academics. The imagery effect—visualizing an object or goal—can trigger the reward system by making the goal more tangible. In other words, imagining yourself crossing the finish line makes you more determined to actually complete the race.

More effective than even visualization, though, is actually being able to see the fruits of your labor—showing somebody the actual reward or providing a tangible equivalent. We are bad at grasping esoteric concepts but easily motivated when we actually see the reward right in front of us.

Dan Ariely, a behavioral economist at Duke University, asked a group of male Harvard students to build models out of Bionicle Legos. The first time each subject built one of the models—forty pieces, with instructions—he was paid two dollars. If the subject decided to build a second Lego model, he was paid $1.89—eleven cents less than the first time. The reward for the third model was eleven cents less than the second reward ($1.78) and continued to descend until the reward reached two cents. All of the Lego sets were identical.[23]

What the subjects didn't know was that they were divided into two groups: Meaningful and Sisyphus. Students in the Meaningful camp were asked to place each completed Lego model on the desk in front of them before they were given a new box of Legos. The models would pile up on the table as they built more. The subjects in the Sisyphus condition, however, only had two boxes of Legos. Each time a subject completed a set, it was disassembled in front of him by the experimenter while they worked on the other box. In other words, the models didn't accumulate on the table like the students in the Meaningful condition.

What do you think happened? Despite the task being completely identical for both groups, the subjects in the Meaningful condition built an average of 10.6 Lego sets—a reward of $14.40. The Sisyphus camp, however, stopped building far earlier than the first group.

They built an average of 7.2 sets before quitting—a reward of just $11.52. Just the mere presence or destruction of their work changed their behavior. Subjects who could see the fruits of their labors focused significantly longer on building Bionicle Lego sets, and watching their work get destroyed deterred them from building further.

In this example, there was an extrinsic and an intrinsic reward. The extrinsic reward was a cash prize, but the intrinsic reward was the sense of accomplishment each group felt after completing a Lego set. The Sisyphus group didn't get much time to feel that sense of accomplishment, though, because their creations kept getting disassembled. This clearly drained them of their motivation to work longer. Reminding people of what they have accomplished or what they can accomplish is another way of helping them visualize an intrinsic reward and drive attention further.

As for the extrinsic reward: I suspect that if Ariely had added money to a pile on the table each time a group completed a Lego set, the subjects would have been more motivated to build additional Lego sets. This would have helped subjects visualize what they were earning. The more visually enticing or concrete the reward you present—whether it's an extrinsic reward like food or money, or an intrinsic one like achievement—the more motivation people feel to capture that reward. This, in turn, leads to more attention.

Applying Ariely, Rajaram, and Hamilton's research in social and business contexts is a different story, of course. But the masters of attention have learned how to do just that.

How to Get People to Walk Through Your Doors

Las Vegas—the city of sin—is not the place it used to be. For the latter half of the twentieth century, tourists embarked to Vegas because of the cards, slot machines, shows, and Frank Sinatra's crooning voice. And while the live shows and the countless gambling options are still big attractions in Las Vegas, the twenty-first century has seen a new type of customer begin to dominate. This customer, the clubber, is coming to Vegas for the food, the liquor, and the DJs who rock the Pure and Marquee Nightclubs in high heels and sports coats.

This shift has changed the way casinos attract customers and build out their revenue. At Caesars Entertainment—which owns Bally's, Flamingo, Paris, Planet Hollywood, Caesars Palace, and many more casinos and hotels worldwide—it's been up to Tariq Shaukat, its chief marketing officer, to figure out how to not only survive the change, but thrive in it too.

"We're very big believers in the idea that you should try to identify and focus on persuadable customers," Shaukat said. According to Shaukat, a persuadable customer is somebody who is in the market for something at a particular time, but looking. Imagine you're on the strip and you're in the mood for Italian, but you don't know which restaurant to pick. "At the moment they're thinking about it, that's when they're in a persuadable moment," the Caesars CMO said. "We focus on being in front of them in those moments in time."[24]

In other words, Caesars focuses on getting in front of consumers when they crave rewards the most. If Caesars knows that you like to play poker, don't be surprised when someone from VIP calls you to offer you a seat. If you're more of the clubbing type, though, Caesars might help you out with that first bottle before you have a chance to hop to a rival casino's club.

How does Caesars get in front of consumers at the right time? First, Shaukat said, Caesars focuses on "being present." It utilizes advertising, Google searches, magazines, and unique publicity to remind its target audience of their favorite things about Caesars, its hotels, and its casinos. As we've already learned, showing people a visual representation of a reward increases their motivation and attention for that reward. If you live for live shows, Caesars will make sure you know which one is being featured with images of its performers suspended on billboards.

The second way Caesars gets in front of its customers is through identifying when its customers are most likely to want and desire the rewards it offers. This level of targeting has only recently been possible, thanks to the proliferation of mobile devices. Caesars is using social media and mobile apps to reach out to consumers when they are actually interested. If you post a picture of the Britney show on Twitter, for example, you might get a message from the Caesars social team about the club party she's hosting—they know this is a reward you will jump at the chance to acquire.

Caesars will even send you discounts and rewards based on your location and tastes. In this respect, Caesars applies a lesson we learned from Brian Wong and Kiip. Instead of trying to change behavior with a reward, Kiip surprises customers with post-action rewards, which creates greater loyalty. It's the difference between a customer and a loyal customer. A customer drops by a restaurant, is satisfied, and doesn't think about it again. A loyal customer comes into a restaurant, receives special treatment they didn't expect, and comes back because they've built a positive relationship with that business.

This is why, Shaukat said, Caesars hosts have a wide scope of discretion. The goal is to give its customers the reward they want at the moment they want it. They focus on building relationships and rewarding existing behaviors rather than making a relationship feel "transactional." Caesars finds a way both to let potential customers know that Caesars has the rewards they want and to surprise its loyal customers with rewards as well.

Balancing Intrinsic vs. Extrinsic Rewards

When McDonald's first introduced healthier items to its menu—Caesar salad, fruit and yogurt parfait, grilled chicken sandwich wrap—it was hailed as an important step toward reducing the consumption of empty calories and the fast-growing problem of childhood obesity. But despite consumer outcry about the traditional menu (thanks to the documentary *Super Size Me*) and demand for the healthier menu, sales of its salads and healthy items have remained flat. Why?[25]

Certainly, one reason is that people don't go to McDonald's to get a salad—they go to get a Big Mac and fries. But Dr. Gavan Fitzsimons, a marketing and psychology professor at Duke's Fuqua School of Business, found another interesting reason why healthy items at the fast food giant didn't sell. Fitzsimons and his collaborators recruited 104 students, measured their level of self-control, and asked them to look over a menu of food options, each of which was the same price. One group had a menu with French fries, chicken nuggets, and a baked potato. The other group had an extra menu item: a salad.[26]

Students in the first group chose the fries (rated by the students two weeks prior as the least healthy option) about 50 percent of the time if they had low self-control and 10 percent of the time if they had high levels of self-control. The second group—the one with the salad on the menu—was a different story, though. Individuals with high levels of self-control actually chose the fries *more often* than their counterparts. When given a menu with a healthy option, students with high levels of self-control chose the fries nearly 50 percent of the time. Adding a healthy option to the menu actually *increased* the likelihood that the students would choose to eat the French fries. Not only that but Fitzsimons and his colleagues also found that the amount of time and attention the students with high self-control gave toward the fries increased significantly when the researchers added a salad to the menu.

Healthy menu options can actually backfire. Add a salad to a menu and you'll pay attention to the least healthy option more. The reason, Fitzsimons and company concluded, is something he calls "vicarious goal fulfillment." Oftentimes, we have to make a choice between an intrinsic reward and an extrinsic one. We derive pleasure from the salty taste of fries (this is tangible, so it's an extrinsic reward), but we also seek to lose weight and feel good about ourselves when we wear our swimsuits at the beach (the positive and intangible feelings of accomplishment and self-satisfaction are intrinsic rewards).

In the case of the McDonald's experiment, our wanting for each reward—extrinsic pleasure from tasty food and intrinsic pleasure from healthy eating—are mutually exclusive: very few people can lose weight on a diet of French fries and Big Macs. But the brain can be tricked into thinking it can have its cake and eat it too. When a healthy option appears on a menu filled with junk food, our brain feels a sense of accomplishment for having just the opportunity to accomplish our intrinsic goal of healthy eating. Merely having the *option* to accomplish a goal is enough of a reward that we are more likely to indulge in an extrinsic reward. Offering a choice actually becomes counterproductive if your goal is to get somebody to choose a healthier option.

I find the results of this study fascinating because they exemplify the different motivators we have to achieve extrinsic and intrinsic rewards. A study conducted by researchers from the University of Chicago determined that, if you show somebody healthy and unhealthy foods, they will immediately prefer the unhealthy option, but as time passes and they have time to think about it, their preference will switch to the healthy option.[27]

Extrinsic rewards like fries and unhealthy food motivate us on a short-term basis and affect our short-term attention and decision making. We ignore the long-term implications of eating fries (weight gain, heart disease, and so on) and focus on the salty, fatty taste that gives so many of us immediate satisfaction. Our brain, sensing that it can achieve an immediate, extrinsic reward through fries, focuses its efforts on achieving that short-term reward at the cost of the long-term, intrinsic reward of self-satisfaction. It can take a lot of self-control to resist the temptation of a short-term reward.

Our brain is wired to find the path of least resistance to a reward when possible. This is why extrinsic rewards are ideal for immediate and short attention and why so many of us succumb to our cravings for McDonald's. On the other hand, if we can exhibit self-control, our attention and decisions will focus on long-term intrinsic rewards. This is why intrinsic rewards are a tool for capturing long attention.

Throughout this chapter, we've discussed the power of dopamine, which gives us motivation and "wanting" for specific rewards. And we've discussed the two types of rewards and the impact they have on all three levels of our attention.

The rewards that motivate us differ from person to person, but in the end, it really does come down to one thing: a reward has to solve somebody's problem. In the immediate term, money and extrinsic rewards solve problems like hunger, short-term pleasure, and the ability to buy your wife something nice. But over the long term, our motivations are intrinsic. Will I be successful? Will I find love? Will I get the respect that I deserve?

The key to capturing attention with the Reward Trigger is using extrinsic and intrinsic rewards in the right situations and discovering the motivations your audience have for achieving those rewards. Finding the right balance between extrinsic and intrinsic rewards means the difference between happy employees who stick with your company and disgruntled ones who never achieve their potential. The key is helping solve people's short-term problems while giving them the opportunity to better themselves in the long term.

Chapter 6

Reputation Trigger

●

Before July 2013, nobody had heard of war veteran Robert Galbraith and his first crime fiction novel, *The Cuckoo's Calling*. When it was first released in April of the same year, it received raving reviews, but it sold a paltry fifteen hundred print copies and only a few thousand more on e-book. Glowing reviews from *USA Today*, *Slate*, and *Publishers Weekly* did little to push the sales of Galbraith's first book.

That all changed on July 13. The *Sunday Times*, following a bread-crumb trail of clues, revealed that Robert Galbraith was actually the pseudonym of J. K. Rowling, the fantastically popular author of the Harry Potter series.[1]

"I had hoped to keep this secret a little longer because being Robert Galbraith has been such a liberating experience," Rowling told the *Sunday Times*. "It has been wonderful to publish without hype or expectation, and pure pleasure to get feedback under a different name."

She may not have been happy about the reveal, but I'm guessing that her publisher didn't mind. In the moments after Galbraith's identity was revealed, sales of the book jumped . . . by 156,866 percent. It rose from 4,709 on Amazon's list of best-selling books to number one. And all it took was a name.

Well, not exactly.

The Reputation Trigger

When you hear the name Stephen Hawking, what comes to mind? I suspect *genius* or *scientist* pops into your head. How about *McKinsey & Company*? For those of us in the business world, simply having that name on a résumé makes us more likely to pay attention.

We don't have time to evaluate the merits of every person, company, or idea we encounter, so we use shortcuts to direct our scarce attention. Perhaps the most useful and most powerful of the shortcuts we use on a daily basis is reputation.

When I use the term *reputation*, I'm not talking about the kids trading gossip in a hallway or coworkers bad-mouthing each other at the water cooler. Reputation is simply the sum total of our beliefs about a person, company, product, or idea. Labels like *genius, narcissist,* or *important* are quickly assigned by our society, and these labels provide the shortcuts we use to choose the products we buy and the people we follow on social media.

Take J. K. Rowling. When you hear her name, you likely have an immediate set of knowledge, judgments, and opinions that come to the surface. You know her name, and for millions of people, simply learning that she is the author of a new book is enough of a reason to buy it. This is because Rowling has built a stellar reputation as a writer and storyteller. We know instantly that she is worth our attention. Her name acts as an attentional shortcut. But reputation doesn't just affect which people capture our attention—it also determines which music we buy and which musicians we follow.

I want you to pretend you're a music recording exec for one of the major labels. Your boss has tasked you with predicting who will be the next music sensation out of a list of a thousand up-and-coming artists. What do you think are the three most important qualities to predicting the next Lorde or Beyoncé? Now write them down.

If I had to venture a guess, I'd bet "talent" topped your list. You might have also written down "stage presence" or "attractiveness" as the most important qualities in predicting an artist's potential popularity.

But you would be wrong. Yes, if you have Adele's voice, you have a better chance of becoming a platinum-selling musician. However, talent is *not* the best predictor of popularity. Dr. Duncan Watts, principal researcher at Microsoft and former sociology professor at Columbia University, asked 14,341 participants, divided into nine groups, to listen to a set of forty-eight songs from eighteen bands, all unknowns. Once participants listened to a song, they were asked to rate it from one star (worst) to five stars (best). Participants could then download the song if they chose.[2]

Group one, the "independent" group, simply rated and downloaded songs, while groups two through nine, the "social influence" groups, were given a critical piece of additional information—the number of downloads each song had received from other participants of their group.

If you believe that quality is the largest determination factor of popularity, it's reasonable to assume that the nine groups would end up downloading the same songs and rating them similarly. But in fact, the opposite happened. In the social influence groups, the most popular songs were *significantly* more popular than any song ever became in the independent group. It was clear from the data that social proofing was driving the popularity of songs.

Perhaps what was more surprising about Watts's experiment was that *completely different songs* became popular in each of the eight social influence subgroups. If a song already had a few downloads, it would continue to acquire more at a faster and faster rate until it shot to the top of the charts. It didn't really matter what song, because the bandwagon had taken over.

Quality had an impact on the rankings—the songs that participants rated as the best generally never did badly and the "worst" songs never made it to the top of the charts—but it was impossible to predict where any individual song would fall in the rankings for any particular group.

Watts's experiment demonstrates that the best predictor of popularity is *what other people think is popular*. Quality matters, but reputation is more powerful when it comes to predicting popularity. This is because we make an automatic assumption that the crowd is usually right. Downloads are an indicator of quality and help to make the choice of which song to download easier. We do this all the time in real life, whether it's browsing restaurant ratings or buying the latest book recommended by Oprah. In the case of J. K. Rowling, the quality of the book didn't make it a best seller— the reputation behind the author's name did.

We rely on reputable sources to direct our scarce attention, and thus we pay more attention to those sources in the process. These reputable sources are individuals, groups of people, or organizations that have developed well-known reputations for their work, their knowledge, or their expertise. The Reputation Trigger is the leveraging of reputable sources and figures to direct attention. By either establishing yourself as a reputable figure, such as an expert, or receiving the endorsement of a reputable source, you can shift attention toward you and your message remarkably quickly.

In fact, the reputation effect accelerates as a reputation becomes stronger, which is why reputation matters when it comes to attention. In the Watts experiment, the number of downloads effectively established the reputation of each musical act within each social influence test group. More importantly, the impact was disproportional: a small increase in downloads early on resulted in huge download numbers by the end of the experiment. This is why reputation is so important—even a little boost creates a big ripple effect on how much attention others will give to you.

Throughout the rest of this chapter, we will explore our reliance on reputation and how to harness the Reputation Trigger by using three types of reputable sources—experts, authority figures, and the crowd—to capture attention and build your own reputation. But before we can dive into how to capture attention, we need to understand why reputable sources are so influential on our attention.

Want to Turn Your Brain Off? Talk to an Expert

Our over-reliance on the reputation and perceived authority of others is well documented. Dr. Greg Berns, a neuroeconomist at Emory University, wanted to understand how the brain functions when it weighs the advice of experts during decision making. Berns and his team placed twenty-four college students under an fMRI—a device that tracks blood flow in the brain in order to measure brain activity—and gave them a scenario where they had to make a decision: to take a guaranteed amount of money or to roll the dice for a higher payout.[3]

One group received no advice on which way they should decide, while the second group received advice from Dr. Charles Noussair, an economist at Emory University. His advice to the second group was simple: take the money and run. It didn't matter how bad his advice was or how stacked the odds were in the students' favor—Noussair would always advocate the conservative approach.

In the first group, the students showed significant activity in the decision-making centers of the brain, especially the anterior cingulate cortex and the dorsolateral prefrontal cortex. This was to be expected—the students were weighing the odds and their options in regards to an important decision.

It's the second group that shocked researchers. The fMRI showed that the students who had received the expert's advice had almost no brain activity in these key decision centers. It was as if their brains had shut down and offloaded the work of making hard decisions to the expert.

Famed psychologist Robert Cialdini likes to call this phenomenon "directed deference." If a doctor diagnoses you with an illness and prescribes a concoction of medications, you're unlikely to dispute him because he's the authority on the subject. The same holds true if a math professor tells you that your quadratic equation is wrong or Jay-Z tells you that your rap skills are off the charts.[4]

According to Cialdini, we're susceptible to directed deference because we're conditioned to respect and follow the edicts of an authority figure. We've learned that defying an authority figure can lead to punishment, while compliance often leads to rewards. If you do your chores, your parents will give you an allowance; defy your boss and you can kiss that promotion goodbye.

We rely on these authority figures for directing our scarce attention. I have a fashion designer friend who has spent her entire life studying fashion trends, following fashion news, and selecting outfits for others. I, on the other hand, know absolutely nothing about the top designers and their labels. So when it comes time to choose new clothing and assemble outfits, I always direct my attention toward the ensembles she picks out.

Each of three types of reputable sources we rely on daily for directing our attention—experts, authority figures, and the crowd— has a different but profound effect on our attention. Establishing yourself as one of these reputable sources—or receiving an endorsement from one of them—is essential to building trust with your audience and is crucial for retaining long attention.

Why You Should Dress like an Expert

Outside of our closest friends and families, there aren't a lot of figures that we're willing to trust. In 2012, a surprising majority of Americans trusted their government—53 percent, in fact. But less than a year after Edward Snowden lifted the veil on the NSA's massive spying apparatus, trust in the U.S. government plummeted by an astonishing 16 percent. American citizens trusted officials who worked for the government even less than the government itself. And this isn't just an American phenomenon: citizens of France and Hong Kong had even less trust in their respective national governments.

So we don't trust our government—this probably doesn't come as a surprise to most. How about CEOs? Only 43 percent of the public trust what CEOs have to say. We have a little more trust in the media (52 percent) and in people who are similar to us (62 percent), but according to research conducted by public relations giant Edelman, none of these figures are considered credible or trustworthy as an expert.

When Edelman surveyed more than thirty-one thousand people, it found that the public trusted academics and experts the most when it came to information about companies or the market. About 67 percent of the public trusted experts and academics, and 66 percent trusted technical experts. Year after year, experts consistently rank as the most trustworthy messengers.[5]

Our trust of experts goes deeper, though. The association is so powerful that *just wearing a white lab coat* improves your own attention. Adam D. Galinsky and Hajo Adam, professors of business management at Columbia University and Rice University, respectively, theorized that wearing a white lab coat—the kind worn by doctors, laboratory researchers, and forensic specialists on TV shows like *NCIS*—would improve somebody's attention and improve their accuracy because the white lab coat symbolizes expertise, attentiveness and carefulness in many cultures.[6]

In their first experiment, Galinsky and Adam tested the selective attention of fifty-eight students, specifically probing their ability to spot out-of-place stimuli. Here's the kicker: half the students wore street clothes while the other half wore white lab coats. The second experiment tested the sustained attention of seventy-four students, asking them to spot minor differences in pictures placed side by side. The catch of the second experiment was that students were asked to wear a doctor's coat, a "painter's coat" that was actually identical to the doctor's coat, or regular clothes while looking at a doctor's coat.

The white coat had a major impact . . . if the students thought it was a doctor's lab coat. In the first experiment, students who wore the white coat had half as many errors as their casually dressed counterparts. The second experiment, however, made it clear it wasn't just the coat that improved attention—it was the coat's association with expertise. Students who wore an identical white coat thought to belong to a painter didn't perform anywhere near as well as the students who thought the coat belonged to a doctor. Galinsky and Adam also found that students had to wear the coat to receive its attention-improving benefits—students who just looked at a doctor's coat didn't show any improved ability to spot the changes in the images.

We trust experts, and because we trust them, we are comfortable relying on them to tell us who or what we should pay attention to. In the "Framing" chapter, I shared the story of one of the most successful antiperspirants from the last century: Odorono. Its founder, Edna Murphey, doubled sales of Odorono simply by emphasizing that a doctor developed its antiperspirant. When an expert talks, we listen.[7]

"One of the most popular posts that we've ever seen on influencers was Bill Gates talking about three pieces of advice he got from

Warren Buffet," LinkedIn CEO Jeff Weiner once explained to me, as we discussed the power of experts and influencers on LinkedIn's platform. "It generated a million page views in less than forty-eight hours. In a world where there's an increasing amount of information, they turn to trusted brands. They turn to trusted people. . . . Bill Gates and Warren Buffet are trusted by individuals."

But the same attention-directing power is also true of the second type of reputable source: the authority figure.

How a Roman Hero Succeeded in Recruiting Soldiers

In his heyday, Lucius Septimius Flavianus Flavillianus (whew!) was admired in Oenoanda—an ancient Greek and Roman city in present-day Turkey—and across Rome. He was the modern-day equivalent to MMA's Chuck Liddell. He stood above his peers as a champion in wrestling and pankration, an incredibly bloody Greek combat sport where the only rules were no biting and no eye gouging.

Because of his championships, he had the rare distinction of notability and celebrity. Ancient statues in his honor were found in 2002, including inscriptions hailing the city's "champion athlete." But more interesting is evidence found in an excavation at Oenoanda that describes how the Romans leveraged his authority and celebrity to successfully recruit countless young men to become soldiers in the Roman army and bring them to Hierapolis, one of Rome's most prominent cities.

Thanks to his status, Flavillianus was successful at recruitment. In fact, he "proved to be so successful as a military recruiter that it was decreed that he be made a 'cult figure in the band of heroes' after he died, with each tribe of the city erecting statues in his honor," according to *LiveScience*.[8]

Flavillianus became an adept recruiter not only because of his celebrity status but also because of his unquestionable authority when it came to combat. This leads us to the second type of reputable figure that commands our attention: the authority figure.

Unlike experts, who command attention because of their perceived knowledge and wisdom, authority figures command attention because of their power and their ability to command obedience from others. We seek to avoid the consequences that result in not paying attention to them. If you're not listening to your professor's review lecture, you might fail her class. When Vladimir Putin's forces stormed Crimea in Ukraine, the world quickly started paying attention because of the potential geopolitical consequences. Ignore him and you risked Putin marching farther into Ukraine.

Most psychology students are familiar with the most famous experiment in the area of obedience to authority: Stanley Milgram's shock experiment. In his famous and controversial 1963 study, he demonstrated that the majority of us are willing to harm our fellow human beings when ordered to do so by an authority figure. When an authority figure told subjects to keep administering shocks to an unseen actor who would scream each time subjects administered punishment, subjects obeyed. Approximately 63 percent, in fact, administered the highest level of pain, despite the screaming and a "Danger: Severe Shock" label on the dial.[9]

Milgram's experiment helps explain why so many people have been willing to participate in crimes against humanity. It's hardwired into our behavior and ingrained in our culture to listen to and obey authority figures. And while obedience and attention are not the same, one often leads to the other. If an authority figure, like your boss, tells you to read a book or file a report—or even if he just suggests a product—it's more likely to register in your working memory.

Not all authority figures are equal, though. Famed sociologist Max Weber divides authority into three types: rational-legal authority, traditional authority, and charismatic authority. Let's start with the first two. Rational-legal authority is an authority that derives its legitimacy from the formal rules of the state, like constitutional governments. Presidents and police commissioners are examples of rational-legal authority. Traditional authority, on the other hand, derives power from customs and social structures—monarchies and emperors are classic examples.

These two types of authorities command attention because defiance results in punishment. This makes them effective tools for capturing attention because we will do what we need to do in order to avoid unpleasantness or punishment, which includes paying attention to the authority figure that can potentially punish us. However, the ability of these two types of authorities to capture attention only lasts as long as they have power over you.

In the workplace, an overbearing authority (an angry and mean boss) can lead to dissension among employees. This often leads to employees making the choice to leave in order to find better working conditions. Once they leave, the power the boss had over those former employees dissipates and the authority figure no longer commands attention. In politics and government, submission eventually turns to rebellion. Once an authority figure no longer has power over others, the attention they control dissipates. That's why neither of these forms of authority are the most effective when it comes to capturing attention in a prolonged, sustained way.

There is a third type of authority, though: charismatic authority. According to Weber, charismatic authority gains its power and legitimacy by demonstrating some type of exemplary trait—heroism, strength of character, holiness, leadership, etc.—that turns into respect and devotion by others. Thus, as long as others feel devotion or respect for the authority figure, he or she will maintain authority—and thus attention.

In his book *Power: A Radical View*, Steven Lukes—a professor of politics at NYU—argues that authority figures exercise their power in three ways. They can force you to do something against your wishes, they can stop you from doing something, and they can alter the way you think.[10] Charismatic figures do the latter—they use power to alter the way you think and perceive. They have the capacity to alter the way we direct our attention by the sheer force of their gravitas and ideas.

We see the power that charismatic leaders and authorities wield over our attention every day with figures like Bill Clinton, Warren Buffett, the Dalai Lama, and Nelson Mandela. They wield their authority to not only capture attention for themselves, but they also direct attention toward the issues they care about. This effect spreads—even if you don't follow Bill Gates or his newest initiative to eradicate another disease, his ideas will almost certainly reach you through the power of news and social media. These examples show two of the captivation triggers in action: their reputations (Reputation Trigger) have the power to set the social agenda (Framing Trigger).

Charisma isn't some abstract superpower that only the chosen few command, though. In her eloquently written book *The Charisma Myth*, Olivia Fox Cabane makes a compelling argument that charisma is a learned trait and not necessarily inherent. A charismatic figure simply needs to demonstrate, to some degree, three qualities: presence, warmth, and power. The Dalai Lama is primarily a warm figure, while a warrior like Flavillianus draws his charisma from power. All you have to do, Cabane suggests, is focus on and develop strength in one of these three areas.[11]

It's clear that we pay attention to authority figures and direct our attention toward what they deem important out of either fear or respect, depending on the type of authority they wield. But I believe a third type of reputable source trumps authority, because it can command both our fear *and* our respect. When it comes to reputable sources that we rely on daily for directing our attention, the crowd is perhaps the most powerful and the most difficult to harness.

The Wisdom of the Crowd and the Power of Conformity

For Americans, the constant deluge of opinion polls in politics is just a fact of life. But in Britain, polls have been a controversial subject since their introduction in the 1950s. Some people in Britain have called for restrictions or even outright bans on the release of opinion poll data during campaigns, as their neighbors in Spain and France have done. In fact, 30 percent of Britain's MPs (Members of Parliament) are in favor of banning opinion polls for a set period of time before general elections.[12]

Do opinion polls really influence our voting behavior, though? Are we more inclined to back the underdog with our votes or to jump on the bandwagon of the likely victor?

Political scientists Ian McAllister and Donley Studlar wanted to find the answers to these questions. They gathered Gallup exit poll data from British general elections in 1979, 1983, and 1987. Voters who reported hearing at least one opinion poll before election day (between 68 percent and 74 percent) were significantly more likely to vote for the winning party. In the 1979 election, voters who believed the Conservatives had a large lead rather than a small one were 18 percent more likely to vote for the Conservatives and 14 percent less likely to vote for Labour. No wonder opinion polls are controversial in Europe.[13]

You may already know why voters in British general elections were more likely to herd toward the winning side rather than risk alienation from the crowd. It's an attention-driving phenomenon most commonly known as the bandwagon effect. Duncan Watts's music download experiment described at the beginning of this chapter demonstrates the bandwagon in action. Asked to rate and download music from unknown artists, participants overwhelmingly chose to download songs that they could see already had a higher number of downloads—songs that were popular. Once it was clear the crowd was favoring a specific song, the rest of the group quickly followed suit.

There are two explanations for why voters in British general elections jumped on the bandwagon. They are the same reasons why the crowd has the power to direct our attention. The first reason has a rational basis: we tend to trust in the crowd's judgment because it is a collection of knowledge. The second reason has its roots in our need for social belonging: we don't want to risk social alienation by swimming against the crowd—even if we know the crowd is wrong.

Why do we trust the crowd's judgment? Perhaps part of the reason why is because, more often than not, the masses are actually right. In his book *The Wisdom of Crowds*, James Surowiecki of *The New Yorker* argues that crowds often make better decisions than experts, especially when there is a clear right or wrong answer. When a group of fifty-six students in a finance class were asked to estimate the number of jelly beans in a jar (a task I attempted and failed at multiple times as a kid), their guesses averaged at 871. Only one student out of fifty-six students made a guess closer to the actual number—850.[14]

Unlike authority figures and experts, the crowd has fewer gaps of knowledge. One person can be wrong or biased, but when 850 people download a song or give a restaurant a five-star rating, it becomes impossible for us to deny its reputation. The larger sample size makes us feel more confident in the crowd. We think, *How can 850 people be wrong?* An expert is convincing, but the crowd is, by definition, what determines a reputation.

Since we trust in the crowd, we use it as an attentional shortcut to figure out what else deserves our attention. A study by Harvard's Michael Luca discovered, for example, that a one-star increase on Yelp can boost a local business's revenue by 5 to 9 percent.[15] In another recent study, two Berkeley economists found that a half-star increase in a restaurant's rating on Yelp improved its chances of having all of its seats sell out by an astounding 49 percent.[16]

Both studies demonstrate the crowd's ability to direct attention. When the crowd approves of a restaurant (in the form of a high rating), we are far more likely to dine there. Little swings in a business's rating on Yelp can make or break a business. If something isn't receiving mass adoption, it isn't going to capture our attention.

Sony understands the power of the crowd better than most. In the late 1970s, it waged war against JVC and its Video Home System format—the VHS. Sony's videotape cassette standard, Betamax, boasted superior quality and resolution but lacked the recording length of VHS. While Betamax could only record sixty minutes, VHS could record 120 minutes (and eventually 240). Betamax also proved to be more costly than VHS, driving consumers away. As the crowd continued to embrace VHS, Sony had no choice but to abandon the fight for Betamax.[17]

Sony learned its lesson, though. In the mid-2000s, Sony found itself in yet another video format war. This time its goal was to make the Blu-Ray Disc the successor to the DVD. Standing in its way was the HD DVD, backed primarily by Toshiba. Once again, a format war was unavoidable.

To quickly generate traction for Blu-Ray, Sony pushed hard in multiple directions to speed up consumer adoption. First, it launched advertisements that declared Blu-Ray "entertainment like no other" in order to sway consumers. Second, it included Blu-Ray in the PlayStation 3, one of Sony's most popular assets. And third, Sony forged alliances with major manufacturers and studios in order to drive up consumer demand for Blu-Ray. It enlisted LG, Samsung, Pioneer, Panasonic, Dell, HP, and 20th Century Fox to its side, along with Sony Pictures. Consumers began to choose Blu-Ray because many popular movies like *The Fifth Element* and *50 First Dates* were being released exclusively for Sony's Blu-Ray standard. As a result, traction quickly began to erode for HD DVD, resulting in companies like Target dropping the format and eventually leading to its demise.

Consumer adoption—not quality—determined the outcome in both the VHS and the Blu-Ray format wars. We rally around those we perceive to be the winners or eventual winners. The crowd becomes a self-fulfilling prophecy.

We may trust the crowd's judgment in some situations, but in others it isn't its wisdom that we pay attention to—it's the social pressure it exerts. We begin to pay attention because we're supposed to pay attention. Perhaps you've heard of the Asch conformity experiments. In the 1950s, Polish-American psychologist Dr. Solomon Asch conducted a series of classic experiments on conformity. In a typical Asch conformity experiment, one test subject (usually a male college student) is placed in a room with a group of five to ten other college students—all actors—and is asked to participate in a perception task. The group is shown a card with a vertical line and then shown a second card with three lines of different lengths labeled A, B, and C. All subjects are asked to say aloud which line—A, B, or C—matches the length of the vertical line from the first card.[18]

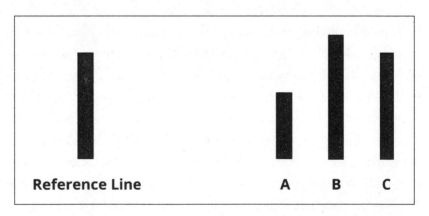

When the participant does this activity alone or is asked first in the group, he almost always gets the answer right with an error rate less than 1 percent. But when the actors go before the participant and pick the same answer, the participant very often picks that answer as well—even if it is completely and obviously wrong. Under group pressure, the participant accepts the crowd's judgment more than one-third of the time.[19]

Our tendency to make decisions—even irrational ones—when we're facing group pressure is known as normative social influence. We conform to the crowd because we begin to doubt our judgment, and we fear the social repercussions of going against the majority. This is why poll booths are private and also why North Korea installs loudspeakers in every home with propaganda that can't be turned off. One study at the University of St. Andrews in Scotland found that vervet monkeys will switch the foods they eat to fit in with a new social group. Even whales adapt their behaviors to the crowd. It's instinctual for many animals to herd—humans included.[20]

This isn't to say the crowd always wins—when Asch implanted a vocal dissenter in one variation of his conformity experiments, the unwitting participant was far more likely to go against the group as well. We are willing to fight against popular opinion, but only if we don't feel like we're standing alone.

We may think of Rosa Parks—the gentle protester who became a symbol of America's civil rights movement—as a lone wolf who quietly fought against racism and oppression by refusing to move from the front of the bus, but that's only part of her story. She wasn't alone; just five months before her famous refusal to give up her seat to a white passenger, she received training at the Highlander Folk School in Tennessee, where she was taught how to react when confronted with a situation like the one she eventually ended up in. She knew going in that she had a support group that would back her up, and indeed it did. Civil rights leaders used Parks's protest to organize the Montgomery Bus Boycott just three days later.[21]

The crowd sways our attention because we believe it makes wise judgments, and the crowd keeps us captivated because we want to belong to a social group and feel supported by others. Combined, these two factors make the crowd a potent reputable source for capturing attention. But in order to harness the crowd for attention, you have to give it the power to participate.

Connecting with the Crowd

In 2009, before Kickstarter became an international phenomenon and when crowdsourcing was in its infancy, Vitaminwater—the popular energy drink—embarked on an experiment to find its next flavor. Instead of using traditional market research and focus groups, it opened up almost every aspect of creating the next flavor of Vitaminwater to the crowd.

To facilitate the power of the crowd, the brand released a Facebook app called the Flavor Creator. It wasn't your typical Facebook app. At first, it allowed its Facebook fans to follow chatter on potential new flavors from not just Facebook but also Twitter and other networks. The more chatter generated for a flavor, the more likely it would end up in a top-ten list that became a ballot for the next flavor. (50 Cent, an early investor in Vitaminwater, also had a say.) That wasn't all, either. Vitaminwater even crowdsourced the design of the bottle using the Flavor Creator. Fans could submit their designs for the next label and let the crowd vote on their designs. More than forty thousand people submitted designs in hopes of winning the five-thousand-dollar grand prize and a lot of Internet points.[22]

In 2010, Vitaminwater released the crowdsourced flavor—Connect—a black cherry and lime concoction. The Flavor Creator campaign was an enormous success, not only in generating a flavor and product the people wanted but also in attracting attention from millions of consumers and dozens of press outlets. The Flavor Creator succeeded because it utilized the crowd as both an expert and an authority figure. It utilized its expertise to pick a flavor, and it was given the authority to turn that flavor into something you could actually find on store shelves.

In its own way, the crowd acts as both an expert and an authority figure, and this is why the crowd is so crucial to directing attention. But this is also what makes it potentially dangerous. What happens when groupthink invades real life? Just days after the horrific Boston Marathon bombings, the community at the online juggernaut Reddit collectively identified a young Indian student, Sunil Tripathi, as a suspicious character near the scene of the crime. He had recently gone missing, and he looked similar to a person with a backpack in the grainy photos.[23]

Unfortunately, as we know now, the student wasn't involved at all in the Boston bombings. Tripathi was found dead in the waters off of Rhode Island, likely having passed away before the bombings ever occurred. The intense attention and scrutiny his family received after the Reddit crowd pointed the finger toward Tripathi was the last thing a grieving family needed.

The crowd can direct the spotlight like nobody else can, right or wrong. This is because the crowd is susceptible to the other two types of reputable sources: experts and authority figures. Researchers at the Cajal Institute in Madrid used a mathematical model to discover that thinkers "who are confident in their own opinion" can significantly influence independent thinkers within a group to their side. In other words, confident and charismatic thinkers can steer the crowd's judgment in directions the crowd wouldn't have gone otherwise.[24]

The crowd is both powerful and shockingly accurate when it acts as a collection of individual thinkers, but it's potentially dangerous when an individual or two push their own agenda with their charisma and confidence. The crowd is at its best when it is decentralized and the opinions of the individuals are collectively put together, like what you see with review sites like Yelp. However, if a crowd is being led by a few individuals, we should be wary of automatically believing its conclusions.

We've analyzed our strange and sometimes irrational relationship with the three main types of reputable figures—from the perceived wisdom of experts to the power of authority figures to the trust and conformity of the crowd. But we still haven't fully answered a key question: How do you harness the power of the Reputation Trigger? Or, perhaps more poignantly, how do you build a reputation that commands attention?

To find answers, let's step back from flavored water and tackle a tastier treat: ice cream.

Building Your Reputation

Despite being in business for nearly forty years, complete with an acquisition by one of the world's largest consumer goods conglomerates, the values that have driven Ben & Jerry's ice cream business haven't changed.

In 1985, the business had already become bigger than its founders, Ben Cohen and Jerry Greenfield. They feared the idea of losing their identity as ice cream people and becoming businesspeople. So the company did what any other company would do: It started a foundation that began donating 7.5 percent of its pre-tax profits to charities worldwide. It began a profit-sharing program with its employees and instituted a salary cap that drove away some talent but attracted the type of philanthropic-minded people the company wanted for its culture. And even back in 1989, Ben & Jerry's fought against the use of growth hormones in cows.[25]

More recently, the company—now a quasi-independent division of Unilever—became the first major ice cream manufacturer to certify all of its ingredients as fair trade, making sure that the farmers it buys from receive a fair price and work in ethical conditions. It has also committed to making its products GMO-free.

Consumers have rewarded Ben & Jerry's for its consistency and values. The brand has some of the highest social media engagement, especially on Facebook, where the ice cream maker has north of 7.5 million fans. More importantly, Ben & Jerry's ice cream continues to sell hundreds of millions of dollars of ice cream annually and has only grown since its inception.

Ben & Jerry's demonstrates the three key elements needed to build a long-term reputation and become worthwhile of somebody's attention: consistency, personality, and time. Experts, for example, build their reputations by creating personal content on a regular basis, whether it's blog posts or scientific papers. This is why top YouTube celebrities, many of them experts in niches like celebrity culture or science, often put their videos out on a weekly fixed schedule. Their audiences know when to tune in, and these You-Tubers deliver. It can take months and years, but eventually these people grow audiences with millions of followers, subscribers, and fans.

Take my old profession—journalism—as an example of how consistency, personality, and time can build reputations. Traditionally, journalists have been taught to report the facts and keep their opinions out of the news, but in the modern era, the star reporters are the ones who aren't afraid to opine and show off their unique personalities. The world's best-known journalists—thinkers like FiveThirtyEight's Nate Silver, Re/code's Kara Swisher, Vox's Ezra Klein, and longtime *Washington Post* journalist Bob Woodward share their opinions thoughtfully and liberally. They write books, tweet their ideas, and engage their readers. The same is true of experts in every field—science communicator Neil deGrasse Tyson and investor Marc Andreessen are just two more examples.

Ben & Jerry's follows this formula to build its reputation as well. Much of its success lies in its mix of posts on ice cream, humor, and news on topics like GMO foods and fair trade. You will always find new content on a daily basis on its Facebook page—it takes the lesson of consistency to heart. And its personality and values are always on display—you won't mistake a Ben & Jerry's post for some other ice cream company's status update.

Expertise is built by knowledge and insight, but reputations are built with consistency, personality, and time. If you share your knowledge and personality on a consistent basis, you will eventually start building an attention-grabbing reputation of your own.

Of course, building a reputation takes time, and you likely have a project or creation you want to catch the public's eye sooner rather than later. Luckily, there is a shortcut to capturing attention using the Reputation Trigger if your reputation is still nascent. I call it the credibility rule.

The premise of the credibility rule is simple: whenever you are trying to get somebody to pay attention to your ideas—whether you're pitching a journalist or a potential client for your company—you need to lead your pitch with at least one validator—a reputable person or company that the person you're pitching recognizes or trusts.

Let's go back to journalism for a moment. Journalists are a cynical, overstressed bunch that has limited amounts of time to write stories and read pitches. I received hundreds of e-mail, Twitter, and Facebook pitches daily when I was at *Mashable*, and I know many other journalists with the same problem. Their attention is even scarcer than most.

That's why it's no surprise that, when most startups pitch journalists to write about their businesses, they get no response. It's because inexperienced entrepreneurs tend to do one, some, or all of the following:

- Cold e-mail or, even worse, cold call (Tech journalists do not enjoy cold calls at all—I know.)

- Write ten paragraphs in the body of an e-mail explaining their startup and its virtues (The journalist never gets past the first paragraph, and often, not even past the headline.)

- Fill their e-mail with buzzwords like *synergy, game-changing, next-generation,* and *never before seen* (No. Please no.)

- Buy Facebook ads that target specific journalists to convince them to write a story about their startup (This really happens, and it always backfires.)

- Send mass, un-targeted pitches (Sending a consumer app to an enterprise reporter demonstrates a lack of research. Getting the reporter's name wrong gets you blacklisted.)

- Send a press release (No journalist reads through press releases anymore.)

A few startups avoid the journalism brick wall, however, by leveraging the credibility rule. Because the attention of journalists is so scarce, they need an immediate way to discern that the pitch they've received is legitimate and worth their time. Validators capture their attention—short phrases like "backed by Mark Cuban," "funded by Google Ventures," or "started by ex-Microsoft execs" makes a world of difference. It's a signal that a startup and its founders have been vetted and the article will generate more traffic because of the recognizable names involved.

In the best-case scenario, the validator that captures the attention of the journalist comes in the form of a personal introduction and recommendation from a respected mutual friend, but the validator can also come in the form of a brand-name investor or advisor in the e-mail subject line. The credibility rule works in other industries as well—you're far more likely to get a second corporate customer for your consulting firm if you already have a happy customer like Sears or Kraft on board.

The credibility rule isn't ironclad by a long shot, though. In the wrong context, it becomes name-dropping—an unsavory, irresponsible, and ultimately destructive way to capture attention. Compare these two hypothetical e-mail pitches:

> We're launching our product next week and announcing our funding from Google Ventures, Gary Vaynerchuk, 500 Startups, the founders of YouTube, and DominateFund. We're a group of former engineers and designers from Motorola, Facebook, and Genentech. Would you be interesting in writing about our launch?

> We were having a chat with Mark Zuckerberg, and he suggested we talk with you! We've worked with everyone from Larry Page at Google to the founders of YouTube. You should totally write about us.

The credibility rule only works if a reputable person has actually put their money where their mouth is. Talking about who you're friends with carries no weight, and the credibility rule only works if the somebody can call the people and companies you mention and get nothing but a positive response. It's the same reason why you shouldn't list faint acquaintances or fake references on your résumé—eventually somebody will call them and your dream job will go out the window. Common sense and the truth are your best friends, which leads us to the problems that arise when you lie to build your reputation.

The Easy Way to Destroy Your Reputation

A few years ago, Elizabeth O'Bagy was a rising star in the Washington political scene. By the time she was twenty-six, she was writing op-eds for *The Atlantic* and *The Wall Street Journal*. One op-ed she wrote for *WSJ* was even cited by Arizona Senator John McCain during a U.S. Senate hearing on the Syrian war. While an undergraduate at Georgetown, O'Bagy studied Arabic—a result of seeing her high school classmates pick on an Arab boy right after the September 11 attacks. She lived in Cairo for a few years before taking up an internship with the Institute for the Study of War (ISW) as she sought a dual master's and Ph.D. from Georgetown on Arabic Studies. A year later, she became an analyst for the ISW.[26]

O'Bagy also had a second job, outside of her internship—she was working with the Syrian Emergency Task Force (SETF), a nonprofit group that helped the moderate wing of the Syrian opposition to Syrian President Bashar al-Assad. This gave her access to Syria itself, and she traveled there often enough to be considered an expert on the subject.

Of course, if O'Bagy's story had ended there, it wouldn't have been all that attention grabbing. Her expertise made her very popular in political circles and within the media. She was a regular on the cable television shows, and quickly became one of Washington's leading experts on the ground operations of Syria. By 2013, she was claiming that she had successfully defended her dissertation. There was just one problem, though—she wasn't a Ph.D. student at Georgetown working on Arabic Studies. She had never even been accepted into the program.

Part of O'Bagy's credibility was her research ties to Georgetown and her supposed doctorate. But none of that was true. When her August 2013 op-ed in *The Wall Street Journal* made headlines and was referenced by the likes of McCain and Kerry, it didn't take long for the media and the ISW to figure out that O'Bagy had padded her credentials. A few days later, O'Bagy was fired by the ISW. The credibility of her findings went up in smoke.

O'Bagy certainly isn't the first person to pad her credentials—some people are tempted to add titles and awards they've never earned in order for others to take them more seriously. But in the era of Google Search, it's easier than ever for lies to be revealed. Scott Thompson, the former CEO of Yahoo, is keenly aware. After a career at Visa and a successful tenure as president of PayPal, he was hired in 2012 to fix Yahoo after the firing of former CEO Carol Bartz.[27]

However, not long after he had Yahoo sue Facebook for patent infringement, an activist investor found that Thompson had lied about his education credentials. Thompson claimed to have received degrees in both accounting and computer science from Stonehill College, but in reality he never studied computer science. This is a major lie when it comes to running a technology company that employs thousands of engineers. A few weeks later, he was fired and eventually replaced with former Google star exec Marissa Mayer.

It's impossible to capture attention without receiving some scrutiny as well, and now that so much of credentialing is verifiable online, that scrutiny can quickly expose anything that doesn't add up. While it's not impossible to crawl back from a fall from grace (O'Bagy eventually became a legislative assistant for McCain), you burn many bridges in the process. More importantly, you open yourself up to the wrong kind of attention—instead of your audience focusing on your message, they focus on you.

O'Bagy and Thompson destroyed their reputations by engaging in deception. This is the first of two ways a reputation can be tarnished. When you lie about the credentials that make you credible, somebody will eventually call you out publicly on your error, your lie, or your lie by omission. O'Bagy, Thompson, and many others have learned this the hard way. The best practice is to always tell the truth, and quickly.

If you do make an error or a misstep, though, the next best response is a swift and truthful apology. The second worst thing you can do is wait—thanks to the power of social media to drive awareness, the era of having something "blow over" is over. Still, nothing is worse than lying to cover up your lie, as former Congressman Anthony Weiner learned when he tweeted out his genitals and claimed it was the work of a hacker. Had he, instead, immediately apologized and never done it again, people might have forgiven him.

There is a second way that a reputation can be hurt, though: misconception. This is when somebody criticizes you for something that is either untrue or a misunderstanding. Years ago, when I was at *Mashable*, I wrote a story about Laura Ling and Euna Lee, two American journalists with Current TV (now Al Jazeera America). Several months before, the North Korean government had captured them, "violently dragged" them across the ice to a North Korean army base, and interrogated them.

The two journalists had just released their first statement since being released. I wrote an article and shared their lengthy statement in its entirety, which I found on Current TV's website. Other sites, including the *Los Angeles Times*, had done the same. Not long after I published my article, a prominent blogger accused me, publicly, of plagiarizing from the *LA Times*. He had seen the statement on the *LA Times* website and assumed I ripped off the statement from there without credit.

I was faced with three choices—ignore the allegations, e-mail the journalist privately and explain the situation, or respond publicly to stop the misinformation about my journalistic integrity from spreading further. I decided to swing back—quickly and publicly. I posted a response on Twitter and a social network called FriendFeed (acquired by Facebook in 2009), and the journalist and I discussed the story at length on both social networks for over an hour until the issue was explained, misconceptions were erased, and my reputation was reestablished. No harm was done to our friendship.

With the proliferation of information, it's always wise to respond quickly but thoughtfully with facts if you truly believe that your character is being unreasonably attacked. The longer you allow a misconception to linger, the more likely it is to stick, even when you eventually clear the air. The key is to respond as quickly as possible, lay out the facts, and be forceful in defending your reputation without resorting to attacks on your accuser. Focus on the accusations, not the person making them.

Your reputation means everything. Nobody will pay attention to your ideas if you've been publicly discredited before. Maintaining trust and credibility is vital to swaying audiences, growing attention, and standing out from the crowd. Perhaps famed investor Warren Buffett put it best: "It takes 20 years to build a reputation and five minutes to ruin it. If you think about that, you'll do things differently."[28]

One Last Lesson on Reputation

A reputation is the embodiment of a person, company, or idea's credibility and worthiness. It is this credibility and worth that determine whether something is worth our time and long-term interest. That's why reputations are important shortcuts for quickly determining who is worthy of our attention. When simply hearing your name makes people pay attention, you have become a master of attention.

Throughout this chapter, we've analyzed our strange and sometimes irrational relationship with the three main types of reputable figures that are at the heart of the Reputation Trigger—from the perceived wisdom of experts to the power of authority figures to the trust and conformity of the crowd. Each has its role in our attentional system. But just as J. K. Rowling's name can quickly summon best-selling status, the fall of a reputable figure who lies his or her way to the top can capture attention—albeit the wrong kind of attention.

Perhaps that's the final lesson we should take away from the Reputation Trigger. Our trust in experts, authority figures, and the crowd is incredibly strong, and sometimes that blinds us from making informed decisions about where our scarce attention should be placed. But these people are still people—humans who can and do make mistakes. Never be afraid to make your own independent judgments.

Chapter 7

Mystery Trigger

●

As a writer for Hearst Corporation newspapers, Russell Birdwell had a fascination with stories. But while he reported on the major stories of his day, such as the 1928 execution of murderer Ruth Snyder, he was always more interested in creating stories, especially ones that others would cover. Perhaps that's why famed PR agent Mark Borkowski declared that, "without [Birdwell] the modern publicity industry would be a very different monster."[1]

A handsome man with slick, black hair combed backward, despite his receding hairline, Birdwell was a force of nature who loved turning nobodies into international superstars. In the late 1930s, Birdwell decided to switch from the press to publicity. He joined bespectacled producer David O. Selznick's motion picture studio. Birdwell's first major project was the 1938 version of *The Adventures of Tom Sawyer*. Birdwell and Selznick together instigated a nationwide search for the man who would play Mark Twain's iconic protagonist. They eventually settled on Tommy Kelly, a thirteen-year-old Irish-American boy from New York with a down-to-earth family that was perfect material for the press.[2]

Birdwell's first attempt at engineering publicity and attention around a star search succeeded in terms of grabbing headlines, but ultimately it didn't succeed at driving box office sales. *The Adventures of Tom Sawyer* flopped, but long before the film had even hit theaters, Birdwell was already refining his techniques for *Gone with the Wind*.

You see, Selznick had, just a few years prior, purchased the film rights to the classic book. Soon after the news broke, letters began to pour in from thousands of fans of the book with suggestions about casting. Selznick wanted the *perfect* actress to play the role of Scarlett O'Hara. By the end of the year, Selznick decided he wanted a fresh face, rather than an established actress, to embody the role.

"Well-known personalities are liable to be identified with their previous roles, whereas a new personality will be accepted, provided they are sufficiently talented and properly cast as Scarlett and Rhett," Selznick explained to Birdwell in an office memo.

Birdwell was tasked with helping manage what became known as the Search for Scarlett and the publicity around it. Birdwell and Selznick began the hunt at the end of 1936 with auditions being set up in New York City and at dozens of universities across the southern United States.

Women showed up in droves to audition for the part. By the end of 1936, over five hundred women had tried out. The team hit Baltimore; Washington, D.C.; Atlanta; Savannah; New Orleans; Charleston; and many other cities. Birdwell, for his part, constantly fed gossip and rumors about the search to local and national press. By 1937, the Search for Scarlett was making headlines across the country. The anticipation was palatable.

The public had bought into the mystery. Who would become Scarlett? Would the studio give up and choose an established actress, or would Birdwell and Selznick find their fresh face? This mystery constantly made the rounds in the press, thanks to Birdwell's masterful management. Every little detail of the search drove interest in the film further. Everyone from Katharine Hepburn to

Lucille Ball was linked to the role. Every new audition became a plot twist in the Search for Scarlett.

By the end of 1938, over fifteen hundred women had auditioned for the part to no avail—until a twenty-five-year-old actress, Vivien Leigh, showed up in Hollywood and secured a screen test, thanks to her agent, Myron Selznick—David's brother. "She's the Scarlett dark horse and looks damn good," David O. Selznick told his wife in a correspondence after the screen test.

By the time Vivien Leigh had beat out Joan Bennett, Paulette Goddard, and Jean Arthur in the Search for Scarlett, thousands of articles had been written about the search—many of them because of Birdwell—not to mention the countless hours of watercooler talk. But more importantly, with new faces Vivien Leigh and Clark Gable headlining the film, it went on to become one of the highest grossing films of all time.

The Search for Scarlett had all the elements of a great mystery. It had compelling characters you could root for or despise (depending on who you wanted to land the role). It had suspense and anticipation for the final decision that made people follow the search until the very end. It had plot twists, thanks to the cast of characters who desperately wanted the part. Katharine Hepburn is said to have demanded a meeting with Selznick, even supposedly telling him, "The role is practically written for me. I am Scarlett O'Hara!"

The Mystery Trigger

Most of the time, when people hear the word *mystery*, they think about crime novels, Sherlock Holmes, and the big reveal in the final pages of a book or the final minutes of a film. It's ingrained in our culture. The United States has author Dashiell Hammett and *The Maltese Falcon*. Italy has Andrea Camilleri and his inspector, Commissario Montalbano; Sweden has author Henning Mankell and his character Kurt Wallander; Japan has Shizuko Natsuki and *Murder at Mt. Fuji*. China has He Jiahong and *Crime De Sang*. The appeal of mystery is universal.

But mystery isn't just about solving the murder. Mystery simply refers to something that we don't yet understand. In other words, a mystery is a puzzle we have to solve, a secret we have to uncover, or a storyline we have to finish. It's an enigma.

We love a good mystery, but we are especially captivated by a mystery that's incomplete. When we watch *Orange Is the New Black* or *Breaking Bad*, we don't stop with the first episode—we binge watch an entire season. We want to know what will happen to our favorite characters. Every episode leaves us with yet another cliff-hanger to be resolved, reeling us in for another episode. Perhaps that's why more than 60 percent of Netflix's users watch more than two episodes of a TV series in a single sitting.[3]

In other words, we have what I call the compulsion for completion. The compulsion for completion is our nagging obsession with unsolved mysteries, riddles, and puzzles. This compulsion, driven by our need for closure and our love of puzzle solving, makes us pay attention to a mystery or an enigma until it's resolved, which makes it a powerful tool of attention. Imagine if you weren't allowed to read the last thirty pages of any book or watch the last thirty minutes of any film for the rest of your life. I don't know about you, but they'd have to send me to a mental institution.

Harnessing the compulsion for completion is essential to capturing attention, which leads us to the next captivation trigger— Mystery. The Mystery Trigger is the tactical use of unfinished mysteries to captivate the attention of others. By creating the right amount of mystery, suspense, and uncertainty, you can activate your audience's compulsion for completion and get them to pay attention to you and your ideas right until the very end.

Not all mysteries are equal, though. Some mysteries and puzzles are more compelling than others. That's why successful use of the Mystery Trigger really lies in four components: suspense, emotional buy-in, plot twist, and cliff-hanger. We will discuss each of these components in detail throughout the chapter and learn how to combine them to create an attention-grabbing idea or story. Before we can dive deeper into the Mystery Trigger, though, we need to answer two important questions: 1) Why does an unresolved mystery capture our attention? and 2) Why do we feel compelled to solve mysteries and puzzles in the first place? To discover the answers to these questions, we need to turn to a Soviet psychologist and her observation of the selective memory of waiters.

The Compulsion for Completion

Back when I was a kid, I was obsessed with *Ragnarok Online*, an online role-playing game similar in many ways to *World of Warcraft* or *EverQuest*, but with cuter characters and a whimsical Korean flair. Every day during the summer, I'd log on and kill slime monsters, trade my goods in towns, beat up bosses, and embark on quest after quest. I couldn't stop thinking about my halfway-completed quests or how I only needed to take out just a few more orc warriors to level up.

Even now, there are times when I can't put down a game. For a short while, I couldn't stop playing *Disco Zoo*—an iPhone game where you rescue animals by unlocking their patterns—until I had caught all the animals in the game. Once I did, though, the task was complete, and it was suddenly easy for me to delete the app forever. It's the same reason people can't stop playing *Candy Crush Saga*—there's always a new stage to unlock or level to beat. But if you do manage to make it to the end, the game loses all of its appeal.

The dopamine reward we receive for achieving a new level is part of the reason these games are so addictive, but there's a different reason why these games stay on our mind, even when we aren't playing them. It explains why we need to watch the next episode of *Game of Thrones*, why a half-completed puzzle bothers us, and why unfinished tasks stick in our mind and continue to grab our attention until they're completed.

According to some accounts, Bluma Zeigarnik, a beautiful raven-haired psychologist of Latvian and Soviet descent, once sat at a restaurant in the 1920s and observed that the waiters had an incredibly detailed memory when it came to orders that had yet to be fulfilled. She also noticed that, as soon as these orders were delivered, waiters would immediately forget them—flushed completely out of working memory. This intrigued her: Why did these waiters remember unfinished orders so well and finished orders so poorly? Was it the recency of the orders, or was it something about the unfinished orders that glued themselves into their memories?

Zeigarnik decided to investigate this phenomenon. She gathered over two hundred students, teachers, and children for a series of experiments to test whether unfinished tasks were more memorable than finished ones. She gave subjects a series of puzzles and other tasks—approximately twenty in total. The catch: she interrupted half the puzzles and tasks that each participant worked on, making those tasks effectively unfinished.[4]

Afterward, she asked subjects about the tasks. The results were astonishing. She found that the first thirty-two subjects—all adults—had an "average memory advantage" of 90 percent when it came to recalling interrupted tasks. Not only were interrupted tasks better remembered, but they were also often the first tasks that subjects recalled. Children performed even better. For all the participating groups, the incomplete tasks were on the top of their minds.

This inability to forget unfinished tasks is known as the Zeigarnik effect, and you see it implemented all the time in everyday life. A show like *Lost* ends on maddening cliff-hangers, assuring that the story is unfinished. If you've bought into the story and its characters, you simply must know what happens to them, and you're willing to wait a week or six months to complete the loop in your mind. This effect even translates to advertising. A 1970s study by researchers at Purdue University found that the Zeigarnik effect had a major impact on recall when it came to commercials cut short—52.4 percent of subjects had improved recall of unfinished commercials after one week.[5]

The Zeigarnik effect doesn't work for every task, though. If a person hasn't had sufficient time to emotionally buy into the task, interrupting the task doesn't have any effect. Would you really care about the end of a TV show you've only watched for three minutes? This is the exact reason why the Zeigarnik effect works so well for the Mystery Trigger, though. The best mysteries know not only how to build in anticipation and suspense but also how to develop compelling characters and an emotional charge that makes a mystery worth solving.

Our compulsion for completion drives us to finish the storyline—not doing so makes us feel uncomfortable and unsettled. We do not enjoy the uncomfortable feelings that come with uncertainty, so we do everything possible to reduce uncertainty in our lives.

Take, for example, how we try to reduce uncertainty in our dating lives. Pretend you're Alice, a twenty-five-year-old law student at the University of California, Berkeley. A few months ago, you broke up with your long-distance boyfriend of two years after you two began drifting apart, and now you're ready to return to the dating scene. You don't get out much, though—after all, you're a second-year law student at Cal—so you decide to turn to online dating for the first time in years.

You're not looking for a hookup, so you decide to skip a trendy new dating app for now and start with a more traditional dating website like Match.com or OkCupid. You upload a single picture of yourself and put up some general information about yourself, being careful to leave out any specific details that would lead back to you. Submit.

Your profile is there for thousands of guys in the Bay Area to find. You go to sleep and wake up the next morning with sixty-five messages—*Wow,* you think, *How am I going to sort through all these guys?*

Most of them are instant throwaways—creepy guys with creepy messages. Why does a fifty-three-year-old man think you're going to respond to a message declaring that his . . . well, that one's trashed, as are all the others. This goes on for two more days until finally you get a message from a decent-looking guy who writes a sweet poem to introduce himself. You learn that he's a developer whose main hobby is skiing down the slopes. Luckily for him, you love to snowboard. Oh, he grew up in Colorado!! You're from Colorado!! Okay, you decide to message him back.

Over the next few weeks, you two message. It starts small—your hobbies, where you grew up, your favorite restaurants in Berkeley. You're trying to find out if this guy is legit. He could secretly be a creeper. You had one guy completely lie about being from Colorado (and being a doctor) until you snuffed him out on the third date. But you Google this guy, and everything checks out. He even started a nonprofit while he was studying engineering at Northwestern. It begins to get more serious as you two reveal more to each other. The relationship becomes more comfortable.

When you first meet someone you may want to date, whether it's through an online dating website or at the bar, you try to learn all you can about the other person. You want to know what you're potentially getting yourself into. While we like to romanticize the thought of a mysterious lover, the reality is that we do everything we can to reduce uncertainty when we first meet someone. In the case of Alice, she's trying to predict whether a guy is simply looking for a hookup or a more serious relationship. After that, she's learning what she can to determine whether the guy she's talking to is a potential match.

We are constantly gathering information about strangers because we dislike uncertainty and uncomfortable situations—and for many people, meeting a stranger can be uncomfortable. We engage in small talk to help us find common ground and figure out whether we want to get to know this perfect stranger further—or at least find something to nullify the awkwardness. And when we find something in common, even when it's something benign, we get overly excited!!! (See what I did there?)

When we first interact with a stranger, we seek information about that person in order to reduce uncertainty in the relationship—this is the uncertainty reduction theory. The theory, first proposed by Charles Berger of Northwestern University, states that we're uncomfortable when we can't predict the actions of others. We feel compelled to reduce this uncertainty when we meet somebody for the first time. Uncertainty reduction theory is why we try to find common interests when we have to talk to strangers, why we're more comfortable with friends of friends, and why we Google the people we date.

Uncertainty reduction theory helps explain our obsession with mysteries that haven't been resolved and why we pay attention to those mysteries. We find uncertainty unpleasant, and thus we are compelled to reduce that uncertainty by gathering more information. In the case of the Mystery Trigger, this comes in the form of resolution and completing an unsolved mystery or puzzle, thus freeing us from our compulsion for completion.[6]

The Zeigarnik effect and uncertainty reduction theory both demonstrate why we pay attention to incomplete ideas, tasks, and mysteries. That's why the Mystery Trigger is essential to capturing our long attention. But as I said earlier, not all mysteries are made equal. So what makes for a compelling mystery?

What Makes for a Great Mystery?

It begins with a surprise going-away party. *We'll Miss You, Rob!* is inscribed on a banner hanging in an apartment filled with people. A friend with a video camera is capturing everybody's reaction to their friend's departure. "Rob, have fun in Japan," a raven-haired woman says. "Rob's awesome. I'm going to miss him," another woman says to the camera.

Rumble. Roar! An earth-shattering cry shakes the apartment and everyone in it. Rob's party suddenly stops. "What was that noise?"

Everybody rushes to the TV for news, but, coming up with nothing, the party moves to the roof to see what's going on. "What animal sounds like that?" The roar fills the sky again, but this time it comes with an explosion in the heart of Manhattan. The shock on everybody's faces lasts for only a moment. Flaming jets streak from the explosion. Fireballs are falling from the sky. Everybody panics and runs onto the streets. "It's alive, it's huge!"

Rob and his friends hear the roar again, followed by another large object hurtling toward them. They evade its pounding collision with the street, the sound of metal now grating against the concrete. It's the Statue of Liberty . . . or at least her head. The screen fades to black before a single line appears: "From Producer J. J. Abrams."

This was the mysterious debut trailer for *Cloverfield*, a clever sci-fi film that made six times its modest $25 million budget. Its trailer didn't spoil the film like the majority of film trailers seem to do these days. It didn't even include the title, and this launched a flurry of speculation over the film and its plot. What was the film about? Nobody knew—J. J. Abrams and Paramount had done a spectacular job at not letting anything about the film leak. Some thought it was a live-action adaptation of *Voltron*. Others thought it was the film extension of Abrams's wildly popular TV show *Lost*. Maybe it was a new *Godzilla* film? Speculation had run rampant, which only generated more headlines, buzz, and attention for the film.[7]

Director J. J. Abrams is among the elite when it comes to bringing a compelling mystery to life. The famous TV show *Lost* is essentially a string of mysteries placed within a larger mystery. It gained an international following during its six-year run; its final season attracted north of 11 million viewers weekly. Abrams's success as a master of mystery can be traced to his abilities as a storyteller. His characters are flawed human beings with personal struggles that hook us into the story. The suspense and anticipation of what will happen to them next keeps us riveted. His plot twists shock us out of complacency. And as fans of *Lost* can attest, his cliff-hangers are simultaneously breathtaking and frustrating. (It's the Zeigarnik effect—our propensity to remember incomplete tasks—at its best.)

How does J. J. Abrams do it? Well he, like many great mystery writers before him, instinctively follows a formula that creates a compelling and captivating mystery. More specifically, there are four key elements that must exist for a mystery to capture attention until the very end. The Mystery Trigger first requires suspense to keep our short attention captivated. What's going to happen? Will our protagonist succeed or falter? It continues with the emotional buy-in—a hook early on that makes us care about the mystery's conclusion. Without the suspense and emotional buy-in, the Zeigarnik effect never kicks in.

Suspense is nothing if it's predictable, though—that's where the plot twist comes into play. It makes us believe the story is going down one path and then suddenly changes the direction of the story, which disrupts our expectations. When we can't predict the outcome, we are forced to pay attention until we've reduced uncertainty. And finally, to capture long attention and make us come back for more, a great mystery needs a cliff-hanger.

These elements—suspense, emotional buy-in, plot twist, and cliff-hanger—activate the compulsion for completion and the attention-retaining capabilities of the Mystery Trigger. And they don't just apply to books and films—these rules apply to our everyday lives and influence everything from the ads we favor to which charities receive our attention.

Suspense, or How a Tasteless Tweet Kept Twitter on Pins and Needles

PR exec Justine Sacco, a sharp-tongued blond woman in her mid-thirties, was great at generating lots of attention for some of the Internet's biggest brands. For years, she ran public relations for IAC, the company that owns Match.com, the *Daily Beast*, Ask.com, Lending Tree, About.com, and OkCupid.

Unfortunately, her experience in PR couldn't save her from becoming the subject of the unrelenting wrath of the Twitter community. At 10:19 A.M. on a Friday in December 2013, just before she boarded a flight from London to Cape Town, South Africa—an eleven-hour flight to visit her family—Sacco published this tweet:

Going to Africa. Hope I don't get AIDS. Just kidding. I'm white![8]

Sacco's tasteless joke caught the attention of a blogger who, three hours later, published a very short post about the tweet. Sacco had just around two hundred followers at the time, but that didn't stop the tweet from spreading. Journalists from *The Wall Street Journal* and other publications, many of whom follow each other, started noticing the tweet and posting their disbelief. It didn't take long for their followers to start tweeting about Sacco and her inappropriate tweet.

As the minutes passed by, the calls for Sacco's head started rolling in like a raging thunderstorm. Some took it too far—"Justine Sacco should get fired . . . and get AIDS," said one Twitter user. Publications like *BuzzFeed* started publishing stories about the tweet that went viral. And all the while, Sacco's tweet remained: she was still on her flight, blissfully unaware of the firestorm building around her.

At around five thirty P.M., a little more than seven hours after her tweet, the hashtag #HasJustineLandedYet started gaining momentum. In a few short hours, it became a global trending topic. Intrepid Twitter users figured out which flight Sacco was on and tweeted out links to track when she would land. Within a few hours, everyone from Kerry Washington to Gogo Inflight Internet to Aid for Africa was tweeting about #HasJustineLandedYet. The latter was clever enough to buy JustineSacco.com and redirect it to its fund-raising page. But the question on the tip of everybody's tongue was the same: What would Sacco do when she finally landed? The anticipation had built up to irreversible levels.

By the time Justine Sacco landed, it was too late to reverse the damage. Deleting her tweet didn't fix the problem. One Twitter user even spotted her in the airport, tweeting not only a picture of Sacco but also the scolding she was receiving from her father. Within twenty-four hours, Twitter users had tweeted #HasJustine-LandedYet more than a hundred thousand times. IAC soon fired her for her insensitivity and lack of judgment. The next day, Sacco issued an apology to ABC News.

> This is my father's country, and I was born here. I cherish my ties to South Africa and my frequent visits, but I am in anguish knowing that my remarks have caused pain to so many people here; my family, friends and fellow South Africans. I am very sorry for the pain I caused.

The #HasJustineLandedYet saga was unfortunate for everybody involved. Sacco's tweet was tasteless, but nobody can justify the death and rape threats she received. It's not as if she's the only person to tweet a racist joke. In fact, during the heart of the Sacco saga, Steve Martin tweeted the following when a follower asked him how to spell "lasonia":

It depends. Are you in an African-American neighborhood or at an Italian restaurant?[9]

Why did Sacco go viral but Steve Martin, a far more notable public figure, didn't? The answer is remarkably simple: Martin didn't allow for suspense to develop. Within minutes, he deleted his tweet and posted an apology. The storyline was open and closed long before anybody could buy into a saga.

But Justine Sacco? There was plenty of time for people to speculate, prognosticate, and anticipate. Without Internet access, the former PR exec couldn't perform any form of damage control. And so the story continued to build momentum until the suspense about how Sacco would react—what would she say?—became so strong that thousands of Twitter users were staying awake for the moment of truth when she would land and be forced to react to the Twitter mob.[10]

Suspense is the emotional state of excitement, apprehension, and tension we experience when faced with a mystery that has yet to be resolved. By building apprehension and anticipation toward a resolution, you can create the feeling of suspense that will captivate others.

Mystery writers do this by leaving clues that push their stories and plots forward while leaving the eventual conclusion uncertain. In the case of Justine Sacco, for example, suspense built up as new information came to light while she was still on the plane. A few Twitter users found other examples of inappropriate tweets from her past while others figured out which flight she was on and when it would land. Each of these developments kept the story salient and present in the Twitterverse.

But just as suspense helps capture our attention and keeps us captivated, giving away too much too soon—the opposite of creating uncertainty—can kill your audience's interest. It may seem obvious, for example, that you shouldn't give key pieces of story away in a trailer, but some studios simply haven't gotten the message. A trailer for *Man of the Year*, in which the late Robin Williams plays a Jon Stewart–type character who suddenly decides to run for president, reveals the answer to the movie's biggest mystery halfway through the trailer: his character wins the election. You know what's going to happen, *there's no suspense*, so why watch the film? The film disappointed, barely breaking $40 million on a $20 million budget (not counting marketing expenses). *Terminator: Salvation*, *Green Lantern*, and *The Sum of All Fears* are just a few of the other many movies that made this fatal mistake.[11]

On the other hand, the trailers for the film *Captain America: The Winter Soldier* never revealed much about the Winter Soldier, the main antagonist of the film. We never even saw his face in the trailers. There was never a trailer spoiling the *Game of Thrones* in-famous Red Wedding sequence. The trailers for *The Empire Strikes Back* never unveiled the movie's big plot twist. In fact, George Lucas only told Mark Hamill, the actor who played Luke Skywalker, of the big plot twist moments before they shot the famous scene.[12]

Suspense is the snowball of the Mystery Trigger—the longer it lasts, the more attention it sucks in. As a mystery lingers in the public, people start pushing every theory and idea they can to allevi-ate their uncertainty. But suspense alone doesn't capture our atten-tion—we have to have an emotional investment in the story as well.

Emotional Buy-In, or Why We Love Emotional Roller Coasters

Malaysia Airlines Flight 370 is an unfortunate case that exemplifies the captivating power of an unsolved mystery. The now-famous passenger flight seemed to disappear from the face of the earth. We don't expect planes to disappear, and when they do, we expect to find their wreckage. Planes do not disappear.

When, after a few days, no trace of the plane could be found, though, speculation about the plane's fate grew rampant. There was worldwide interest in the mystery of MH370. Every new piece of information resulted in hundreds of articles. Every conspiracy theory—hijacking, electrical fires, and the pilots being in league with terrorists—became hours of fodder for the cable news networks. The major networks aired stories about the 227 passengers and the agony their families experienced as they awaited word on the fates of their loved ones. CNN especially went wall-to-wall with its coverage, boosting its ratings but also resulting in an embarrassing amount of speculation to fill airtime.

Eventually, of course, as the months passed with no new developments, the story began to fall off the public's radar and other stories with new developments came to the forefront. Without new developments or clues, a story loses its suspense and thus loses the attention it has accumulated.

This leads us to discussing emotional buy-in, a fundamental component of mystery. In order for a mystery to be effective, we have to care about some aspect of the mystery we're being presented. We have to emotionally invest in the mystery and its outcome. In the case of MH370, audiences were invested emotionally in the outcome of the story: Was there a chance that the passengers could be alive? How are the families of the passengers holding up? Could the same thing happen on my next international flight?

The reality is that the captivating power of a mystery doesn't lie in its ending, but in the emotional roller coaster we take to get there. Despite the fact that we dislike uncertainty and actively seek to reduce it (uncertainty reduction theory), suspense itself is an emotion that actively gives us enjoyment. A study conducted at Indiana University found that people's appreciation of a dramatic story increased consistently as the story's suspense increased.[13]

Mysteries are a bit of a paradox: we dislike uncertainty yet enjoy the emotional rush of suspense. This is true even when we're aware of the eventual outcome. After all, we still re-read our favorite books and fret about whether the date from last night will text back, even though she made it clear she wants to go out again. Famed contemporary philosopher Noël Carroll believes that during a suspenseful story, our attention doesn't wander beyond the moment we're in.

"In this case, we focus our attention on the relevant, available information in the story up to and for the duration of the interlude in which suspense dominates," Carroll states in an article about suspense. He claims that our attention is riveted "to the unfolding of the story on a moment-to-moment basis." In other words, a great mystery makes us live in the moment. Instead of thinking about how the story is going to end, we're engrossed in the action happening right now.[14]

The science shows that it's the emotional investment in this moment-to-moment aspect of suspenseful stories that attracts us to them. It's even true in advertising. Robert Madrigal and Colleen Bee, professors of marketing at the University of Oregon and Oregon State University, respectively, asked thirty-six subjects to watch four TV commercials twice. Each time, they were instructed to turn a Perception Analyzer dial to rate how much hope or fear they felt for the protagonist of each commercial, on a scale of 0 to 100. Two commercials were filled with suspenseful moments, while the others weren't.[15]

Madrigal and Bee found that subjects felt both hope and fear when watching suspenseful commercials. What was surprising, though, was the *amount* of hope and fear each subject experienced just by adding a little suspense. Suspenseful commercials received a sky-high score of 80 on the fear factor and nearly 60 on hope during their most suspenseful moments. The other commercials simply resulted in ambivalence—none broke a 50 emotion score for either hope or fear, and hope barely averaged a 10 for the nonsuspenseful commercials.

In another study, the same researchers found that TV viewers had a much more favorable reaction to ads when they appeared immediately after a suspenseful basketball game. Their fear, excitement, and emotional buy-in all transferred to the ads.[16]

Director Steven Soderbergh puts the emotional roller coaster of mystery into context. "The audience has a certain expectation, and in a macro sense, wants [a story] to go in a certain direction," Soderbergh said when I interviewed him in his New York apartment. "And I guess what you're trying to do is continually sort of fool them on a micro level so that moment to moment they feel like they know what's going to happen. But they're comfortable in a macro sense with where [a story] is basically going."[17]

The key to capturing attention through mystery is providing uncertainty, but the key to locking in that attention is providing an emotional roller coaster for your audience. The best way to do this is to always have new developments and information whenever you utilize the Mystery Trigger. Your audience needs to feel like the story you're providing them—whether it's a play, an ad, or a presentation—is progressing toward a resolution, even if in the back of their heads, they're aware of the eventual outcome.

To do this, you always need to provide novel information. For products and Kickstarter campaigns, this comes in the form of updates. For stories, it's leaving bread crumbs and adding material that helps the protagonist get closer to solving the mystery. Even the news media used new developments in the Malaysia Airlines Flight 370 story to create emotional buy-in (though they sometimes took it too far by rehashing the same developments, but with different experts and angles that didn't actually provide any new information about the mystery).

So long as you make your audience feel like the mystery you've given them is progressing, they will continue to buy into the mystery, feel the suspense of the mystery, and pay attention. But unpredictability is still vital to keeping your audience's attention focused on you, which is why every great mystery needs a plot twist.

Plot Twists, or Why We Love March Madness

For three weeks every March, millions of Americans obsess over their television screens, brackets, and betting pools, thanks to the college basketball championship—the NCAA basketball tournament, which culminates in a Final Four showdown of the country's four best college basketball teams. ESPN analysts, regular Joes, and even the president of the United States make bold predictions about which teams will be knocked out early, which team will be this year's underdog story, and which team will win it all.

For many, the tournament is serious business: Americans bet approximately $12 billion in bracket pools, and the sixty-eight-team NCAA tournament costs businesses somewhere between $1.2 and $2 billion per year in lost productivity. But regardless of whether you bet thousands on the games or just enjoy basketball, it's hard not to get swept up in March Madness. If you're a hardcore fan of the Kentucky Wildcats (like my father is), you've built a piece of your identity based on associating with that team and the community around it. In some ways, their success is your success. For others, the draw is the drama of close games and upsets by teams seeded twelfth against teams seeded fifth. For others, it's a matter of rooting for their predictions to come true so they can win their office pool.[18]

The NCAA basketball tournament—and most high-stakes sporting championships—has all the elements of a great mystery. There's the suspense over each close game and wondering which teams will make it to the Final Four. There are the cliff-hangers—waiting a week to see your team take the court again can be torture. But what really makes the NCAA tournament one of the best three weeks on television are the upsets.

Upsets are the plot twists of sports—what nobody sees coming. The story of 2013 was fifteenth seed Florida Gulf Coast University upsetting powerhouse Georgetown 78–68 and then going on to disrupt expectations again by trouncing San Diego State 81–71. In 2014, the tournament was an amazing series of upsets, with eleventh seed Dayton reaching the Elite Eight, eighth seed Kentucky reaching the championship, and seventh seed UConn winning it all. Upsets like these are the wrinkles to conventional thinking. Like plot twists, they violate our expectations and delight us, because who doesn't love a good underdog story?

Plot twists capture our attention at a fundamental level. In one study, researchers at the University of Illinois tracked the eye movements of subjects as they read stories. They found major changes in eye movement when readers came upon the plot twists. The number of eye fixations increased dramatically, indicating that, when subjects hit surprising plot twists, their attention stopped because they had to reread the text. Not only that, but the eye fixations also lasted longer. There is something inherently captivating about a good plot twist.[19]

One reason may simply be that plot twists keep us on our toes and, as we learned from the Reward Trigger, surprise activates our dopamine reward systems. They assure that we never take our predictions or conclusions for granted, which may be why we tend to reread or rewatch major plot twists in our favorite books and shows. *Ender's Game* was one of my favorite books as a child. It had a compelling story set in space about an underdog overcoming adversity, but it was the fact that I did not see the story's plot twist coming that won me over. After that moment, I couldn't get enough of *Ender's Game* and I quickly became hooked on the series of books. The plot twist heightened the emotional intensity of the story for me and millions of others, and has made *Ender's Game* a very popular sci-fi series.

Not all plot twists are created equal, though. While the plot twist in *Ender's Game* floored me, I could see the plot twists of the 2004 film *The Village* a mile away, and it killed the story for me. This leads us to the first and most important rule to remember about plot twists: they have to be surprises. Make it too obvious and you will spoil the surprise. Most of the time, this happens because you either 1) provide too much warning or foreshadowing or 2) let the plot twist leak. The trick is striking the fine balance between dropping enough clues to build up suspense but not so many that your audience can figure out what you're going to do before it happens.

Apple's Steve Jobs was remarkably adept at executing the plot twist while avoiding the spoiler. At the end of Apple's big presentations and product launches, when it seemed like Jobs had finished his presentation, he would come back with three little words: "One more thing. . . ." When he said those words, the crowd would go wild and Jobs would unveil one more surprise product. In 2012, he launched FaceTime for face-to-face conversations. In 2005, his "one more thing" was the iPod Shuffle, which went on to become a best seller. And in 2006, he unveiled iTV (now Apple TV) before another surprise—bringing John Mayer on stage to perform "Waiting on the World to Change." And, more often than not, the world didn't see these products coming—Jobs was legendary for tamping down on leaks during his second tenure as CEO. Even when some product details leaked in the media, he would use other unannounced features to blow away the crowd.

The other rule to keep in mind when using plot twists is that they also have to be believable and significant with your audience. In many ways, the plot twist is an extension of the Disruption Trigger, which relies on simplicity, surprise, and significance to be effective. When a plot twist becomes unbelievable, it loses its significance and your audience will tune out. People expected Steve Jobs to unveil a new technology product when he said, "One more thing . . . ," but had he strayed from that formula too much and, say, announced his own line of clothing, thousands of Apple fans would have been confused and disappointed (unless black turtlenecks are your thing, of course).

We've covered three elements of the Mystery Trigger thus far: suspense, emotional buy-in, and the plot twist. They are all key elements of capturing attention using the Mystery Trigger. But it's the final element—the cliff-hanger—that makes us do more than just pay attention—it makes us come back.

The Cliff-Hanger, or Why Chicago Fell for Kathlyn

In 1913, Kathlyn fever swept Chicago. "Young Ladies: Watch your Sweethearts. Kathlyn is coming!" the *Chicago Daily Tribune* declared. Audiences were captivated by the beautiful blonde's jungle adventures, escapes from prisons, brushes with death, and her constant struggle with Umballah, a villainous figure whose desire for Kathlyn went unrequited.[20]

The Adventures of Kathlyn wasn't your typical film, at least for its time. It was the second movie serial ever developed by an American film studio—but more importantly, it was considered by many to be the first serial to ever employ the cliff-hanger. Not only was it divided into thirteen parts, but each episode also often ended with Kathlyn Hare in the midst of some sort of daring escape or mortally dangerous situation. In one episode, Kathlyn, her father, and her other companions hooked metal chains to the bars of Umballah's ancient prison and, using the might of an elephant, broke the metal bars from their sockets. And then . . .

. . . And then captivated viewers had to wait two weeks for the next installment. Each episode was released biweekly, both on film and in print form in the *Chicago Daily Tribune*. The twenty-six-week saga boosted circulation of the *Tribune* by 10 percent. It spawned a book, a feature-length movie in 1916, collectible post-cards, the Kathlyn cocktail, a clothing line, and countless imitators.

The cliff-hanger is when an installment of a story or idea ends with an unfinished mystery. Sometimes it ends one storyline only to launch a new one. It leaves an audience in suspense—enough so that they feel compelled to come back for the next installment. This is because our compulsion to complete an unresolved mystery demands that we pay attention until the story comes to its conclusion. If the story isn't complete, it becomes an obsession.

This makes the cliff-hanger a powerful tool of serial film and television. It's a major reason why viewers came back for episode after episode of *Lost* and why viewers anticipate the return of a show like *House of Cards*—the end of each episode or season raises new questions that can only be answered by watching the next episode or season.

The cliff-hanger is more specific than general suspense though. Suspense is an emotional state that keeps people captivated. The cliff-hanger is the element of the Mystery Trigger that *brings people back*. Bringing people back is especially important if your goal is to capture long attention—our long-term interest in people and ideas that can last weeks, months, and years.

Television show writers and mystery novelists aren't the only ones who need their audiences to return for multiple installments. Teachers—whether they're professors or yoga instructors—need students to come back for the second, third, and fourth classes. Entrepreneurs need users to return for second and third visits. Sales-people need their prospective customers to agree to second and third meetings.

There are plenty of other stories that end in cliff-hangers that don't become sensations like *The Adventures of Kathlyn*. So why do some cliff-hangers work and others don't?

Capturing attention like *The Adventures of Kathlyn* did requires three tactics: ending by launching a new mystery, delivering on the promise of the cliff-hanger, and moving the story forward. There has to be a sense of progression. If you don't deliver on all three things—if you keep your audience hanging for too long—their curiosity can quickly turn to anger.

In March of 2013, Reddit user dont_stop_me_smee posted five images of a locked, person-size safe he found in a friend's basement. "A friend of mine moved into a former drug house and found this HUGE safe. How do we get it open?" he titled the post.[21]

It caused a sensation on the site, all centered around one question: *What's in the safe?!* It quickly gained forty-seven thousand upvotes and six thousand comments. The user even created a subreddit dedicated to what was in the safe, gaining more than sixty thousand members in just two days. Post after post about the safe dominated the front page. Any day now, everyone would know what was in the safe . . . right?

The days passed, and . . . nothing. After a while, dont_stop _me_smee stopped posting updates about the safe. This angered the Reddit community, which had become obsessed with the contents of the safe. It lived on as a meme. More safes popped up, reaching the top of Reddit as well. But finally, after months of silence, the Reddit user with the safe finally came back and delivered. Perhaps unsurprisingly, his photos of the contents of the safe—a disappointingly empty room with a big-ass spider—also became one of Reddit's most popular posts of all time with 155,000 upvotes and 12,000 comments. The audience simply had to know and share the answer to the mystery no matter how humdrum it might be.

The lesson here is that you need to always deliver on the promise of your mystery. You can only leave your audience hanging for so long before their suspense turns into anger.

How to End a Crisis: A Lesson in Closure

In 2011, my friends at Airbnb—the popular website for renting out homes and apartments—were struck by controversy. A San Francisco resident known as "EJ" wrote a blog post about how her apartment had been decimated by the people renting it through Airbnb. "They smashed a hole through a locked closet door, and found the passport, cash, credit card and grandmother's jewelry I had hidden inside. They took my camera, my iPod, an old laptop, and my external backup drive filled with photos, journals . . . my entire life," she said in her blog post.[22]

Airbnb's CEO quickly issued a response, but it didn't directly address EJ's concerns—instead, it felt like a lawyer wrote it. *Tech-Crunch* called it "diplomatic but tepid." Talking about how they were "working closely with the authorities" and held "the safety of our community members as our highest priority" didn't cut it. The victim responded a few days later with more information, specifically that Airbnb had not been supportive of her situation, instead focusing on addressing her blog post. The uncertainty and mystery around the story grew as journalists published even more stories.

After another week, the crisis ended. Why? Brian Chesky, Airbnb's cofounder and CEO, directly addressed the issues EJ brought up and truly owned up to the company's mistakes. "With regards to EJ, we let her down, and for that we are very sorry," he said in a blog post. "We should have responded faster, communicated more sensitively, and taken more decisive action to make sure she felt safe and secure. But we weren't prepared for the crisis and we dropped the ball. Now we're dealing with the consequences."

In the same post, Airbnb instituted a fifty-thousand-dollar guarantee for protecting its hosts from property damage and launched an in-house task force for trust and safety. These are some of the best decisions the company has ever made, and now Airbnb is bigger than ever—it's worth over $10 billion now.

Airbnb's mistake was not making a direct, personal response to the crisis. Chesky's first response—tepid, noncommittal, and vague—didn't provide any *resolution* or *closure* to the EJ saga. Without that closure, the story was allowed to thrive—the suspense remained. How would EJ respond? What would the authorities say? And what would Airbnb say next on the matter?

Airbnb allowed the Mystery Trigger to snowball out of control, but it fixed this mistake a week later by directly addressing EJ's concerns, providing far more resolution and closure for both her and the story at large. This closure is what completed the cycle, and thus attention dissipated.

If you or your company are faced with a crisis where the media and the public are watching your next move, the number-one thing you want to do is provide closure, because closure and resolution end the cycle of the Mystery Trigger. If you leave a tiny crack for a cliff-hanger with either no response or a weak response that doesn't directly address the story, people will keep calling you and writing about your crisis.

Airbnb has learned how to dissipate attention by providing closure quickly. When an Airbnb user found that his place had been used for an orgy in early 2014, it took less than twenty-four hours for Airbnb to change the user's locks, put him up in a hotel room, and wire him $23,817. It had already practiced its response to this scenario. By providing immediate resolution and closure, it quelled a controversy that could've become much bigger.[23]

When you want attention, you want to find ways to keep your audience in suspense. But when you have a crisis and you want the attention to end, the one thing you have to do is provide closure. When the mystery is solved, your audience will move on to the next one.

The Innate Appeal of Mystery

"It's one of the basic human instincts to be attracted to mysteries and to look for the solution to them," award-winning mystery writer Tana French once said in an interview with NPR.[24]

French couldn't be more right. A great mystery activates our curiosity and makes us uncomfortable enough to seek out an answer. A great mystery sticks in our mind and demands our attention until it is solved. I hope you've learned that mystery is more than just sleuths solving crimes; it's tied into the everyday unsolved questions of life. We are driven to seek answers to unsolved riddles, not just from the stories we read but also from questions about the universe itself. Here's how Isaac Newton summarized his life:

> I do not know how I may appear to the world, but to myself I seem to have been only like a boy, playing on the sea-shore, and diverting myself, in now and then finding a smoother pebble or prettier shell than ordinary, whilst the great ocean of truth lay all undiscovered before me.[25]

Mysteries are fundamental to human nature, and thus they are fundamental to our attention. "Mystery is a good thing," director Steven Soderbergh told me. "I think it's a good thing in life; I think it's a good thing in narrative." Soderbergh and Newton both understood just how important mystery is to our lives, and thus why the Mystery Trigger is a fundamental tool for commanding our long attention.

In the last chapter, we will learn about one final piece of human nature that directs our attention in strange, powerful, and ultimately empowering ways.

Chapter 8

Acknowledgment Trigger

●

Kina Grannis, a woman with a petite physique and a voice as smooth as silk, used to dream of touring the world and making music her life. She certainly had the voice and the talent—when you hear her play her guitar and sing with her sweet and melodic tones, it's hard not to drift away into a happy place. It's the same feeling you get when you listen to Norah Jones.

Grannis, like many artists, was looking for her big break. But she took far more initiative with her career than most. In 2007, she entered the Doritos "Crash the Super Bowl" contest. The grand prize was a chance for a musical artist to make his or her debut in a Doritos commercial seen by tens of millions of people nationwide. You couldn't buy that kind of exposure without being a multimillionaire.

Grannis's talent helped her get into the top ten. She was faced with a new challenge, though—she had to convince the public to vote for her song and music video, "Message from Your Heart." She started by releasing a new song every day on YouTube. It was mildly successful, but it wasn't the big pop she needed to reach the upper ranks of the Doritos contest.

"We started thinking, *How do we get in front of many more people who are not in my current bubble?*" Kina explained to me while grasping a cup of tea in a Los Angeles coffee shop. Kina then explained that she and her sisters had an idea. "Digg was huge at the time, and my sisters and I were big Digg fans, so we thought, *Well maybe we write a tribute to Digg song*."[1]

Digg, the popular news-sharing website and "homepage" of the Internet at the time, could make or break a website. The "Digg effect" could send so much traffic to a site all at once that it literally shut down some sites' servers. So Grannis wrote a tune, "Gotta Digg," that was essentially a love ballad to the website. It wasn't just a ploy to get attention, though—that would've failed. Her lyrics made it very clear that she *got* the Digg community and what it was all about:

> The fanboys can be tiresome, they always are outspoken.
> And if you're listening, Kevin Rose, the comment system is
>   broken!
> I know Digg isn't perfect, but be thankful for what we've got.
> It's just like Daddy always says, "At least it's not Slashdot!"[2]

Within a few hours, the video skyrocketed to the top of the Digg charts, pushing Grannis's fan base to new levels and helping her reach the top three of the Doritos contest. Grannis engaged her newly enlarged fan base with a new cover or original every single day. One element remained the same in her videos—she interacted with her fans. She answered questions, made creative shout-outs, and didn't try to portray anybody but herself.

"One thing I learned that was helping me was that I was trying to be as human as possible," Grannis tells me.

When the day of the Super Bowl came, Grannis was in Phoenix with the other two finalists, not knowing who had won the contest. But when the Doritos commercial began and the music started playing, Grannis's familiar guitar strumming, soulful voice, and wavy locks of hair made their debut to nearly 98 million people.

Why did tens of thousands of people rally for Kina? What motivated them to turn a complete stranger into an overnight star?

Our Quest for Acknowledgment

Dr. Thomas de Zengotita—an expert in anthropology and media—and Adrian Grenier—best known for portraying Vincent Chase in HBO's hit TV show *Entourage*—understand why fans are obsessed with Grannis and other celebrities better than most. In 2010, this unlikely duo teamed up to create the documentary *Teenage Paparazzo*, a critically acclaimed documentary about the life of a fourteen-year-old paparazzi photographer, the struggle between celebrities and the media, and the role that celebrity plays in our culture.

Grenier, de Zengotita, and I discussed at length why we as a society care about celebrities. While there is no single reason why celebrities captivate us, one concept kept coming up over and over as the key driver: acknowledgment.

"Attention figures first on the list of specifically nonmaterial needs," Dr. de Zengotita said as we began our joint interview at NASDAQ's headquarters in the heart of New York City. "All mammals want attention. Only human beings need *acknowledgment*."

According to de Zengotita, acknowledgment is our deep-seated need to be recognized, validated, and understood by others. "If you forget your dog's name, she won't be insulted—she's ecstatic if you pat her on the head and play with her. But if you somehow forget your longtime friend's name, your friend is going to be upset."

I define *acknowledgment*—at least in the context of attention—as an umbrella term that describes our innate need for recognition (Do you know my name? Do you know I exist?), validation (Do you think I'm special, unique, or important?), and empathy (Do you feel what I feel? Do you care about me? Do you understand me?). Our desire to have these three needs met increases in intensity as we develop a connection with a person, product, or idea.

You've almost certainly experienced the desire to have these three needs—which constitute the overall need for acknowledgment—met in your personal life. Maybe you've thought about what it would be like to be famous, or maybe you've changed what you wear to catch the eye of your crush (both exemplifying our need for recognition). Maybe your heart jumped for joy when your boss told you that your latest project was an excellent piece of work (our need for validation). Or perhaps you fell in love with somebody because he or she listened to your problems instead of trying to criticize you (our need for empathy). When met, these three needs are the foundation of trust. And as we already learned from the chapter on the Reputation Trigger, when we trust somebody, we pay attention to whatever he or she has to say.

In one study conducted by researchers at the University of Virginia and the University of Wisconsin, sixteen married women had electrodes strapped to their ankles and were threatened with electric shock. During each of the experiments, the women received either a safety signal that indicated they were not going to get shocked or a threat signal that indicated they had a 20 percent chance of being shocked.[3]

The researchers, led by Dr. James Coan, wanted to measure their brain activity under duress. But sometimes the women received support. In some cases, they were allowed to hold the hands of total strangers. In others, the women held the hands of their husbands. But in yet another case, the women weren't permitted to hold anybody's hand.

As you might expect, the experiment was stressful and resulted in elevated brain activity. Activity was highest when the married women had no hand to hold and lowest when the women held the hands of their husbands. But what was most startling was that brain activity was also correlated with the quality of their marriage. They were the calmest in the face of danger. The women with the greatest satisfaction with their relationship and strongest bond with their husbands showed the least brain activity when threatened with shock.

Coan's study demonstrates that strong bonds help us shift our attention away from stressful situations and toward the comforting figures in our lives. It's no wonder why we tend to pay attention to the people, communities, and ideas that meet our need for acknowledgment—they provide us with the emotional comfort we need. This is why, among all seven captivation triggers, the Acknowledgment Trigger is the most powerful at capturing long-lasting attention.

The premise of the Acknowledgment Trigger is simple: we pay attention to the people and ideas that recognize, validate, and empathize with us in some way. If somebody starts flirting with us, we naturally pay attention because we appreciate, enjoy, and even crave positive reinforcement and affection from others. Or perhaps more succinctly, if you pay attention to someone, that person will pay attention back. When attention is given by one party and then returned by another, it becomes reciprocal attention. Reciprocal attention is the basis of the Acknowledgment Trigger's captivating power.

For Kina Grannis—our soulful musician—her rise to popularity validated Digg's community and its power to propel somebody to fame. But as she started making more and more videos, she started developing empathy for and an understanding of who her fans were and why they appreciated her genuine, quirky nature. Grannis loves her fans, and in return, her fans—who call themselves Kinerds—love her back.

In the rest of this chapter, we will explore the three needs that, when met, activate the Acknowledgment Trigger. We'll look at why we seek acknowledgment from others and how you can meet your audience's need for acknowledgment to capture their attention at the deepest level possible.

To start, let's explore our need for recognition and the real reasons we actually crave fame.

The Quest for Recognition and the Fame Formula

Richard Heene and Mayumi Iizuka had a craving for fame. The married couple appeared on the reality show *Wife Swap* in 2008, and before that they unsuccessfully pitched a reality show concept— *The Psyience Detectives* (they did pitch William Shatner, though). Unfortunately for them, they wanted more.[4]

Heene and Iizuka did eventually achieve their goal of recognition and fame. However, it came with a heavy price. You probably heard about their story in 2009, when the couple claimed their six-year-old son, Falcon, had taken to the skies in a balloon-laden device Heene had built. Millions of people watched the news track the balloon contraption soar seven thousand feet into the air with Falcon inside. The story of the "balloon boy" captivated audiences.

Of course, we know today that Heene and Iizuka were simply con artists who had fooled the public and the media. Their son, Falcon, never took to the skies—he had been hiding in the family's attic. The emotional outpouring of suspense and support turned into anger, especially after an interview between the family and CNN's Wolf Blitzer, where the six-year-old said he purposely didn't come out of the attic because of a show. "You guys said that . . . we did this for the show," he said on air. The judge didn't take too kindly to Heene and Iizuka's hoax—Heene was sentenced to ninety days in jail and four years of probation, with his wife given a lighter sentence. The judge also ruled that the couple could not profit from the hoax in any way for four years.

Heene and Iizuka went to extremes to achieve fame, but they certainly aren't the only ones to crave recognition from their peers. Surveys conducted in Germany and China found that approximately 30 percent of adults daydreamed about being famous. Even crazier is that more than 40 percent believed they would achieve some sort of fame someday in the future. And the numbers skyrocketed with teenagers. In fact, one study found that children ages ten to twelve listed fame as their top future goal.[5]

We clearly have an innate desire for others to recognize us and be aware that we exist. But why are we motivated by fame? The answer lies in acknowledgment and our desires for others to acknowledge us and accept us. Dr. Dara Greenwood, a psychologist at Vassar College, and her colleagues found that individuals with a greater need for "belongingness" were more drawn to fame than others. Even just fantasizing about fame could make these subjects feel better about themselves. The visibility and status that fame provides is simply a path to gain a sense of belonging.[6]

Recognition is the acknowledgment that you and your message exist, while fame is based on the amount of recognition and awareness you achieve for something notable you do. Or, put more simply, when we express recognition, acceptance, and belonging to people, we make them famous. The Acknowledgment Trigger is about harnessing our audience's fundamental desire for acceptance by offering them recognition.

Our desire for recognition helps explain why we pay so much attention to fame and the things that can help us achieve it. Thus, providing recognition or the opportunity to be recognized is a powerful motivator that can be harnessed to capture attention. The desire for recognition is the reason why shows like *The Voice* and *American Idol* have had such strong appeal and ratings worldwide; it's not just the fact that they have celebrities as coaches or that the rising artists they feature are talented; it's also that you or someone you know could be next to achieve recognition. This is especially true of *The Voice*, whose entire premise is around becoming a superstar based on your talent and not your looks.

Creating recognition isn't a simple matter of calling attention to yourself, though. Waving and yelling, "Me, me, me!" lead to the kind of backlash the balloon boy hoaxers received from the public and the media (not to mention the judge). Instead, you have to gain awareness for something of substance—for your achievement or what you stand for.

"Popularity is gained by what [people] do to earn it," said Dick Guttman, the PR mastermind behind Jay Leno, Barbra Streisand and dozens of Hollywood's elite. "Popularity is a function of what you do to please other people."[7]

Celebrities like George Clooney or Will Smith, for example, don't call attention to themselves for their own sake; they use the recognition they've built to call attention for their work. That's why people are able to pay sustained attention to them rather than the fleeting attention many washed-out stars once received.

Of course, recognition is an even more powerful tool when it is reciprocated. When people recognize you for your work, it opens the possibility for you to demonstrate that you recognize them and acknowledge your gratitude that they paid attention to you. This mutual or reciprocal attention leads to capturing people's sustained, long attention.

Recognition is an important need that drives our attention, but it isn't our only need. Just as we desire recognition from our peers, we also desire the validation that who we are and the things we accomplish are worthy and worthwhile. This leads us to the next need of the Acknowledgment Trigger.

Validation, or Why Is *BuzzFeed* So Popular?

BuzzFeed's office in the Flatiron District of Manhattan is a sprawling sea of white—the color of the walls and furniture—and yellow—the color of giant circular LOL, CUTE, FAIL, and WTF signs that permeate the office's walls. It's filled with the bustle of hundreds of writers, editors, developers, and salespeople. You can almost feel the imminent creation of a new list about adorable animals or reasons why the nineties was the best decade.

BuzzFeed is the viral content engine of the Internet. Since it was cofounded in 2008 by *Huffington Post* cofounder Jonah Peretti and Eyebeam founder John Johnson, *BuzzFeed* has grown exponentially year after year. It tripled its audience between 2011 and 2013. In 2014, tens of millions visited the site monthly for their fill of news, entertainment, and viral lists. I was here to learn the site's secret sauce for capturing so many eyeballs and keeping them there.

Jonah Peretti is part mad genius and part savant. The baby-faced CEO has been generating viral hits since the nineties with sites like Black People Love Us!, a crude-looking parody website where a white couple posts about how black people love them (complete with hilarious testimonials). Peretti's also famous for an e-mail chain with Nike in which he attempted to get the word *sweatshop* custom printed on his sneakers.

As I sat with Peretti in his office—three walls made entirely of crystal-clear glass in the center of the entire floor—he told me that, while there was no silver bullet, there were three main factors to *BuzzFeed*'s success. The first is the science behind *BuzzFeed*—an internal viral engine that calculates the spread of any piece of content on the web.

"We use a simple equation from epidemiology," Peretti told me. "The math used for the spread of disease can be applied to the math of sharing and content." This model lets the *BuzzFeed* team predict how any piece of content will spread. His team takes lots of factors into account to improve the chance that something will go viral. Peretti himself has spent the last ten years learning the structure of networks and human behavior "to have slightly better odds of success."

The second factor is novelty—the key to short attention. "Novelty is one of the most important things for what takes off," Peretti said. *BuzzFeed*'s reporters are constantly scanning the web for new content to post. The result is a never-ending stream of new content and new takes on old content.

The third factor—the one with the most captivating power—is validation. "Emotion matters a lot more for sharing than IQ," Peretti said. He used Minnesotans as an example.

One *BuzzFeed* article, "38 Things Minnesotans Are Too Nice to Brag About," featuring Minnesota staples like Bob Dylan, Juicy Lucy (a cheeseburger within a cheeseburger), and Target, broke a million page views. But what intrigued Peretti was how the article went viral. When the article was first posted, Minnesota lit up like a beacon. Thousands of Minnesotans shared the article, which spurned more Minnesotans in other states and countries to share the article as well. The article wasn't just cool facts about Minnesota—it was a statement. Minnesotans shared the article because it validated an important piece of their identity.

BuzzFeed's active attempt to appeal to the various identities of its audience is apparent in its content. Here are the headlines from a few popular *BuzzFeed* lists:

- "21 Questions Asian People Are Sick of Answering"

- "23 Problems Only Kids of Immigrant Parents Will Understand"

- "48 Pictures that Perfectly Capture the '90s"

Recognize a pattern here? *BuzzFeed* understands its audience. But more importantly, *BuzzFeed* acknowledges the unique identities and experiences that define different groups of people. Sure, only a relatively small number of people are from Minnesota, but you can bet they're going to share an article that validates their association with Minnesota, which in turn validates their identity as people from Minnesota.

We naturally seek and direct our attention toward anything that affirms our identity, uniqueness, or extraordinariness. In other words, we seek validation and, in return, pay attention to the things that give us that validation. It's reciprocal attention in action.

That's why *BuzzFeed*'s quizzes and lists are so popular: they emphasize the uniqueness and extraordinariness of *BuzzFeed*'s audience. Its articles provide validation for multiple identities. Perhaps you're not from Minnesota, but *BuzzFeed* also has articles that validate Chicagoans, Hispanic culture, people who grew up during the nineties, etc. Almost every article finds a way to provide validation for the site's audience. One of the site's most popular articles, "19 People Who Are Having a Way Worse Day than You" (20 million-plus views), is actually a validation that your life, despite all its problems, is a good one. After all, your day could be a lot worse.

Part of the reason why validation captures people's attention is because everyone worries all the time about being validated: Will my boss recognize my good work? Will the cute guy or gal I met at the bar last week call me back? Validation—our need for positive affirmation—is a constant driver of our attention. We don't often talk about our desire for validation, though. It's taboo to draw attention to yourself or to want to be popular. Validation is supposed to come to you if you put your head down and do good work. If we've learned anything throughout this book, however, it's that taking the attitude that "if you build it, they will come" doesn't work in the modern world.

While our quest for validation is universal, the type of validation we seek is unique from person to person. Some of us love seeing ourselves in the newspaper or envision ourselves on the campaign trail, courting adoring crowds. Some of us turn to psychics to validate that we have an extraordinary future ahead. Many of us just want to hear a few validating words from a close friend or lover and would rather not be the center of attention. If you're an introvert, you're more likely to seek validation for your work than for yourself. Will people like my art? Will people share my blog posts?

The universality of our quest for validation can be plainly observed in how we use social media. In 2012, I wrote about a concept I called the validation society. I argued that social media has created a society where we covet constant validation from others, mostly in the form of likes, retweets, favorites, and comments. We get a rush when one of our tweets goes viral, and we're disappointed when nobody comments on our witty Facebook post.[8]

The rise of retweets and likes has made validation easier than ever to obtain. The result of the growth of the validation society is that lots of status updates are calculated attempts to amass likes and favorites rather than genuine expressions of our personalities and our lives. Perhaps my friend Jenna Wortham of the *New York Times* puts it best:

> That validation that your contribution is important, interesting or worthy is enough social proof to encourage repetition. Many times, that results in one-upmanship, straining to be the loudest or the most retweeted and referred to as the person who captured the splashiest event of the day in the pithiest way.[9]

Facebook isn't the most popular social network in the world solely because you can connect with your friends. We pay attention to it because it's the place where friends will pay attention to *us*. In other words, we pay attention to it because it meets our need for validation. Just check your Facebook on your birthday or count the likes and comments your friends receive when they announce their engagement.

The companies, products, ideas, and communities that validate us or facilitate others validating us are the ones we inevitably pay attention to. We covet followers—even if we don't know them—because it supposedly says something about the quality of our content or our popularity.

"*Follow* is the magic verb," said Josh Elman, a partner at Greylock Partners and former product manager at Facebook, Twitter, and LinkedIn. Elman explained that more and more companies have focused on adding features that let you "follow" others, rather than "friend" other friends because it provides a greater amount of both validation and attention. He believes that both media and social media will be "dependent on the follow model." Facebook adding "followers" to profiles was just the beginning, as other companies like Foursquare have done the same and added follower features to their apps in recent years.[10]

Elman is right—there are simply more opportunities for validation with "followers" versus "friends." The more followers you have, the more validation you receive. And while you can't pay attention to every person who is favoriting your tweets, you certainly are going to pay attention to Twitter if you're getting lots of interactions. Adding features that provide validation to users—whether it's likes, favorites, followers, or something else—greatly improves the amount of attention they will give to a product.

But meeting someone's need for validation isn't the only tool that activates the Acknowledgment Trigger. Even more than being validated, we want others to empathize with us—and we want to empathize with them.

Batkid, Rokia, and the Identifiable Victim

Life hasn't done any favors for Miles Scott. When he was just eighteen months old, doctors diagnosed him with lymphoblastic leukemia—cancer of the white blood cells. Untreated, lymphoblastic leukemia takes over the bone marrow before spreading to the rest of the body. It's a painful condition, especially for a kid.[11]

Miles is a fighter, though. It took three years of constant chemotherapy treatments, but eventually his cancer went into remission. During his treatment, the Make-A-Wish Foundation—a nonprofit that helps grant the wishes of children with life-threatening illnesses—offered to grant his wish. His reply:

"I wish to be Batkid."

Make-A-Wish's San Francisco chapter e-mailed its supporters, asking for volunteers. The request was simple—show up to cheer on the Batkid. The plan was to have a few hours when Miles would fight crime dressed as his favorite superhero. San Francisco was chosen as the location, since Miles and his family lived in Northern California. Make-A-Wish hoped a few hundred volunteers would show up for the closing ceremony.

They underestimated the power of social media and the empathy of thousands of people. Make-A-Wish's request spread like wildfire. Instead of three hundred volunteer pledges, Make-A-Wish got over twelve thousand. By the time Batkid made his debut in November 2013, all of San Francisco was talking about his epic fight against crime.

For their part, Make-A-Wish and San Francisco put on one hell of a show. In tandem with (an actor dressed as) Batman, the Batkid rode through the streets of San Francisco in the Batmobile (a donated Lamborghini). Batkid saved a damsel in distress, disabled a (fake) bomb, foiled a bank robbery by The Riddler, and rescued San Francisco Giants mascot Lou Seal from the clutches of The Penguin. San Francisco's chief of police gave Batkid instructions all along the way and, when it was all over, the mayor gave Batkid the key to the city. President Obama even sent a Vine video congratulating Miles on "saving Gotham."

By the time Batkid's adventures in San Francisco had concluded, more than twelve thousand people had shown up to cheer Miles Scott on. On Twitter, users generated more than four hundred thousand tweets in support of Batkid. Every major news outlet covered the story—even international papers as far away as India wrote about how an entire city transformed into Gotham.

Why did Batkid go viral but thousands of other causes can't even get in the news? Why does Make-A-Wish seem more worthy of our attention than starving children in Africa? The answer has to do with empathy, the final need that, when met, activates the Acknowledgment Trigger.

"The flip side of acknowledgment is understanding," Dr. Thomas de Zengotita said to Adrian Grenier and me as we were wrapping up our conversation at NASDAQ. "The deepest human need—not sex, not food, not sleep—is to be understood. [It's] the greatest feeling in the world. That's a deeper form of acknowledgment."

Empathy is our capability to understand the needs and concerns of others and demonstrate compassion for them. More than someone simply recognizing us or validating our identity, empathy creates the connection that leads us to listen more intently to the words of the people we love, whether it's our friends, our family, or a public figure. We can't help but feel for Miles Scott: What if it was our kid who had cancer? And so when Make-A-Wish asked people to turn out and show their support, they came out by the thousands (hundreds of thousands if you count social media).

"There's something to be said about feeling the sense of connectedness with the rest of humanity," Jeff Weiner, CEO of LinkedIn, told me when I interviewed him. "When people are able to touch on that, when people are able to connect with that feeling, I think those things go viral almost immediately."

Part of the reason why empathy is so powerful is our innate ability and need to understand and connect with others—even if we don't know them personally. Consider the following two appeals for charitable donations:

1. Food shortages in Malawi are affecting more than three million children. In Zambia, severe rainfall deficits have resulted in a 42% drop in maize production from 2000. As a result, an estimated three million Zambians face hunger. Four million Angolans—one-third of the population—have been forced to flee their homes. More than 11 million people in Ethiopia need immediate food assistance.

2. Any money that you donate will go to Rokia, a seven-year-old girl who lives in Mali in Africa. Rokia is desperately poor and faces a threat of severe hunger, even starvation. Her life will be changed for the better as a result of your financial gift. With your support, and the support of other caring sponsors, Save the Children will work with Rokia's family and other members of the community to help feed and educate her, and provide her with basic medical care.

Which pitch is more likely to get you to donate? Dr. Deborah Small of the University of Pennsylvania's Wharton School, an expert in human decision making, asked 121 students to fill out a short survey about their use of technology products in return for five dollars. The survey was a red herring, though. The real experiment was in the blank envelope that Small and her team gave to each participant. In it were a receipt, a charity request letter, and five one-dollar bills.[12]

The letter informed students about an opportunity to donate the money they had just earned to Save the Children. Half of the students received a letter with a "statistical victim" appeal. The letter featured factual information about the plight of children in Africa ("three million Zambians face hunger") to convince them to donate. The other students received a letter with an "identifiable victim" appeal, profiling a short story about Rokia, a little girl starving in Africa, and a picture of her to convince the students to donate.

The exact letters Small gave to her subjects are the ones you just considered above. The first letter, the statistical victim letter, solicited a measly median donation of $1.17. However, the letters that focused on Rokia—the identifiable victim—boosted donations to an astounding $2.83, a whopping 142 percent increase.

Small and her team call this the "identifiable victim effect." Personal identification intensifies emotional empathy, which in turn increases generosity and attention. We also believe that we can directly affect Rokia's situation. On the other hand, we can't empathize with a statistic, even if it is a horrendous statistic. Telling the story of a starving girl or a heroin addict who lost everything forces us to put ourselves in their shoes.

In the same study, Small gave students the same two charity request letters, but this time they were given a lesson on how "people typically react more strongly to specific people who have problems than to statistics about people with problems." Giving students this lesson actually increased donations in the statistics pitch from $1.17 to $1.26—a minor improvement. But it had a massively negative impact on donations for those who got the Rokia letter—the donations from these subjects dropped from $2.83 to a far less charitable $1.36.

Finally, giving somebody a story about a victim along with the statistics doesn't help. In fact, it hurts your cause. Small and her team found that hearing a story just about an identifiable victim led to a median donation of $2.38, but adding statistics to that same story dropped the median donation to $1.43.

The lesson here isn't that you should throw out statistics in your next pitch but that building a connection (and thus attention) requires that your audience have enough information to empathize with you or the story you're telling. This is most successful when the content or information is about a person and not a statistic. It's easy for your audience to root for the Batkid, but it's far more difficult for them to empathize for the thousands of faceless children suffering through cancer.

You have to make it easy for your audience to visualize themselves in the situation. The more you show, the more your audience will understand. The nonprofit charity: water, which builds wells for communities that don't have clean water in developing countries, makes a point of sending all the donors on a particular well the story of the people whose lives were transformed by the well that their money built. They do this through positive media—photos of the actual citizens drinking from the well, videos of the girls who can now go to school instead of fetching water, and GPS tracking so they know exactly where their well is if they ever want to visit it. "We're storytellers. We are always looking for positive, redemptive stories [potential donors] can engage in or participate in," explains Scott Harrison, founder of charity: water. "If you have an incredible story, you can command attention."[13]

We seek empathy from others, but we also seek people to empathize for. Like everything else in the Acknowledgment Trigger, empathy creates reciprocal attention. Meeting all three needs of awareness, validation, and empathy to harness the Acknowledgment Trigger is easier said than done—especially when you need to capture the attention of millions. But there are some, like the pop group AKB48, who have figured out how to scale acknowledgment.

The Secret Formula of the World's Most Popular Band

When the Japanese pop group AKB48 takes the stage, thousands of fans erupt in a roar of euphoria and joy. When they release a single, it flies to the top of the charts. In fact, the group has released over twenty consecutive number-one singles in Japan since 2009. To say AKB48 is popular would be a massive understatement. In just eight years, it has become one of the best-selling musical acts in the world, generating over $225 million in total sales revenue in 2012.

How has this J-pop group become one of the most popular groups in the world?

AKB48 isn't your typical musical act. The Japanese pop group doesn't have a lead singer—at least not one that stays with the group for very long. Members tend to graduate from the group in their early to mid-twenties. AKB48 also happens to have more members than the Eagles, U2, One Direction, the Black Eyed Peas, and Arcade Fire . . . combined. Its all-female membership fluctuates between eighty and ninety-five members and holds the Guinness World Record for the world's largest pop group. The members of AKB48 are known as "idols"—a term that refers to the young Japanese pop stars that are pushed into the public eye and expected to be *kawaii* (cute and adorable) and act as proper role models.

Because of its size, the group is actually divided into four main teams—Team A, Team K, Team B, and Team 4—along with satellite groups and a trainee group. The teams tour across Japan and the globe, although one team always performs daily at the AKB48 Theater in Tokyo's Akihabara district. It's part of the group's mission of having "idols you can meet everyday."

"I think the closest comparison is with die-hard baseball fans—they go to the key games no matter what it takes," Yasushi Akimoto, the fifty-six-year-old Japanese media mogul who created the group, told *The Wall Street Journal* in 2011. "It's the same kind of feeling with AKB48." Akimoto goes on to explain that fans of AKB48 don't just watch the shows, but they also care about whether their favorite singers have improved their skill or changed their hairstyles. Like baseball, fans of AKB48 root for their favorite "players" and feel a strong sense of loyalty and solidarity with the band.

AKB48's upbeat and catchy songs, adorable image, and cutesy costumes are certainly a major factor in their popularity. The sexualization of AKB48's performers is a factor as well, but sexualization is not unique to Japanese culture. The depths of AKB48's popularity can't be explained by just the women's looks or the group's songs. So what has made AKB48 the most popular music group in the world?

According to Grenier and de Zengotita, we idolize people who reflect our personalities or values in some way. We love—or hate—certain figures, especially celebrities, and use them as placeholders for who we are or who we want to be.

"In order to cut through all of the media that strives for our attention, we look for the [celebrities] that we like . . . the people that we say—'they reflect my values,'" Grenier explained to me during our interview.

"It's more and more about people expressing themselves through the choices they make, in terms of what they pay attention to," de Zengotita added. "They are finding themselves in various ways in celebrity culture. It's like a gigantic set of mirrors."

When people find celebrities who exemplify their values and validate them as human beings, they build a powerful connection with them. They aspire to be as successful or beautiful as these figures. And they do so despite the fact that the vast majority of people have never met a celebrity, much less become friends with one. For many people, these connections to celebrities feel real and genuine, even if they are one-sided. That connection is a big part of a celebrity's appeal, and it explains why AKB48 is so successful. There's a term for this unique interaction between public figures and the public: the *parasocial relationship*.

A parasocial relationship is a relationship in which one person knows a lot about another person, but the other doesn't know anything about the first person. The most common type of parasocial relationship (or interaction) is the one that celebrities and public figures have with their audience. Celebrities like Jennifer Lawrence and Kim Kardashian—or Batkid, Rokia, and corporations like Apple, for that matter—will probably never know who we are, but that doesn't stop us from tracking everything they do through blogs, television, and social media.

In the 1950s, Donald Horton and Richard Wohl—the researchers who coined the term *parasocial interaction*—observed that great actors have a knack for building an intimacy with their audience despite the fact it's "inevitably one-sided" and a relationship can't be directly reciprocated—only suggested.[14] This type of parasocial interaction is the thing that AKB48 excels at most. The Japanese pop sensation is cleverly designed to harness the power of parasocial relationships to build a deep connection between the singers and their fans at every turn.

"They go on a lot of variety shows that show their personality so people feel closer to them," my friend Mona Nomura, a Tokyo-based digital strategist, told me. "And the girls always make guys feel special—the way they look into the camera, it's like they are looking at them."[15]

The group regularly holds events called *akushu-kai*—literally "handshake meeting." Fans get the chance to meet their favorite performers in person and connect—it's reciprocal attention between the performers and their millions of fans. Fans don't even care that they only get a few seconds to shake their favorite idol's hand—getting any form of attention from someone they admire is more than enough.

The lyrics of AKB48's songs also play into this parasocial interaction. One of the group's most popular songs, "Heavy Rotation," is a tune about finding true love. Its lyrics are clearly and unabashedly directed at its audience. The chorus, "I want you! I need you! I love you!" is repeated in English over and over. These lyrics create a fantasy for the listener that they are somehow involved in an intimate relationship with AKB48's performers. Nearly everything AKB48's performers do is meant to propel this fantasy forward, which further develops the parasocial relationship between them and their fans. In fact, in AKB48's quest to further promote the idea that its performers are attainable, the performers aren't allowed to date anybody while they are members of the group.

The parasocial relationship even permeates AKB48's concerts. Japanese concerts are different than ones in the West, especially for groups like AKB48. The audience is far more involved. They are cheering, dancing, and performing in sync with AKB48's performers—it's known as the *wotagei*. The energy of the crowd's chants and cheers sweeps over you—the same feeling you get when you're cheering on your home basketball or football team with all the other fans in the stadium.

What makes AKB48 truly genius, though, is the *sousenkyo*—or "general election"—which gives its fans the power to support their favorite performers. Sometimes, when fans buy the group's newest single, they receive a ballot, which they then use to vote on which performers will participate in the next single. Twelve to twenty performers are chosen through this voting process. In 2013, 2.6 million people voted in the *sousenkyo*. That's more than 2 percent of the entire Japanese population.[15]

The secret formula of AKB48—and subsequently the Acknowledgment Trigger itself—is its ability to meet its fans' needs for awareness, validation, and empathy. AKB48 simply knows how to scale this parasocial yet personal connection with millions of people simultaneously. I call this phenomenon connection at scale, and no one is better at it than my friend Gary Vaynerchuk.

Scaling the Unscalable

On a crisp April evening in New York City, I received a piece of advice I will never forget. It came from Gary Vaynerchuk, three-time best-selling author and founder of Vaynermedia and Wine Library TV, as we shared a bottle of chilled white wine and chatted about the ingredients for a best-selling book.

After creating a successful business and web series around wine, Vaynerchuk launched a multimillion-dollar creative agency and hit the best-seller list with *Crush It!* Not only that, but his business acumen also helped him become an investor in everything from Tumblr (acquired by Yahoo) to Twitter.

His advice to me, as we chatted on the corner of 75th and Lexington, was simple. "Scale the unscalable," Vaynerchuk said succinctly.

In the tech industry, we talk constantly about scaling. The reason many investors put their money into a digital startup like Instagram and not into a brick-and-mortar business is because a digital startup can grow bigger and faster with fewer employees than a brick-and-mortar can. Starbucks employs over a hundred thousand people in its many locations—this requires tremendous amounts of capital, management, and time to scale into a global business. Facebook, on the other hand, has a significantly higher valuation on the public market with fewer than ten thousand employees because it requires far less manpower and fewer resources to generate more profit. Heck, Instagram had fewer than fifteen employees when it was acquired for nearly $1 billion by Facebook.

Part of the reason why Facebook is worth significantly more than Starbucks on the stock market is because it's easy to scale technology and it's difficult to scale people. A thousand people can use the same product, but a thousand people can't talk to the same person. Perhaps that's why so many people believe that personal relationships aren't scalable. But AKB48 and Vaynerchuk prove this logic shortsighted.

Vaynerchuk is a master at scaling relationships with his fans. He has over a million followers on Twitter because he finds ways to interact and even help his followers. In one viral interaction, Vaynerchuk posted a simple tweet: "Good morning everyone—need anything?" One of his followers, Daniel Bentley of mobile news startup Circa, quickly responded: "Eggs, I'm out of eggs." While most celebrities would ignore a tweet like this, Vaynerchuk asked Daniel for his address and, less than an hour later, Daniel got eggs. Two hundred forty eggs. Daniel blogged about his experience with Vaynerchuk, and the story spread like wildfire.[17]

Vaynerchuk acknowledges the importance of every person who follows him by offering to help them out whenever possible. Using social media, he has found a way to build a rapport with his audience at scale. Even if you don't ask Vaynerchuk for help, you know that he's willing to hustle if you actually do need help one day. Media—whether it's social media, television, or news—has the power to help you quickly build parasocial relationships with your audience and amplify your positive (and—beware!—negative) actions.

So one of the ways in which we can scale relationships and reciprocal attention is to give acknowledgment and attention to just a few fans. As other fans recognize that you are the kind of person who will acknowledge them directly should the occasion arise, they will start tuning in to you and reciprocating attention, even if they weren't the direct recipients of your attention.

Another way you can scale relationships and reciprocal attention is by giving your audience the power of participation. During the 1940s and '50s, three of the largest brands in baking and home cooking battled viciously to become the king of the cake mix market. Pillsbury started the war in 1948 when it released its first chocolate cake mix. Three years later, Duncan Hines unleashed a triple flavor mix that captured half of the cake mix market in less than a month. Betty Crocker opted to roll out five flavors from 1952 to 1955.[18]

None of these products turned cake mix into a household necessity, though. Women weren't lining up to buy the cake mixes. The big three couldn't figure out why—after all, Betty Crocker's Bisquick was huge. So General Mills, the owner of Betty Crocker, turned to Dr. Burleigh Gardner and Dr. Ernest Dichter to figure out the problem and a potential solution.

The answer, it turns out, was eggs. Most cake mixes in the forties and fifties contained powdered eggs—just add water and poof!—you have a cake. This didn't appeal to the market, though. It was almost . . . too easy. There was nothing special that home chefs could add. There was no creative contribution. There was no participation.

Gardner, Dichter, and General Mills thought about this problem for a while and decided to try something: Why not let customers add the eggs themselves? General Mills removed the dried eggs and used this in its marketing: "Betty Crocker Cake Mixes bring you that Special Homemade Goodness," one ad read, " . . . Because You Add The Eggs Yourself."

The campaign worked beyond their wildest expectations. Betty Crocker quickly dominated Duncan Hines and Pillsbury, even winning over First Lady Mamie Eisenhower. Consumers purchased nearly a billion pounds of cake mix by 1951, most of it from Betty Crocker. And ever since, we've been adding eggs to our cake mixes and every other type of popular mix on the market.

This classic story is popular among marketers because it demonstrates the impact that participation and contribution can have on attention and sales. Products like Kickstarter and Medium give consumers buy-in and a sense of acknowledgment because they invite consumers to participate. It's true of advertising campaigns as well—you may remember from the chapter on the Reputation Trigger how Vitaminwater gave consumers a chance to create their own

Vitaminwater flavor through the Flavor Creator Facebook app. By giving consumers the power to shape their products, Vitaminwater acknowledged the trustworthiness and wisdom of its audience. Even the simple act of acknowledging somebody's comment or feedback creates a stronger connection between a brand and a consumer— something Vaynerchuk harnesses daily.

If you want to build attention through acknowledgment, you have to give your audience a way to contribute. You have to acknowledge that they matter to you through awareness, validation, and empathy.

If You Care About Us, We Will Care About You

My friend Kina Grannis is an extraordinary musician. After Grannis won the Doritos Super Bowl contest, she charted on the Billboard Hot 100 (despite a not-so-amicable breakup with Interscope Records) and has since amassed over a million subscribers to her growing YouTube channel. One of her most popular music videos, "In Your Arms," surged past 10 million views in a few days because of its pure novelty. The entire music video used 288 thousand jelly beans animated into stop-motion blustering snowflakes, arching rainbows, flying birds, and Grannis floating in a jelly bean spacesuit. She's also performed on the stages of *The Ellen DeGeneres Show* and *Jimmy Kimmel Live!*

The reason why she's received these opportunities is because she has built a loyal audience by harnessing the Acknowledgment Trigger. Her fans promote her music, share her videos, and create fan sites dedicated to her—they're loyal. You see this type of loyalty among the fan bases of all the major superstars. Justin Bieber's fans are Beliebers. Lady Gaga's fans are Little Monsters. Beyoncé's fans are the BeyHive. These superstars all know how to go one step beyond capturing attention—they know how to build lasting fan bases that feel acknowledged and turn into loyal fans.

You may be wondering, *How did Grannis build her fan base?* The answer lies in her ability to scale relationships with her audience. Grannis not only made countless video replies and posted shout-outs to all of the fans supporting her during her Doritos campaign, but she also gave her fans the ability to contribute. During the promotion of her first album, Grannis created the Street Team. She would send her biggest fans a Street Team packet with an ID card, a T-shirt with their ID number, swag, and promotional material to post and share. Her fans all across the world would post flyers about her album on bulletin boards and libraries and put the swag on their websites, amplifying the noise around her album. She gave extra attention to her Street Team and provided them the tools they needed, and they returned the favor by showering her with attention and recruiting new people to become fans.

More than anything, Grannis attributes her success to the connection she has with her fans. "I hate being in front of a camera," Grannis explained to me as we finished our drinks. "People saw it: 'She's a normal person.' 'She's not a superstar.' 'She's awkward, and I can relate to that.'" She acknowledges her fans and her admiration for them, and her fans return the favor.

We all want to be acknowledged. Our long attention is at its peak when we feel like we've found somebody or something that recognizes, validates, or understands us. This is true of our closest friends, our favorite products, and even our most popular celebrities.

Or, as *TechCrunch* editor Alexia Tsotsis once told me, "The world cares about the people who care about it."[19]

Conclusion
The Influence of Attention

In 1993, my entrepreneurial mentor Mark Achler became president of a small game software company called Kinesoft. The company had created a technology called Exodus, a video game development environment that allowed developers to port Sega and Nintendo scrolling action arcade games to the upcoming Microsoft Windows 95 platform.

Two years later, Kinesoft made the journey to the first E3—to get game publishers to use Exodus to port their games to Windows PCs. There was plenty of competition for attention at E3, though, and Kinesoft was just a small startup. Achler and his team wondered: How are we going to get publishers to buy into a technology they didn't think was possible from a company they had never heard of?

The solution they came up with was unique: invite the publishers to a wedding. Before the show, Kinesoft sent a series of beautifully crafted wedding invitations to the CEOs of all the major game publishers. These wedding invitations, handwritten by a calligrapher, invited the CEOs to the "marriage" of Sega and Nintendo games with Windows 95 and requested a meeting at E3.

"We sent out 81 wedding invitations," Achler told me. "We ended up booking 71 meetings. It was an incredible show and a truly inspired way to break through the clutter and noise and accomplish our very specific goal—which was to set up meetings with the CEOs at the trade show."[1]

The invitations certainly captured attention, and we know why, thanks to the captivation triggers. The wedding invitations acted as powerful and distinctive visual cues—the Automaticity Trigger. They stood out like a sore thumb among the mail these CEOs received. In addition, we as a society are trained to pay attention to wedding invitations because they represent something important and worth our attention—the Framing Trigger. This was how Kinesoft sparked the attention of the game publishers. The bonfire of attention was ignited.

The invitation itself, with its handwritten calligraphy and unique marriage announcement, also violated the expectations of what a meeting request should look like—the Disruption Trigger. The result was that over 87 percent of the CEOs who received the wedding invitation read the invitation, responded, and set up meetings with Kinesoft. My mentor and his team used enough kindling to capture the attention of these CEOs and secure meetings.

When the game publishers finally sat down for their meetings with Kinesoft, Exodus blew them away. Seeing the actual product in action demonstrated clearly the upside and potential rewards if the publishers partnered with Kinesoft (the Reward Trigger), and many publishers quickly agreed to use Exodus to run their games on Windows 95. Top-selling games such as *Pitfall: The Mayan Adventure, Earthworm Jim,* and *Gex* all used Exodus to bring their games to the PC. Eventually, it caught the attention of Microsoft and, together, the two companies created DirectX, the underlying platform Microsoft has now been using for Windows games for over a decade. The bonfire of attention.

Kinesoft's success is a powerful example of how the captivation triggers—in isolation or in combination—can take a product or idea from zero awareness to being used by millions. Had my mentor and his company taken a more conventional route, DirectX probably wouldn't even exist. Attention is the conduit through which we experience our world. If you don't have somebody's attention, no amount of effort you put into your product, music, art, lesson plan, or project will matter.

Throughout *Captivology*, I have used scientific research and the stories of masters of attention, like Mark Achler, to illuminate how the captivation triggers affect our attention everywhere, every day. My goal in writing this book has been to show you how to harness those triggers to get your ideas noticed. With this knowledge, your ideas will have a better chance of rising above the noise that dominates our media-rich world.

But I've also had another goal with this book: I wanted to help you become more aware of your own attention and the subtle biases that guide it. Hopefully you have a better understanding now why some ideas and ideologies are so compelling and why other ideas simply don't capture your attention, even if you know they should.

The lessons of this book apply everywhere, from teaching to entrepreneurship to your personal relationships. Use *Captivology* to not only capture the attention of others but to improve the quality of your own life as well. You have the tools and the knowledge to build long-lasting attention. Now go and use them.

Acknowledgments

●

C aptivology is the culmination of the knowledge and friendship of hundreds of people. The support I've received throughout this project has been overwhelming.

I'd like to first thank David Vigliano, the best literary agent in the business. His wisdom, insight, and friendship have been invaluable throughout this process, and I couldn't have been luckier to end up with The Vig as my agent. A special thank you to Philip Kaplan for the introduction.

I had a lot of offers for this book, but the HarperOne team stood out as the people who truly understood the kind of book I wanted to write and provided the support and guidance that turned this thing into a reality. A special thanks goes out to my editor, Genoveva Llosa, whose straight-shooting and no-nonsense approach transformed *Captivology* from a good book into a *great* one.

Another special thank-you to the people who helped in the promotion and strategy around this book. Melinda Mullin of HarperOne is a total badass, and the same is true of Claudia Boutote, Carol Kleinhubert, Terri Leonard, Kim Dayman, and Hannah Rivera of the HarperOne team. Marcy Simon, who helped me with so much in the beginning, is a true hero. Ryan Holiday is a marketing mastermind, and his innovative ideas made promoting this book an absolute blast. Sara Walker-Santana and Laura Mignott of DigitalFlash transform every event they touch—including my book tour—into incredible, mind-blowing experiences. There are others who helped with the book's launch I will have to add in the next edition of the book, I am sure. I was lucky enough to write this book in some amazing places. A special thanks to Russ and Debbie Reiner for allowing me to use their beautiful lakeside home in seclusion to write the first part of this book, and thank you to Rocky Slaughter for setting it up.

I couldn't have done this without the friends who read my work and sent me unvarnished feedback. They helped me craft the best story possible. Thank you, Hilary Karls, Matt Schlicht, Alex Wilhelm, Nathalie Nuta, Luke Ryan, Julie Pearne, Ryan Holiday, Chloe Condon, Megan Berry, Tina Hui, Phil Libin, Amanda Stiles, Milana Rabkin, Kristina Matthews, Mark Witte, and my favorite teacher from my childhood, Elaine McVety.

I'm grateful for the people who agreed to the interviews that make this book so extraordinary. Jon Armstrong, Alan Baddeley, Robin Bechtel, Kent Berridge, Mike Bush, Susan Cain, Seija Carpenter, David Copperfield, Mike Dubin, Josh Elman, Nir Eyal, Joe Fernandez, Eli Finkel, Mark Fitzloff, Adam Gazzaley, Kina Grannis, Adrian Grenier, Dick Guttman, Scott Harrison, Grant Imahara, Susan Keser, Franklin Leonard, Rachel Lightfoot Melby, Shigeru Miyamoto, Mona Nomura, Don Norman, Alexis Ohanian, Jeremiah Owyang, Jonah Peretti, Daniel Pink, Michael Posner, Steve Rubel, Sheryl Sandberg, Dietram Scheufele, Tariq Shaukat, Mark Shillum, Carmen Simon, Steven Soderbergh, Brian Stelter, Michael Stevens, John Sweller, Garry Tan, Jeanne Theokaris, Jorge Titinger, Anne Treisman, Alexia Tsotsis, Jeff Weiner, Brian Wong, and Thomas de Zengotita. You didn't have to take time out of your busy lives, but you did anyway.

To Sheryl Sandberg, I want to give an extra shout-out. Despite her incredibly busy schedule in changing the world, she has always made time for me and granted me her insight whenever I have asked for it. She's one of my favorite people on the planet, and I feel humbled to be able to call her my friend.

I owe an immeasurable debt of gratitude to Mark Achler and Troy Henikoff, my entrepreneurial mentors, for the success I've achieved in my life. Troy was the first person to teach me the hard lessons of entrepreneurship, and he continues to do so today. Mark not only gave me my first job, but he also gave me confidence, compassion, and a healthy dose of skepticism. Thank you, both of you.

Thank you to my "Badass Executive Ninja Assistant" Hallie Cooper, who made sure my life was kept in order and that I stayed on task.

Finally, I want to thank the people closest to me. To my business partners and pals, Matt Schlicht and Mazy Kazerooni—you are my brothers for life. The same is true for Hilary Karls, Nathaniel Mc-Namara, Brandon Nyman, Jennifer Van Grove, Jason Baptiste, Aza Raskin, and Elizabeth Young. Julie, you were my rock. To my sister, Teera, and my parents, Ernie and Nid—thank you for loving me and believing in me.

Notes

●

INTRODUCTION: A BONFIRE OF ATTENTION

1. *Up*, directed by Pete Docter (Burbank, CA: Walt Disney Studios Home Entertainment, 2009), DVD.
2. Richard Alleyne, "Welcome to the Information Age—174 Newspapers a Day," *Telegraph* (London), February 11, 2011, http://www.telegraph.co.uk/science /science-news/8316534/Welcome-to-the-information-age-174-newspapers-a -day.html.
3. Adam Gazzaley, interview by author, phone interview, July 23, 2013.
4. Rachel Emma Silverman, "Workplace Distractions: Here's Why You Won't Finish This Article," *The Wall Street Journal*, December 11, 2012.
5. Larry D. Rosen et al., "An Empirical Examination of the Educational Impact of Text Message–Induced Task Switching in the Classroom: Educational Implications and Strategies to Enhance Learning," *Psicología Educativa* 17, no. 2 (2011): 163–77.
6. Eyal Ophir, Clifford Nass, and Anthony D. Wagner, "Cognitive Control in Media Multitaskers," *Proceedings of the National Academy of Sciences* 106, no. 37 (2009): 15583–87.
7. Sanbonmatsu, David M., David L. Strayer, Nathan Medeiros-Ward, and Jason M. Watson, "Who Multi-Tasks and Why? Multi-Tasking Ability, Perceived Multi-Tasking Ability, Impulsivity, and Sensation Seeking," *PloS One* 8, no. 1 (2013): e54402.
8. Adrian Grenier and Thomas de Zengotita, interview by author, personal interview, New York City, July 16, 2013.

CHAPTER 1: THE THREE STAGES OF ATTENTION

1. Joshua New, Leda Cosmides, and John Tooby, "Category-Specific Attention for Animals Reflects Ancestral Priorities, Not Expertise," *Proceedings of the National Academy of Sciences* 104, no. 42 (2007): 16598–603.
2. Addie Johnson and Robert W. Proctor, "Memory and Attention," in *Attention: Theory and Practice* (Thousand Oaks, CA: Sage Publications, 2004), 191–225.

3. Stefanie J. Krauth, et al., "An In-Depth Analysis of a Piece of Shit: Distribution of *Schistosoma mansoni* and Hookworm Eggs in Human Stool," *PLoS Neglected Tropical Diseases* 6, no. 12 (2012): e1969; Ross Pomeroy, "An In-Depth Analysis of a Piece of $%&@," *RealClearScience*, December 27, 2012, http://www.realclearscience.com/journal_club/2012/12/27/an_in-depth_analysis_of_a_piece_of__106431.html.
4. Luis Carretié, et al., "Automatic Attention to Emotional Stimuli: Neural Correlates," *Human Brain Mapping* 22, no. 4 (2004): 290–99.
5. Deborah Wearing, *Forever Today* (Tyne and Wear, UK: Soundings, 2006); *The Mind*, directed by George Page (Alexandria, VA: PBS Video, 1988).
6. Kent C. Berridge and Terry E. Robinson, "What Is the Role of Dopamine in Reward: Hedonic Impact, Reward Learning, or Incentive Salience?" *Brain Research Reviews* 28, no. 3 (1998): 309–69.
7. Adam Gazzaley, interview by author, phone interview, July 23, 2013.
8. John Sweller, interview by author, Skype interview, May 29, 2013.
9. Ronald Gallimore et al., "The Effects of Elaboration and Rehearsal on Long-Term Retention of Shape Names by Kindergarteners," *American Educational Research Journal* 14, no. 4 (1977): 471–83.
10. Alan Baddeley, interview by author, phone interview, May 21, 2013.
11. William James, "Attention," in *The Principles of Psychology* (New York: Dover Publications, 1950).
12. Stephen Silverman, "Beyoncé Releases Surprise Self-Titled Album," *People*, December 13, 2013, http://www.people.com/people/article/0,,20765913,00.html.
13. Andrew Hampp and Jason Lipshutz, "Beyonce Unexpectedly Releases New Self-Titled 'Visual Album' on iTunes," *Billboard*, December 13, 2013, http://www.billboard.com/articles/columns/the-juice/5827398/beyonce-unexpectedly-releases-new-self-titled-visual-album-on.
14. Bob Lefsetz, "Beyonce's Album," *Lefsetz Letter* blog, December 16, 2013, http://lefsetz.com/wordpress/index.php/archives/2013/12/16/beyonces-album/.
15. Nicholas Carlson, "Inside Pinterest: An Overnight Success Four Years in the Making," *Business Insider*, May 1, 2012, http://www.businessinsider.com/inside-pinterest-an-overnight-success-four-years-in-the-making-2012-4.
16. Tom Cheshire, "In Depth: How Rovio Made Angry Birds a Winner (And What's Next)," *Wired*, March 7, 2011, http://www.wired.co.uk/magazine/archive/2011/04/features/how-rovio-made-angry-birds-a-winner.
17. Sweller, interview by author.
18. Jeff Ryan, *Super Mario: How Nintendo Conquered America* (New York: Penguin, 2011).

CHAPTER 2: AUTOMATICITY TRIGGER

1. Julia Gögler et al., "Ménage À Trois—Two Endemic Species of Deceptive Orchids and One Pollinator Species," *Evolution* 63, no. 9 (2009): 2222–34.
2. Daniela Niesta Kayser, Andrew J. Elliot, and Roger Feltman, "Red and Romantic Behavior in Men Viewing Women," *European Journal of Social Psychology* 40, no. 6 (2010): 901–8.

3. J. A. Maga, "Influence of Color on Taste Thresholds," *Chemical Senses* 1, no. 1 (1974): 115–19.

4. Yorzinski, Jessica L., Michael J. Penkunas, Michael L. Platt, and Richard G. Coss, "Dangerous Animals Capture and Maintain Attention in Humans," *Evolutionary Psychology* 12, no. 3 (2014): 534–48.

5. R. Reed Hunt, "The Subtlety of Distinctiveness: What von Restorff Really Did," *Psychonomic Bulletin & Review* 2, no. 1 (1995): 105–12.

6. Nicolas Guéguen, "Color and Women Hitchhikers' Attractiveness: Gentlemen Drivers Prefer Red," *Color Research & Application* 37, no. 1 (2012): 76–78.

7. Andrew J. Elliot and Daniela Niesta, "Romantic Red: Red Enhances Men's Attraction to Women," *Journal of Personality and Social Psychology* 95, no. 5 (2008): 1150–64.

8. Dan McGrady, "How We Improved Our Conversion Rate by 72%," *Dmix* blog, 2011, http://web.archive.org/web/20140413033138/http://dmix .ca/2010/05/how-we-increased-our-conversion-rate-by-72/.

9. "B2B Landing Page Optimization Lifts Lead Generation by 32.5%—Within Strict Branding Guidelines," WiderFunnel Marketing Conversion Optimization, http://www.widerfunnel.com/proof/case-studies/sap-landing-page -optimization (accessed September 12, 2014).

10. Hans-Peter Frey et al., "Beyond Correlation: Do Color Features Influence Attention in Rainforest?" *Frontiers in Human Neuroscience* 5 (2011): 36.

11. Roger T. Hanlon and John B. Messenger, "Adaptive Coloration in Young Cuttlefish (*Sepia officinalis* L.): The Morphology and Development of Body Patterns and Their Relation to Behaviour," *Philosophical Transactions of the Royal Society of London, Series B, Biological Sciences* 320, no. 1200 (1988): 437–87.

12. Mel White, "Why Birds Attacked the Peace Doves in Rome," *National Geographic*, January 27, 2014, http://news.nationalgeographic.com /news/2014/01/140127-white-peace-doves-attacked-birds-rome-vatican-pope/.

13. Michael Aagaard, "How to Design Call to Action Buttons that Convert," *The Landing Page & Conversion Rate Optimization Blog*, Unbounce, May 22, 2013, http://unbounce.com/conversion-rate-optimization /design-call-to-action-buttons/.

14. Adam L. Alter, "Colors," in *Drunk Tank Pink: And Other Unexpected Forces that Shape How We Think, Feel, and Behave* (New York: Penguin, 2013).

15. N. Yoshioka, "[Epidemiological Study of Suicide in Japan—Is It Possible to Reduce Committing Suicide?]" *Nihon Hoigaku Zasshi* 52, no. 5 (1998): 286–93; Keith W. Jacobs and James F. Suess, "Effects of Four Psychological Primary Colors on Anxiety State," *Perceptual and Motor Skills* 41, no. 1 (1975): 207–10; Robert E. Strong et al., "Narrow-Band Blue-Light Treatment of Seasonal Affective Disorder in Adults and the Influence of Additional Nonseasonal Symptoms," *Depression and Anxiety* 26, no. 3 (2009): 273–78.

16. Cliff Kuang, "Infographic of the Day: What Colors Mean Across 10 Cultures," *Fast Company*, April 26, 2010, http://www.fastcompany.com/1627581 /infographic-day-what-colors-mean-across-10-cultures.

17. Patricia Valdez and Albert Mehrabian, "Effects of Color on Emotions," *Journal of Experimental Psychology: General* 123, no. 4 (1994): 394–409.
18. Anton J. M. de Craen et al., "Effect of Colour of Drugs: Systematic Review of Perceived Effect of Drugs and of Their Effectiveness," *British Medical Journal* 313, no. 7072 (1996): 1624–26.
19. Lauren I. Labrecque and George R. Milne, "Exciting Red and Competent Blue: The Importance of Color in Marketing," *Journal of the Academy of Marketing Science* 40, no. 5 (2011): 711–27.
20. Mark Wilson, "Why the Security Bug Heartbleed Has a Catchy Logo," *Fast Company*, April 11, 2014, http://www.fastcodesign.com/3028982/why-the-security-bug-heartbleed-has-a-catchy-logo.
21. Gráinne M. Fitzsimons, Tanya L. Chartrand, and Gavan J. Fitzsimons, "Automatic Effects of Brand Exposure on Motivated Behavior: How Apple Makes You 'Think Different,'" *Journal of Consumer Research* 35, no. 1 (2008): 21–35.
22. Daniel Kahneman, "The Associative Machine," in *Thinking, Fast and Slow* (New York: Farrar, Straus and Giroux, 2011), 50–58.
23. Bill Prady, Steven Molaro, and Jim Reynolds, "The Cohabitation Formulation," *The Big Bang Theory*, season 4, episode 16, directed by Mark Cendrowski, aired February 17, 2011 (New York: CBS).
24. Lawrence E. Williams and John A. Bargh, "Experiencing Physical Warmth Promotes Interpersonal Warmth," *Science* 322, no. 5901 (2008): 606–7.
25. Simon Storey and Lance Workman, "The Effects of Temperature Priming on Cooperation in the Iterated Prisoner's Dilemma," *Evolutionary Psychology* 11, no. 1 (2013): 52–67.
26. Chris Eccleston and Geert Crombez, "Pain Demands Attention: A Cognitive-Affective Model of the Interruptive Function of Pain," *Psychological Bulletin* 125, no. 3 (1999): 356–66.
27. Judee K. Burgoon, "Relational Message Interpretations of Touch, Conversational Distance, and Posture," *Journal of Nonverbal Behavior* 15, no. 4 (1991): 233–59; Glen P. Williams and Chris L. Kleinke, "Effects of Mutual Gaze and Touch on Attraction, Mood, and Cardiovascular Reactivity," *Journal of Research in Personality* 27, no. 2 (1993): 170–83.
28. Kate McCulley, "How I Survived a Mugging," *Adventurous Kate's Solo Female Travel Blog*, October 12, 2010, http://www.adventurouskate.com/how-i-survived-a-mugging/.
29. Carles Escera et al., "Neural Mechanisms of Involuntary Attention to Acoustic Novelty and Change," *Journal of Cognitive Neuroscience* 10, no. 5 (1998): 590–604; Fabrice B. R. Parmentier, "Towards a Cognitive Model of Distraction by Auditory Novelty: The Role of Involuntary Attention Capture and Semantic Processing," *Cognition* 109, no. 3 (2008): 345–62; Dennis P. Carmody and Michael Lewis, "Brain Activation when Hearing One's Own and Others' Names," *Brain Research* 1116, no. 1 (2006): 153–58.
30. Michael Posner, interview by author, phone interview, July 3, 2013.

31. E. Colin Cherry, "Some Experiments on the Recognition of Speech, with One and with Two Ears," *Journal of the Acoustical Society of America* 25, no. 5 (1953): 975–79.
32. Anne M. Treisman, "The Effect of Irrelevant Material on the Efficiency of Selective Listening," *American Journal of Psychology* 77, no. 4 (1964): 533–46.
33. Noelle Wood and Nelson Cowan, "The Cocktail Party Phenomenon Revisited: How Frequent Are Attention Shifts to One's Name in an Irrelevant Auditory Channel?" *Journal of Experimental Psychology: Learning, Memory, and Cognition* 21, no. 1 (1995): 255–60.
34. Megan Garber, "Ghost Army: The Inflatable Tanks that Fooled Hitler," *The Atlantic*, May 22, 2013, http://www.theatlantic.com/technology/archive/2013/05/ghost-army-the-inflatable-tanks-that-fooled-hitler/276137/; *The Ghost Army*, directed by Peter Coyote (Arlington, VA: PBS Distribution, 2013), DVD.

CHAPTER 3: FRAMING TRIGGER

1. Sarah Everts, "How Advertisers Convinced Americans They Smelled Bad," *Smithsonian.com*, August 2, 2012, http://www.smithsonianmag.com/history-archaeology/How-Advertisers-Convinced-Americans-They-Smelled-Bad-164779646.html.
2. Dietram Scheufele, interview by author, phone interview, February 5, 2014.
3. Elizabeth F. Loftus and John C. Palmer, "Reconstruction of Automobile Destruction: An Example of the Interaction Between Language and Memory," *Journal of Verbal Learning and Verbal Behavior* 13, no. 5 (1974): 585–89.
4. Marianne Bertrand and Sendhil Mullainathan, "Are Emily and Brendan More Employable than Lakisha and Jamal? A Field Experiment on Labor Market Discrimination" (working paper, Univ. of Chicago, Graduate School of Business, 2002).
5. Will Wei, "How Pandora Survived More than 300 VC Rejections," *Business Insider*, July 14, 2010, http://www.businessinsider.com/pandora-vc-2010-7.
6. Robert Strohmeyer, "The 7 Worst Tech Predictions of All Time," *TechHive*, December 31, 2008, http://www.techhive.com/article/155984/worst_tech_predictions.html.
7. Gene Weingarten, "Pearls Before Breakfast," *The Washington Post*, April 8, 2007.
8. Nina Verdelli, "The Violin and the Street," *Citizen Brooklyn*, n.d., http://www.citizenbrooklyn.com/topics/fashion/the-violin-and-the-street/.
9. Susan Keser, interview by author, phone interview, July 26, 2013.
10. Alhan Keser, "Why Joshua Bell Failed in the Subway," *Alhan Keser* blog, November 22, 2012, http://web.archive.org/web/20130806230315/http://alhan.co/why-joshua-bell-failed-in-subway/.
11. Press Association, "Rush Hour Traffic Tops Poll of Everyday Stresses," *The Guardian*, October 31, 2000, http://www.theguardian.com/uk/2000/nov/01/transport.world.
12. Keser, interview by author.

13. Adam Wooten, "International Business: Wrong Flowers Can Mean Death for Global Business," *Deseret News*, February 4, 2011, http://www.deseretnews.com/article/705365824/Wrong-flowers-can-mean-death-for-global-business.html.

14. Frank Luntz, *Words that Work: It's Not What You Say, It's What People Hear* (New York: Hyperion, 2007).

15. Tommy Christopher, "How Fox News, CNN, and MSNBC Covered Chris Christie 'Bridgegate' on Wednesday," *Mediaite*, January 9, 2014, http://www.mediaite.com/tv/how-fox-news-cnn-and-msnbc-covered-chris-christie-bridgegate-on-wednesday/.

16. Lynn Hasher, David Goldstein, and Thomas Toppino, "Frequency and the Conference of Referential Validity," *Journal of Verbal Learning and Verbal Behavior* 16, no. 1 (1977): 107–12.

17. Nos. 1 and 4 are incorrect: Tulane defeated Temple in the first Sugar Bowl (20-14). The tallest building outside of New York and Chicago is the Bank of America Plaza in Atlanta.

18. Wesley G. Moons, Diane M. Mackie, and Teresa Garcia-Marques, "The Impact of Repetition-Induced Familiarity on Agreement with Weak and Strong Arguments," *Journal of Personality and Social Psychology* 96, no. 1 (2009): 32–44.

19. Rachel Feintzeig, Mike Spector, and Julie Jargon, "Twinkie Maker Hostess to Close," *The Wall Street Journal*, November 16, 2012, http://online.wsj.com/news/articles/SB10001424127887324556304578122632560842670.

20. Michael Lynn, "Scarcity Effects on Value: A Quantitative Review of the Commodity Theory Literature," *Psychology & Marketing* 8, no. 1 (1991): 43–57.

21. Theo M. M. Verhallen and Henry S. J. Robben, "Scarcity and Preference: An Experiment on Unavailability and Product Evaluation," *Journal of Economic Psychology* 15, no. 2 (1994): 315–31.

22. Associated Press, "Hostess: Twinkies Demand at Record High," *The Huffington Post*, July 18, 2013, http://www.huffingtonpost.com/2013/07/18/hostess-twinkies-demand_n_3615900.html.

23. Stephen Worchel, Jerry Lee, and Akanbi Adewole, "Effects of Supply and Demand on Ratings of Object Value," *Journal of Personality and Social Psychology* 32, no. 5 (1975): 906–14.

24. Josh Elman, interview by author, personal interview, Half Moon Bay, CA, June 17, 2013.

CHAPTER 4: DISRUPTION TRIGGER

1. Nicholas Carlson, "This Post Has All the Black Friday Stats You Need to Sound Smart in Meetings," *Business Insider*, December 13, 2013, http://www.businessinsider.com/2013-black-friday-stats-2013-12.

2. Jeff Rosenblum, "How Patagonia Makes More Money by Trying to Make Less," *Fast Company*, December 6, 2012, http://www.fastcoexist.com/1681023/how-patagonia-makes-more-money-by-trying-to-make-less; Kyle Stock, "Patagonia's Confusing and Effective Campaign to Grudgingly Sell Stuff,"

Bloomberg Business Week, November 25, 2013, http://www.businessweek
.com/articles/2013-11-25/patagonias-confusing-and-effective-campaign-to
-grudgingly-sell-stuff; Kyle Stock, "Patagonia's 'Buy Less' Plea Spurs More
Buying," *Bloomberg Business Week*, August 28, 2013, http://www.business
week.com/articles/2013-08-28/patagonias-buy-less-plea-spurs-more-buying.

3. Marilyn Boltz, Matthew Schulkind, and Suzanne Kantra, "Effects of Background Music on the Remembering of Filmed Events," *Memory & Cognition* 19, no. 6 (1991): 593–606.

4. Judee K. Burgoon and Jerold L. Hale, "Nonverbal Expectancy Violations: Model Elaboration and Application to Immediacy Behaviors," *Communications Monographs* 55, no. 1 (1988): 58–79.

5. Scott Goldthorp, "The 2012 Rosenthal Prize for Innovation in Math Teaching: Hands-On Data Analysis," *MoMath*, 2012, http://momath.org /wp-content/uploads/RosenthalPrize2012_Winning_Lesson_Plan.pdf; Evelyn Lamb, "Award-Winning Teachers Put Math on Hands and Heads," *Roots of Unity* blog, *Scientific American*, May 3, 2013, http://blogs.scientific american.com/roots-of-unity/2013/05/03/math-on-hands-and-heads -rosenthal-prize/.

6. Mark A. McDaniel et al., "The Bizarreness Effect: It's Not Surprising, It's Complex," *Journal of Experimental Psychology: Learning, Memory, and Cognition* 21, no. 2 (1995): 422–35.

7. Igor Bobic, "Todd Akin Just Can't Stop Talking About Rape," *The Huffington Post*, July 17, 2014, http://www.huffingtonpost.com/2014/07/17/todd-akin-rape _n_5595270.html.

8. Tony Thwaites, Lloyd Davis, and Warwick Mules, "Advertisement," in *Introducing Cultural and Media Studies: A Semiotic Approach* (Houndmills, Basingstoke, Hampshire: Palgrave, 2002), 50–52.

9. Farhad Manjoo, "Invincible Apple: 10 Lessons from the Coolest Company Anywhere," *Fast Company*, July 1, 2010, http://www.fastcompany. com/1659056/invincible-apple-10-lessons-coolest-company-anywhere.

10. Jürgen Huber, Michael Kirchler, and Matthias Sutter, "Is More Information Always Better?: Experimental Financial Markets with Cumulative Information," *Journal of Economic Behavior & Organization* 65, no. 1 (2008): 86–104.

11. John Sweller, interview by author, Skype interview, May 29, 2013.

12. Sweller, interview by author.

13. Jeremiah Owyang, interview by author, phone interview, May 14, 2013.

14. Rachel Lightfoot Melby, interview by author, personal interview, San Bruno, CA, April 12, 2013

15. Barb Dybwad, "When Videos Buffer, Viewers Leave . . . in Droves [STATS]," December 11, 2009, *Mashable*, http://mashable.com/2009/12/11/ online-video-buffering/.

16. Lisa Belkin, "Moms and Motrin," *Motherlode* blog, *New York Times*, November 17, 2008, http://parenting.blogs.nytimes.com/2008/11/17/moms-and -motrin/.

17. Seth Stevenson, "The Creatures from the Sandwich Shop," *Slate*, February 23, 2004, http://www.slate.com/articles/business/ad_report_card/2004/02/the_creatures_from_the_sandwich_shop.html.
18. Jane Levere, "A Guy's Guy Tired of Plain Old Soap? Old Spice Is Counting on It," *New York Times*, August 1, 2003, http://www.nytimes.com/2003/08/01/business/media-business-advertising-guy-s-guy-tired-plain-old-soap-old-spice-counting-it.html.
19. Mark Fitzloff, interview by author, phone interview, July 13, 2013; Brenna Ehrlich, "The Old Spice Social Media Campaign by the Numbers," *Mashable*, July 15, 2010, http://mashable.com/2010/07/15/old-spice-stats/; David Griner, "Hey Old Spice Haters, Sales Are Up 107%," *AdWeek*, July 27, 2010, http://www.adweek.com/adfreak/hey-old-spice-haters-sales-are-107-12422.
20. Rick Kissell, "It's Official: 'Game of Thrones' Is HBO's Most Popular Series Ever," *Variety*, June 5, 2014, http://variety.com/2014/tv/ratings/its-official-game-of-thrones-is-hbos-most-popular-series-ever-1201214357/.
21. Ken Tucker, "Why Is Game of Thrones So Popular?" *BBC*, April 7, 2014, http://www.bbc.com/culture/story/20140407-why-people-love-game-of-thrones.

CHAPTER 5: REWARD TRIGGER
1. Leslie A. Perlow, *Sleeping with Your Smartphone: How to Break the 24/7 Habit and Change the Way You Work* (Boston: Harvard Business, 2012).
2. Doug Aamoth, "Study Says We Unlock Our Phones a LOT Each Day," *Time*, October 8, 2013, http://techland.time.com/2013/10/08/study-says-we-unlock-our-phones-a-lot-each-day/.
3. Kent Berridge, interview by author, phone interview, April 16, 2014.
4. Cash, Hilarie, Cosette D. Rae, Ann H. Steel, and Alexander Winkler, "Internet Addiction: A Brief Summary of Research and Practice," *Current Psychiatry Reviews* 8, no. 4 (2012): 292.
5. Brian A. Anderson, Patryk A. Laurent, and Steven Yantis, "Value-Driven Attentional Capture," *Proceedings of the National Academy of Sciences* 108, no. 25 (2011): 10367–71.
6. Richard M. Ryan and Edward L. Deci, "Intrinsic and Extrinsic Motivations: Classic Definitions and New Directions," *Contemporary Educational Psychology* 25, no. 1 (2000): 54–67.
7. Jessica Guynn, "L.A. Startup Looks for the Most Interesting Engineers in the World," *Los Angeles Times*, December 1, 2011, http://latimesblogs.latimes.com/technology/2011/12/la-startup-is-looking-for-the-most-interesting-engineers-in-the-world.html.
8. Daniel Pink, interview by author, phone interview, June 16, 2014.
9. Timothy A. Judge et al., "The Relationship Between Pay and Job Satisfaction: A Meta-Analysis of the Literature," *Journal of Vocational Behavior* 77, no. 2 (2010): 157–67.
10. Gregory S. Berns et al., "Predictability Modulates Human Brain Response to Reward," *Journal of Neuroscience* 21, no. 8 (2001): 2793–98.
11. Brian Wong, interview by author, phone interview, April 17, 2014.

12. Chou, Yu-kai, "The Six Different Contextual Types of Rewards in Gamifica-tion," *Yu-kai Chou Gamification.* November 11, 2013. http://www.yukaichou.com/marketing-gamification/six-context-types-rewards-gamification.
13. Leslie Scrivener, "Terry's Running for the Cancer Society," *Montreal Ga-zette,* April 28, 1980; Leslie Scrivener, *Terry Fox: His Story,* rev. ed. (New York: McClelland & Stewart, 2010).
14. Pink, interview by author.
15. James K. Harter et al., "Causal Impact of Employee Work Perceptions on the Bottom Line of Organizations," *Perspectives on Psychological Science* 5, no. 4 (2010): 378–89.
16. Sheryl Sandberg, interview by author, phone interview, May 13, 2013.
17. Steven Reiss, *Who Am I?: 16 Basic Desires that Motivate Our Actions and Define Our Personalities* (New York: Penguin, 2002).
18. Pink, interview by author.
19. Robert Weisman, "An Iconoclast's Ideas for Redefining Management," *Boston.com,* May 9, 2004, http://www.boston.com/business/articles/2004/05/09/an_iconoclasts_ideas_for_redefining_management/.
20. Amy Sawitta Lefevre, "Bangkok 'Smoking Kid' Lights Up Internet with Quit Message," *Reuters,* June 22, 2012, http://www.reuters.com/article/2012/06/22/net-us-thailand-smoking-idUSBRE85L0E420120622; Ogilvy & Mather Bangkok, "Smoking Kid—Best of #OgilvyCannes 2012 / #CannesLions," YouTube video, June 6, 2013, https://www.youtube.com/watch?v=g_YZ_PtMkw0.
21. Berridge, interview by author.
22. Maryellen Hamilton and Suparna Rajaram, "The Concreteness Effect in Implicit and Explicit Memory Tests," *Journal of Memory and Language* 44, no. 1 (2001): 96–117.
23. Dan Ariely, Emir Kamenica, and Dražen Prelec, "Man's Search for Mean-ing: The Case of Legos," *Journal of Economic Behavior & Organization* 67, no. 3 (2008): 671–77.
24. Tariq Shaukat, interview by author, phone interview, June 25, 2013.
25. Julie Jargon, "At McDonald's, Salads Just Don't Sell," *The Wall Street Jour-nal,* October 18, 2013, http://online.wsj.com/news/articles/SB10001424052702304384104579139871559464960.
26. Keith Wilcox et al., "Vicarious Goal Fulfillment: When the Mere Presence of a Healthy Option Leads to an Ironically Indulgent Decision," *Journal of Consumer Research* 36, no. 3 (2009): 380–93.
27. Ayelet Fishbach and Kristian Ove R. Myrseth, "The Dieter's Dilemma: Iden-tifying When and How to Control Consumption," in *Obesity Prevention: The Role of Brain and Society on Individual Behavior,* ed. Laurette Dube et al. (London: Elsevier, 2010), 353–64.

CHAPTER 6: REPUTATION TRIGGER

1. Josh Levs, "J. K. Rowling Revealed as Secret Author of Crime Novel," *CNN,* July 16, 2013, http://www.cnn.com/2013/07/14/world/rowling-secret-book/; Alex Hern, "Sales of 'The Cuckoo's Calling' Surge by 150,000% After JK Rowling Revealed as Author," *New Statesman,* July 14, 2013, http://

www.newstatesman.com/2013/07/sales-cuckoos-calling-surge-150000
-after-jk-rowling-revealed-author.
2. Matthew J. Salganik, Peter Sheridan Dodds, and Duncan J. Watts, "Experimental Study of Inequality and Unpredictability in an Artificial Cultural Market," *Science* 311, no. 5762 (2006): 854–56.
3. Jan B. Engelmann et al., "Expert Financial Advice Neurobiologically 'Offloads' Financial Decision Making Under Risk," *PLoS One*, 4, no. 3 (2009): e4957.
4. Robert B. Cialdini, *Influence: The Psychology of Persuasion*, rev. ed. (New York: HarperCollins, 1993).
5. "2014 Edelman Trust Barometer," Edelman, http://www.edelman.com /insights/intellectual-property/2014-edelman-trust-barometer/.
6. Hajo Adam and Adam D. Galinsky, "Enclothed Cognition," *Journal of Experimental Social Psychology* 48, no. 4 (2012): 918–25.
7. K. Anders Ericsson, et al., eds, *The Cambridge Handbook of Expertise and Expert Performance* (Cambridge, UK: Cambridge Univ. Press, 2006).
8. Owen Jarus, "Mixed Martial Arts Celebrity Recruited for Ancient Roman Army," *LiveScience*, March 29, 2012, http://www.livescience.com/19354 -martial-artist-recruited-ancient-roman-army.html.
9. Stanley Milgram, "Behavioral Study of Obedience," *The Journal of Abnormal and Social Psychology* 67, no. 4 (1963): 371–78.
10. Steven Lukes, *Power: A Radical View* (London: Macmillan, 1974).
11. Olivia Fox Cabane, *The Charisma Myth: How Anyone Can Master the Art and Science of Personal Magnetism* (New York: Penguin, 2012).
12. George Eaton, "Should Pre-Election Opinion Polls Be Banned? A Third of MPs Think So," *New Statesman*, November 13, 2013, http://www.new statesman.com/politics/2013/11/should-pre-election-opinion-polls-be-banned -third-mps-think-so.
13. Ian McAllister and Donley T. Studlar, "Bandwagon, Underdog, or Projection? Opinion Polls and Electoral Choice in Britain, 1979–1987," *Journal of Politics* 53, no. 3 (1991): 720–41.
14. James Surowiecki, *The Wisdom of Crowds: Why the Many Are Smarter than the Few and How Collective Wisdom Shapes Business, Economies, Societies, and Nations* (New York: Doubleday, 2004).
15. Michael Anderson and Jeremy Magruder, "Learning from the Crowd: Regression Discontinuity Estimates of the Effects of an Online Review Database," *The Economic Journal* 122, no. 563 (2012): 957–89.
16. Michael Luca, *Reviews, Reputation, and Revenue: The Case of Yelp.com*, No. 12-016 (Harvard Business School, 2011).
17. Lance Ulanoff, "Why Sony Won the Format War," *PC*, February 19, 2008, http://www.pcmag.com/article2/0,2817,2264994,00.asp.
18. Solomon E. Asch, "Opinions and Social Pressure," in *Readings About the Social Animal*, ed. Elliot Aronson (New York: Worth, 2004): 17–26.
19. Asch, "Opinions."
20. Seth Borenstein, "Conformity Rules: Social Animals Really Do Exhibit Monkey-See, Monkey-Do Behavior, Research Shows," *Buffalo News*, May 5,

2013, http://www.buffalonews.com/20130505/conformity_rules_social_animals _really_do_exhibit_monkey_see_monkey_do_behavior_research_shows .html.

21. Jeanne Theoharis, interview by Gwen Ifill, "Known for Single Act of Defiance, Rosa Parks Trained for Life Full of Activism," *PBS Newshour*, February 7, 2013, http://www.pbs.org/newshour/bb/social_issues-jan-june13 -rosaparks_02-07/.

22. Marisa Taylor, "Vitaminwater Gets Facebookers Brainstorming on a New Flavor," *Digits* blog, *The Wall Street Journal*, September 8, 2009, http://blogs. wsj.com/digits/2009/09/08/vitaminwater-gets-facebookers-brainstorming -on-a-new-flavor/.

23. Kate Pickert and Adam Sorensen, "Inside Reddit's Hunt for the Boston Bomb- ers," *Time*, April 23, 2013, http://nation.time.com/2013/04/23/inside-reddits-hunt -for-the-boston-bombers/.

24. Gonzalo De Polavieja and Gabriel Madirolas, "Wisdom of the Confident: Using Social Interactions to Eliminate the Bias in Wisdom of the Crowds" (paper, Cornell Univ. Library, June 30, 2014), http://arxiv.org/abs/1406.7578.

25. Genevieve Roberts, "Ben & Jerry's Builds on Its Social-Values Approach," *New York Times*, November 16, 2010, http://www.nytimes.com/2010/11/17 /business/global/17iht-rbofice.html; "Ben Cohen & Jerry Greenfield," *Entre- preneur*, October 10, 2008, http://www.entrepreneur.com/article/197626.

26. Jay Newton-Small, "The Rise and Fall of Elizabeth O'Bagy," *Time*, Sep- tember 17, 2013, http://swampland.time.com/2013/09/17/the-rise-and-fall-of -elizabeth-obagy/.

27. James Stewart, "In the Undoing of a C.E.O., a Puzzle," *New York Times*, May 18, 2012, http://www.nytimes.com/2012/05/19/business/the-undoing-of-scott -thompson-at-yahoo-common-sense.html.

28. Brad Tuttle, "Warren Buffett's Boring, Brilliant Wisdom," *Time*, March 1, 2010, http://business.time.com/2010/03/01/warren-buffetts-boring-brilliant -wisdom/.

CHAPTER 7: MYSTERY TRIGGER

1. Mark Borkowski, *The Fame Formula: How Hollywood's Fixers, Fakers and Star Makers Created the Celebrity Industry* (London: Pan Macmillan, 2009).

2. "Producing Gone with the Wind" (web exhibition, Harry Ransom Center, Univ. of Texas at Austin, through January 4, 2015), http://www.hrc.utexas .edu/exhibitions/web/gwtw/scarlett/.

3. Jason Abbruzzese, "Embrace the Binge: Netflix Viewers Average 2.3 Episodes per Sitting," *Mashable*, December 13, 2013, http://mashable.com/2013/12/13 /embrace-the-binge-netflix-data-shows-viewers-usually-watch-more-than-one -embargo-til-6am/.

4. Bluma Zeigarnik, "On Finished and Unfinished Tasks," in *A Source Book of Gestalt Psychology* ed. Willis D. Ellis (New York: Routledge, 2013), 300–14.

5. James T. Heimbach and Jacob Jacoby, "The Zeigarnik Effect in Advertising," in *Proceedings of the Third Annual Conference of the Association for Con- sumer Research* (1972), 746–58.

6. Malcolm R. Parks and Mara B. Adelman, "Communication Networks and the Development of Romantic Relationships: An Expansion of Uncertainty Reduction Theory," *Human Communication Research* 10, no. 1 (1983): 55–79; Charles R. Berger, "Uncertain Outcome Values in Predicted Relationships: Uncertainty Reduction Theory Then and Now," *Human Communication Research* 13, no. 1 (1986): 34–38; Kathy Kellermann and Rodney Reynolds, "When Ignorance Is Bliss: The Role of Motivation to Reduce Uncertainty in Uncertainty Reduction Theory," *Human Communication Research* 17, no. 1 (1990): 5–75.

7. Anthony Breznican, "Mystifying Trailer Transforms Marketing," *USA Today*, July 9, 2007, http://usatoday30.usatoday.com/life/movies/news/2007-07-08 -abrams-trailer_N.htm.

8. Alison Vingiano, "This Is How a Woman's Offensive Tweet Became the World's Top Story," *BuzzFeed*, December 21, 2013, http://www .buzzfeed.com/alisonvingiano/this-is-how-a-womans-offensive-tweet-became -the-worlds-top-s.

9. Vingiano, "This Is How."

10. Jeff Bercovici, "Justine Sacco and the Self-Inflicted Perils of Twitter," *Forbes*, December 23, 2013, http://www.forbes.com/sites/jeffbercovici/2013/12/23/justine -sacco-and-the-self-inflicted-perils-of-twitter/.

11. Matt Singer, "Ten Movie Trailers that Spoil Their Movie," *IFC*, August 5, 2010, http://www.ifc.com/fix/2010/08/ten-movie-trailers-that-spoil.

12. Dalton Ross, "Secrets and Jedis," *Entertainment Weekly*, September 16, 2004, http://www.ew.com/ew/article/0,,698013,00.html.

13. Dolf Zillmann, T. Alan Hay, and Jennings Bryant, "The Effect of Suspense and Its Resolution on the Appreciation of Dramatic Presentations," *Journal of Research in Personality* 9, no. 4 (1975): 307–23.

14. Noël Carroll, "The Paradox of Suspense," in *Suspense: Conceptualizations, Theoretical Analyses, and Empirical Explorations*, eds. Peter Vorderer, Hans J. Wulff, and Mike Friedrichsen (New York: Routledge, 2013), 71–91.

15. Robert Madrigal and Colleen Bee, "Suspense as an Experience of Mixed Emotions: Feelings of Hope and Fear While Watching Suspenseful Commercials," *Advances in Consumer Research* 32, no. 1 (2005): 561.

16. Colleen C. Bee and Robert Madrigal, "It's Not Whether You Win or Lose; It's How the Game Is Played," *Journal of Advertising* 41, no. 1 (2012): 47–58.

17. Steven Soderbergh, interview by author, personal interview, New York City, July 17, 2013.

18. Eric McWhinnie, "How Much Will March Madness Cost Corporate America?" *Wall St. Cheat Sheet*, March 13, 2014, http://wallstcheatsheet.com /politics/how-much-will-march-madness-cost-corporate-america.html/; Erik Matuszewski, "March Madness Gambling Brings Out Warnings from NCAA to Tournament Players," *Bloomberg*, March 17, 2011, http://www.bloomberg .com/news/2011-03-17/march-madness-gambling-brings-out-warnings-from -ncaa-to-tournament-players.html.

19. Harry E. Blanchard and Asghar Iran-Nejad, "Comprehension Processes and Eye Movement Patterns in the Reading of Surprise-Ending Stories," *Discourse Processes* 10, no. 1 (1987): 127–38.
20. Emily Nussbaum, "Tune In Next Week," *The New Yorker*, July 30, 2012, http://www.newyorker.com/arts/critics/television/2012/07/30/120730crte _television_nussbaum; Harold MacGrath, *The Adventures of Kathlyn* (Indianapolis: Bobbs-Merrill, 1914).
21. Mike Fenn, "60,000 Redditors Want to Know What's in This Safe," *The Daily Dot*, March 18, 2013, http://www.dailydot.com/society/reddit-whatsin thisthing-locked-safe-new-zealand/.
22. Ben Parr, "Startup Crisis Control: 6 Painful Lessons from Airbnb," *Mashable*, July 29, 2011, http://mashable.com/2011/07/29/airbnb-pr-crisis/; Michael Arrington, "The Moment of Truth for Airbnb as User's Home Is Utterly Trashed," *TechCrunch*, July 27, 2011, http://techcrunch.com/2011/07/27 /the-moment-of-truth-for-airbnb-as-users-home-is-utterly-trashed/.
23. Austin Carr, "The Secret to Airbnb's Freakishly Rapid Orgy Response: 'Scenario Planning,'" *Fast Company*, March 17, 2014, http://www.fast company.com/3027798/the-secret-to-airbnbs-freakishly-rapid-orgy-response -scenario-planning.
24. NPR, "How to Write a Great Mystery," *Talk of the Nation*, July 28, 2008, http://www.npr.org/templates/story/story.php?storyId=92995184.
25. Mark Alford, "Isaac Newton: The First Physicist," Washington Univ. in St. Louis, 1995, http://physics.wustl.edu/~alford/newton.html.

CHAPTER 8: ACKNOWLEDGMENT TRIGGER
1. Kina Grannis, interview by author, personal interview, Los Angeles, June 11, 2013.
2. Kina Grannis, "Gotta Digg," YouTube, December 23, 2007, https://www .youtube.com/watch?v=XLLRsn_nr6s.
3. James A. Coan, Hillary S. Schaefer, and Richard J. Davidson, "Lending a Hand: Social Regulation of the Neural Response to Threat," *Psychological Science* 17, no. 12 (2006): 1032–39.
4. Deirdra Funcheon, "Balloon Boy 2012: Three Years After the Hoax, Falcon Heene Fronts a Metal Band," *New Times Broward-Palm Beach*, December 13, 2012, http://www.browardpalmbeach.com/2012-12-13/news /balloon-boy-2012-three-years-after-hoax-falcon-heene-fronts-a-metal-band /full/.
5. Yalda T. Uhls and Patricia M. Greenfield, "The Value of Fame: Preadolescent Perceptions of Popular Media and Their Relationship to Future Aspirations," *Developmental Psychology* 48, no. 2 (2012): 315–26.
6. Jeremy Rifkin, *The Empathic Civilization: The Race to Global Consciousness in a World in Crisis* (New York: Penguin, 2009).
7. Dick Guttman, interview by author, phone interview, May 11, 2013.
8. Ben Parr, "Likes, Retweets, Comments & the Rise of the Validation Society," *Ben Parr's Entrepreneurial Musings* blog, January 24, 2012, http://benparr .com/2012/01/validation-society/.

9. Jenna Wortham, "Valley of the Blahs: How Justin Bieber's Troubles Exposed Twitter's Achilles' Heel," *Bits* blog, *New York Times*, January 25, 2014, http://bits.blogs.nytimes.com/2014/01/25/valley-of-the-blahs-how-justin-biebers-downfall-exposed-twitters-achilles-heel/.

10. Josh Elman, interview by author, personal interview, Half Moon Bay, CA, June 17, 2013.

11. Carol Kuruvilla, "San Francisco Turns into Gotham City for Batkid," *Daily News*, November 16, 2013, http://www.nydailynews.com/news/national/san-francisco-turns-gotham-city-batkid-article-1.1518454; Bill Chappell, "Holy Empathy! Batkid Lives Superhero Dream in San Francisco," *The Two-Way*, NPR, November 15, 2013, http://www.npr.org/blogs/thetwo-way/2013/11/15/245480296/holy-empathy-batkid-lives-superhero-dream-in-san-francisco.

12. Deborah A. Small, George Loewenstein, and Paul Slovic, "Sympathy and Callousness: The Impact of Deliberative Thought on Donations to Identifiable and Statistical Victims," *Organizational Behavior and Human Decision Processes* 102, no. 2 (2007): 143–53.

13. Scott Harrison, interview by author, phone interview, New York City, June 7, 2013.

14. Donald Horton and R. Richard Wohl, "Mass Communication and Para-Social Interaction: Observations on Intimacy at a Distance," *Psychiatry* 19, no. 3 (1956): 215–29.

15. Mona Nomura, interview by author, Instant Message interview, December 18, 2014.

16. Kenneth Maxwell and Andrew Joyce, "The Man Who Made AKB48," *Japan RealTime* blog, *The Wall Street Journal*, December 28, 2013, http://blogs.wsj.com/japanrealtime/2011/12/28/the-man-who-made-akb48/; Tokyo Hive, "Oricon Reveals 'Artist Total Sales Revenue' Ranking for 2012," December 20, 2012, http://www.tokyohive.com/article/2012/12/oricon-reveals-artist-total-sales-revenue-ranking-for-2012/; Michael Cucek, "Japanese Idol," *Latitude* blog, *New York Times*, June 14, 2013, http://latitude.blogs.nytimes.com/2013/06/14/japanese-idol/?gwh=F315862CCB765F470AA0C90C0F44296F.

17. Daniel Bentley, "I Asked for Eggs," *Medium*, May 15, 2013, https://medium.com/this-happened-to-me/i-asked-for-eggs-c9e6fd3ef792.

18. Susan Marks, *Finding Betty Crocker: The Secret Life of America's First Lady of Food* (New York: Simon & Schuster, 2010).

19. Alexia Tsotsis, interview by author, personal interview, San Francisco, June 19, 2013.

CONCLUSION: THE INFLUENCE OF ATTENTION

1. Mark Achler, e-mail message to author, February 9, 2013.

About the Author

•

Ben Parr is the cofounder and managing partner of Dominate-Fund, a strategic venture capital firm that invests in and accelerates the growth of early-stage companies through its expertise in attention, branding, press, marketing, customer and user acquisition, virality, and celebrity partnerships. He is also a columnist for *Inc.* and a regular contributor at CNBC. Previously, Parr was a columnist and commentator for CNET and, before that, was coeditor and editor-at-large of *Mashable*, where he wrote more than 2,400 articles on social media and technology and helped manage *Mashable's* growing editorial team. *Forbes* named Parr one of its 30 Under 30, and his work has been featured in a variety of media, including CNN, Fox News, *The Wall Street Journal*, NPR, and the *New York Times*. He lives in San Francisco, although he remains a die-hard fan of his hometown Chicago Bears.

Want more news, tips, and tricks on the science of attention?

Visit www.Captivology.com and you'll find it.

Got questions about how to promote your
idea, business, art, or cause?

Captivology's community can help you find the
answer: www.Reddit.com/r/Captivology

Index